Herausgeber
Günter Zamp Kelp, Julia Lienemeyer
Universität der Künste Berlin

Redaktion
Julia Lienemeyer

Buchgestaltung
CoDe. Communication and Design, New York
Jenny 8 Del Corte Hirschfeld, Hadrien Gliozzo, Anne Gabella

Fotoarbeiten
Gerhard Braun, Berlin
Artem Koljadynskyj (**Артем Колядинський**), Chernivtsi
Wolodymyr Zytrak (**Володимир Цитрак**), Chernivtsi

Alle anderen Aufnahmen wurden von den Workshop – und Exkursionsteilnehmern sowie Autoren
freundlicherweise zur Verfügung gestellt

Übersetzungen
Deutsch/Englisch
Edith Wunsch, UdK Berlin
Ukrainisch/Englisch
Anna Zubowytsch (**Анна Зубович**), Chernivtsi
Deutsch/Ukrainisch
Oxana Matijtschuk (**Оксана Матійчук**), Chernivtsi

Herstellung
Merkur Druck GmbH & Co. KG

© 2007 Institut für Außenwirtschaft GmbH, Düsseldorf, Germany, www.ifa-d.com

ISBN 13: 978-3-939717-04-1

Bibliographische Informationen der Deutschen Nationalbibliothek
Die Deutsche Nationalbibliothek verzeichnet diese Publikation in der Deutschen Nationalbibliographie;
detaillierte bibliographische Daten sind im Internet über http://dnb.d-nb.de abrufbar.
Sommerakademie, Ausstellung und Buchherstellung wurden gefördert durch:

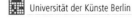

CZERNOWITZ TOMORROW

Dieses Buch entstand anlässlich der "International Summer Academy of Architecture and Urban Regeneration in Chernivtsi 2006" und der Ausstellung: "Czernowitz Tomorrow – Ideas for the city of Chernivtsi", Kunstmuseum, Zentralplatz 10, Chernivtsi vom 14. bis 23. August 2006. This book emerged as a result of the "International Summer Academy of Architecture and Urban Regeneration in Chernivtsi 2006" and the Exhibition: "Czernowitz Tomorrow – Ideas for the city of Chernivtsi", Art Museum, Central Square 10, Chernivtsi from 14th to 23rd August 2006.

TEILNEHMENDE UNIVERSITÄTEN PARTICIPATING UNIVERSITIES:
University of Technology Graz, Polytechnical College Chernivtsi, Ion Mincu University of Architecture und Urbanism Bucharest, University of the Arts Berlin

STUDENTEN STUDENTS:
Bastian Bechtloff, Irina Bogdan, David Bürger, Kostya Chebriy, Sasha Chebriy, Jenica Craiu, Raluca Davidel, Lisa Dietersdorf, Olga Dundich, Konrad Edlinger, Elena Fischmann, Natasha Galyshka, Elisa Hernando Vilar, Konstantyn Komarovskyy, Dirk Krutke, Sebastian Lupea, Joachim Maier, Sven Marx, Inna Palka, Nataly Patraboy, Sigrun Rottensteiner, Vanessa Sartori, Nina Sleska, Dina Sokur, Elena Stoian, Adrian Timaru, Stefan Tuchila, Veronica Tudor, Matthias Tscheuschler, Tanja Vakoliuk, Michael Wierdak

BETREUER UNIT ADVISER:
Oxana Boyko, Prof. Grigor Doytchinov, Stefan Ghenciulescu, Emil Ivanescu, Julia Lienemeyer, Prof. Günter Zamp Kelp

ORGANISATOREN ORGANIZER
University of the Arts Berlin and Chernivtsi National University

Site investigation at the River Pruth on the first day of the Summer Academy

DANK

Die Idee eine Internationale Sommerakademie in Chernivtsi zu veranstalten entstand im Anschluss an unsere Studienreise in die Ukraine im April 2004. Die nächsten zwei Jahre reifte die Idee zu einem realistischen Projekt heran. Wir fanden motivierte Partner vor Ort in Chernivtsi und interessierte Kollegen in Österreich, Rumänien und der Ukraine, die es uns ermöglichten, das Projekt inhaltlich durchzuführen. Die finanzielle Unterstützung einiger großzügiger Sponsoren gab uns letztendlich die Chance, die Sommerakademie im August 2006 zu realisieren. Wir danken dem Präsidenten der Universität der Künste Berlin Prof. Martin Rennert, der Fakultät Gestaltung und der Kommission für künstlerische und wissenschaftliche Vorhaben, dem Deutsch Ukrainischen Forum, der Robert Bosch Stiftung, der Stadtverwaltung Landeshauptstadt Klagenfurt und der Deutschen Botschaft Kiew für die finanzielle Unterstützung und das uns entgegengebrachte Vertrauen. Weiterhin danken wir dem DAAD, der uns durch seine finanzielle Unterstützung zwei wichtige Studienreisen in die Ukraine und nach Rumänien ermöglicht hat.

Für die inhaltliche und organisatorische Unterstützung der Sommerakademie in Chernivtsi bedanken wir uns ganz herzlich bei unseren Partnern vor Ort: Pavlo Koljadynsky und Oksana Matiychuk sowie Kathrin Hartmann und Bernd Böttcher vom Bukowina Zentrum. In Berlin danken wir allen studentischen Mitarbeitern unseres Lehrgebietes GruV, die sich an der Umsetzung der Sommerakademie beteiligt haben, insbesondere Matthias Tscheuschler. Außerdem danken wir Lilly Barbat, Tetyana Berezhna, Heidi Langner, Bo Larsson, Sergij Osatchuk, Rosemarie Paus-Daniel, Oliver Paus, Werner Sewing, Ihor Zhaloba, Alexander Zuckrow und den vielen hier nicht genannten Gesprächspartnern für ihre konstruktiven Ratschläge und die Weitergabe ihres Wissens. Alle haben zur Optimierung und letztendlich zur Durchführung der Sommerakademie wesentlich beigetragen.

Ein besonderes Dankeschön gilt dem Architekten Mykola Felonjuk (**Микола Фелонюк**), der mit seinem Fachwissen bei der Vorbereitung der Sommerakademie unseren Nicht-Architekten-Partnern vor Ort mit Rat und Tat zur Seite stand. Unser Dank gilt weiterhin den Architekten aus Chernivtsi, die ihr fachliches Wissen über die Stadt zusammengetragen haben und mehr als 30 aktuelle Themen zur stadtplanerischen Situation in Chernivtsi formuliert haben, die handfeste Grundlage für unsere Sommerakademie: Switlana Bilenkowa (**Світлана Біленкова**), Oksana Bojko (**Оксана Бойко**), Wjatscheslaw Kischljaruk (**В'ячеслав Кішлярук**), Iryna Korotun (**Ірина Коротун**), Oleksandr Sawaletskyj (**Олександр Завалецький**), Larysa Wandjuk (**Лариса Вандюк**), Wolodymyr Zwyljow (**Володимир Цвильов**)

Wir bedanken uns sehr bei dem Bürgermeister von Chernivtsi, Mykola Fedoruk, für seine bereitwillige Unterstützung und Förderung der Sommerakademie.

Wir sind zuversichtlich, dass das entstandene Netzwerk weiterhin eng zusammenarbeiten und neue Möglichkeiten auftun wird, die begonnenen Projekte fortzusetzen.

Günter Zamp Kelp und Julia Lienemeyer

ACKNOWLEDGEMENTS

The idea to organize an International Summer Academy in Chernivtsi arose following an educational trip in April 2004. Within the succeeding two years, this idea gradually matured into a realistic project. We found motivated partners in Chernivtsi and additionally came across interested colleagues in Austria, Rumania, and the Ukraine, who rendered possible the thematic realization of the project. Several generous sponsors supported us financially, finally enabling the realization of the project in August 2006. We would like to thank the president of the University of the Arts, Prof. Martin Rennert, the faculty of design and the commission for artistic and scientific projects, the German Ukrainian Forum, the Robert Bosch Foundation, the Regional Capital Klagenfurt and the German Embassy in Kiew for their financial support and the offered confidence. Further, we would like to thank the DAAD, which enabled two important educational trips to the Ukraine and Rumania by supporting us financially.

We thank our local partners, Pavlo Koljadynsky and Oksana Matiychuk, as well as Kathrin Hartmann and Bernd Böttcher from the Bukovina Center for the contextual and organizational support with the Summer Academy in Chernivtsi. We are also grateful towards all colleagues of the GRuV who contributed to the realization of the Summer academy, particularly Matthias Tscheuschler. Furthermore we would like to thank Lilly Barbat, Tetyana Berezhna, Heidi Langner, Bo Larsson, Sergij Osatchuk, Rosemarie Paus-Daniel, Oliver Paus, Werner Sewing, Ihor Zhaloba, Alexander Zuckrow and many other conversational partners for their constructive advice and for passing on their knowledge. All those involved have contributed significantly to the optimization and ultimately the carrying out of the Summer Academy.

We are especially grateful for the contributions by the architect Mykola Felonjuk (Микола Фелонюк), who aided all our non-architectural partners with his expertise and knowledge during the organizational phase of the project. We also owe our thanks to the following architects from Chernivtsi who contributed their expertise on the town and formulated theses about more than thirty relevant themes concerning the town planning situation in Chernivitsi, which we could use as a starting point for the Summer Academy. These architects include: Switlana Bilenkowa (Світлана Біленкова), Oksana Bojko (Оксана Бойко), Wjatscheslaw Kischljaruk (В'ячеслав Кішлярук), Iryna Korotun (Ірина Коротун), Oleksandr Sawaletskyj (Олександр Завалецький), Larysa Wandjuk (Лариса Вандюк), Wolodymyr Zwyljow (Володимир Цвильов)

We would also like to express our special thanks to Chernivitsi's mayor, Mykola Fedoruk, for willingly supporting and promoting the Summer Academy.

We are optimistic that the network, which has evolved will continue to work together very closely. Further opportunities for new projects are bound to develop and our commenced projects will continue.

Günter Zamp Kelp und Julia Lienemeyer

CZERNOWITZ TOMORROW

ВІТАННЯ З ЧЕРНІВЦІВ
GREETING FROM CHERNIVTSI

ШАНОВНІ ДРУЗІ!

Ви тримаєте в руках унікальне видання.

Своєрідне архітектурне майбутнє нашого чудового міста. Поки що на папері. Але, сподіваюсь, новаторські цікаві ідеї, мудре та професійно виважене архітектурне бачення «Чернівців- 2030» обов'язково будуть втілені у життя.

Прикметно, що розмаїття пропозицій, які виникли під час літньої архітектурної академії в Чернівцях, притаманні саме молодим перспективним архітекторам з різних країн – Німеччини, Австрії, Румунії та України. Тих країн, кожна з якої вписала свою сторінку в історію нашого міста.

Приємно, що ця унікальна міжнародна літня академія в рамках дослідницького проекту «Зміна архітектури й ідентичності у Центральній та Східній Європі» відбулась саме в Чернівцях – місті з багатими архітектурними, культурними та історичними традиціями.

Через рік Чернівці святкуватимуть поважний ювілей -600-річчя першої письмової згадки про місто.

Безперечно, проекти молодих талановитих архітекторів матимуть продовження і чернівчани пишатимуться тим, що саме столиця Буковини стала плацдармом для нових оригінальних ідей, сміливих пошуків та творчих фантазій.

Успіхів вам та натхнення!

З повагою,
Чернівецький міський голова   Микола Федорук

Dear friends,

You are holding a unique edition in your hands.

It is peculiar architectural future of our wonderful city. Still on paper. But I do hope that innovative ideas, wise and professional architectural vision of "Czernowitz tomorrow" will be made a reality.

It is worth noticing that the variety of suggestions at the Summeracademy of Architecture and Urbanism in Chernivtsi were made by young perspective architects from different countries – Germany, Austria, Romania and Ukraine, the countries that left their traces in the history of our city.

It is nice to realize that this unique international Summeracademy within "Change of Architecture and Identity in Central and Eastern Europe" research project took place in Chernivtsi, a city with rich architectural, cultural and historical traditions.

In a year Chernivtsi will celebrate the significant 600th anniversary of the first written record of the city.

Projects by young talented architects will undoubtedly be realized and Chernivtsi dwellers will take pride in the fact that the capital of Bukovyna is a base for new original ideas, daring search and creative fantasies.

I wish you good luck and inspiration!

Respectfully,
Chernivtsi City Mayor   Mykola Fedoruk

View of Chernivtsi from the northeast

GRUSSWORT AUS BERLIN
GREETING FROM BERLIN

WAS SIND KULTURRÄUME?

Wie hängen ihre Grenzen vom aktuell Gemeinsamen ab, oder ist allein gemeinsame Geschichte Bindeglied genug? Wenn Menschen gehen und eine Sprache oder ein Teil der Bevölkerung verschwindet, was ist mit den Immobilien: bleiben sie Denkmal, Dokument, oder sind sie den urbanen Geist prägende wirksame Hinterlassenschaft?

Welche Fülle an Fragen hat uns die Geschichte Europas im 20. Jahrhundert aufgegeben, Fragen, die in einem nunmehr friedlich zueinander findenden Kontinent neu aufbrechen und gesehen werden müssen, will man tatsächlich eine gemeinsame Sprache finden, die das rein Verbale hinter sich lässt und gute Zukunft ermöglicht.

Die Universität der Künste Berlin stellt sich diesen Problemkreisen – und Chancen! – aus Überzeugung in der ihr gemäßen Art: Mittels der Künste und des durch sie möglichen differenzierten Dialogs. In diese Tradition stellte sich die Internationale Sommerakademie Chernivtsi mit großem Erfolg und dokumentiert einen Anspruch, ohne den keine Nation, keine Region aber eben auch keine Kunst denkbar sein sollte: den Anspruch auf klares Sehen, genaues Erkennen und ehrlichen Austausch.

Prof. Martin Rennert, Präsident der Universität der Künste Berlin

WHAT ARE CULTURAL SPACES?

How do their boundaries depend on the currently shared common grounds? Or does the mutual history itself function as a sufficient common link? When people leave and a language or part of the population disappears, what becomes of the deserted estates? Do they remain as memorials, as a documentation, or is it an effective legacy which characterizes the urban spirit? What abundance of questions has Europe's history imposed upon us? Queries emerge anew and have to be perceived innovatively within this continent, which will – from now on – move together peacefully. This is necessary in order to find a common language, which is able to leave the solely verbal communication behind and enables a promising future.

The University of the Arts Berlin faces these perpetually reoccurring problems – and possibilities! – with a conviction common in its manner: Through the arts and the differentiated dialogue, which the former facilitates. In the light of this tradition, the International Summer Academy Chernivtsi dedicated itself and successfully documented an aspiration without which no nation, no region, but equally no art is imaginable. This is the claim to see clearly, to comprehend in a detailed manner, and to establish a genuine exchange.

Prof. Martin Rennert, president of the university of the arts berlin

Monument of T. Shevchenko, Central Square and town hall, built in 1848

VORWORT
PREFACE
BY *WERNER SEWING*

Die hier präsentierten Resultate einer Internationalen Sommerakademie für Architektur in Chernivtsi 2006, deren Teilnehmer Studenten aus Berlin, Bukarest, Graz und Chernivtsi waren, sind ein weiteres Indiz für eine neue Sicht auf Europa, eine Verschiebung des Interesses nach Ostmitteleuropa. Dabei werden alte kulturelle Topografien und Räume wieder entdeckt und zugleich mit der neuesten Geographie der Globalisierung konfrontiert. Aus dieser Gleichzeitigkeit des Ungleichzeitigen bezieht das Projekt seine Faszination. Wenn unlängst weltweit ein neues Zeitalter, ein Urban Age ausgerufen wurde, so muss dieser Suggestion einer universalen Stadt, gar einer Generis City, eine differenzierte Wahrnehmung historisch ganz unterschiedlicher Stadtkulturen entgegengehalten werden. Reale und fiktionale Geschichte, Bild und Raum gehen in Städten eine eigentümliche Verbindung, oft keine Synthese, ein. Immer noch aber werden sie vom Genius Loci, seiner spezifisch Geschichte und nicht von Hollywood bestimmt. In weiten Teilen Osteuropas gilt dies umso mehr.

Chernivtsi, eine insular gelegene kleine Großstadt in der Bukowina, einem Südwestzipfel der Ukraine, gehört nicht zu den osteuropäischen Metropolen, die wie Budapest, Warschau oder Prag längst Teil der globalen Netzwerkgesellschaft geworden sind. Ihre Randlage am Fuß der Kaparten hängt sie räumlich von den Verkehrs- und Kommunikationsströmen Europas ab. Gleichwohl ist sie unter ihrem alten Namen Czernowitz im kulturellen Fundus Europas ideell hoch präsent. Die Sommerakademie hat versucht, aus dieser Spannung zwischen Mythos und Ort kreative Entwurfsideen zu generieren, Entwicklungspotentiale freizulegen. In der Doppelexistenz der Stadt als virtuelles Bild und als Text und als soziale Stenografie der Stadtgesellschaft findet die Architektur ihr Thema.

Es war die Postmoderne, die das Imaginäre als eigene Realität rehabilitiert hatte. Die postmoderne Architekturtheorie aber hatte der Materialität des Urbanen eine besondere Rolle in der Vermittlung der ideellen mit der sozialen und historischen Welt zugeschrieben. Aldo Rossi sah 1966 in seinem Schlüsseltext "Die Architektur der Stadt" in der Textur des Stadtgrundrisses und in den Objekten und Typologien des

Exhibition of the final results at the Art Museum, Central Square 10, Chernivtsi

The International Summer Academy of Architecture 2006 in Chernivtsi accommodated participating architecture students from Berlin, Bucharest, Graz, and Chernivtsi. With a shift in interest towards Central Eastern Europe, the academy indicated a new European perspective. In the course of this shift old cultural topographies and regions are rediscovered while simultaneously being confronted with the most recent developments in the geographical aspects of globalization. The fascination with this project stems from the simultaneity of the non-simultaneous.

In these days a new age has been declared – the urban age. But the suggestive idea of a universal urbanism - some even talk about a generic city - must be challenged by a precise perception of historically diverse urban cultures. Real and fictional history in cities merge into peculiar relationships, often not in synthesis, but still these are not manufactured by Hollywood scripts but usually reflect a Genius Loci, a specific history in a specific place and space.

Chernivtsi is an insular city of medium size in the western part of the Ukraine, the capital of a county called Bukovina. Unlike large Eastern metropolises like Budapest, Warsaw, or Prague it has not become an integral part of the global network-society. Its peripheral position on the foothills of the Carpathian Mountains sets it apart from the main traffic and communication flows and from the rest of Europe. Nevertheless Chernivtsi is highly present in Europe's cultural memory under its historical name Czernowitz.

The summer academy sets out to generate creative ideas of urban design through the tension between myth and location. Architecture finds its theme in the city's dual existence, as a virtual image and as a text, as a social stenography, as an urban society.

Postmodernism rehabilitated the imaginary as an independent reality. Postmodernist theory of architecture simultaneously ascribed to the materiality of the urban, the physical fabric of the city a special role of mediating between this virtual and the social and historical worlds. In 1966 Aldo Rossi had identified the pivotal function of the city as the embodiment of the collective memory of a community. In his key text at the outset of the post-modern rediscovery of the old city, The Architecture of the City, he analyzed the texture of the ground plan and the objects and the typologies of the built form of the city as the corner stones of historical memory. The historical form of the city guarantees identity through the permanence of the object, such as the monuments of Eternal Rome. Text and space, history and architecture

gebauten Stadtkörpers das kollektive Gedächtnis einer Gemeinschaft verkörpert. Die historische Stadtgestalt verbürgt Identität – so etwa die Monumente des ewigen Rom. Text und Raum, Geschichte und Architektur sind zwei Seiten einer historischen Erzählung. Die spätere Postmoderne tendierte indes dazu, das Gebaute auf Text und Bild zu reduzieren, das Imaginäre gewann die Überhand über Raum und Zeit. Unter den Bedingungen der Medienrealität einer globalisierten Welt aber erweisen sich Mythen und Bilder nun als harte ökonomische Fakten im Stadtmarketing, sie verschaffen Städten Aufmerksamkeit, Interesse, Investoren, Arbeit. Chernivtsi ist noch weit davon entfernt, seinen Mythos zu bewirtschaften, das Potential aber ist da.

In dynamischen Metropolen, man denke an London, werden Geschichte und Mythos zum Teil des Lebens, historisches Erbe und Tourismus sind ein Teil der Stadtökonomie, mehr nicht. In rein touristischen Städten, etwa in Venedig, erstickt die reale Stadt im Imaginären. Venedig, so ein Kenner der Stadt, ertrinkt nicht im Wasser, sondern in Worten.

Chernivtsi ist weder Venedig noch London. Mit dem Fall des eisernen Vorhangs ist die Bukowina, wie der Osten Mitteleuropas insgesamt, als realer Ort wieder in Europa angekommen. Tourismus oder Dynamik, beides steckt noch in den Kinderschuhen. Der flottierende Mythos, - der von Czernowitz etwa lebte in Emigranten- und Intellektuellen-kreisen zwischen New York und Tel Aviv, London und Berlin, wenig in Chernivtsi, kann nun wieder zurückkehren. Macht er noch, machte er je Sinn?

Hier liegt das Faszinosum von Chernivtsi: Zu entdecken ist eine lebendige Stadt in der westlichen Ukraine. Zu entdecken ist auch eine intakte habsburgische Stadt aus der Zeit der vorletzten Jahrhundertwende als bauliches Gesamtkunstwerk. Das kollektive Gedächtnis evoziert eine längst untergegangene Epoche, einen Ort namens Czernowitz, den Aussenposten des habsburgischen Reiches an der Grenze zum Zarenreich. Wir sind am Ursprung des Mythos Czernowitz. Damals schon peripher, eine Kolonialstadt, wurde die Stadt zu einer multikulturellen geistigen Provinz, bevölkert von Deutschen, Juden, Ruthenen, Rumänen, Polen und Moldawiern. Geistiger Mittel-punkt, neben dem Theater und den Kirchen, war vor allem die Universität. Die "Stadt des Westens im Osten", die zugleich als ein "österreichisches Jerusalem" galt, wurde durch ein weltläufiges Bildungsbürgertum geprägt.

Dieses Laboratorium, das seit 1919 rumänisch war, es hiess jetzt Cernauti, ging unter im zweiten Weltkrieg, im Holocaust überlebten von 245 000 Juden gerade 6000. Es ist diese Katastrophe, die jede nachträgliche Verklärung der fast postmodern anmutenden Pluralität der Stadtkultur unmöglich macht. Gleichwohl macht dieser Mythos das Faszinosum der Stadt aus.

Czernowitz ist ein literarischer Topos, ein Ort in den Erzählungen und Gedichten von Paul Celan und Rose Ausländer, Cernauti findet sich bei dem rumänischen Schriftsteller Norman Manea, der heute in den USA lebt. Die Lebenswelten hinter dieser virtuellen Welt indes sind Geschichte. Bruch, nicht Kontinuität ist das historische, soziale und kulturelle Thema der Stadt. Kontinuität aber, hier ist Chernivtsi ein Beleg für Aldo Rossis Theorie des gebauten Gedächtnisses, bietet die bauliche Gestalt der alten Stadt, vollständig bewahrt, im Kontrast zur umgebenden neuen sozialistischen Stadt seit 1945. Das Thema der Rekonstruktion wie in Warschau, Danzig/Gdansk, Breslau/Wroclaw, oder der kritischen Rekonstruktion wie im heutigen Berlin – in Chernivtsi stellt es sich nicht. Der kollektive Stadtkörper ist da, wo aber bleibt das Gedächtnis?

are two sides of a single historical narrative. Later postmodernism tended to reduce the built form to mere text and image, the imaginary gained predominance over time, space and place.

Under the present conditions of a global media reality myths and images turn out to be hard facts of city-marketing, they attract attention to cities and places, draw interest, investment, economy into the city. Of course Chernivtsi is still far away from marketing its myth, yet the potential is given.

In a dynamic metropolis such as London, history and myth are part of life and heritage-tourism, which are merely one asset of the urban economy. In a purely tourism-oriented urban destination, like Venice for example, the city seems to be drowned in the imaginary. Venice is said not to be lost in the water of the lagoon, but rather in a sea of words.

Chernivtsi is neither London nor Venice. With the fall of the Iron Curtain, Bukovina, like most of Central Eastern Europe, has only gradually begun to re-emerge as a real place in Europe. Both tourism and economic dynamics are, at best, in its beginning stage.

The freely floating myth of Czernowitz, which had circulated between emigrants and intellectuals in New York and Tel Aviv, London and Berlin, though not so much in Chernivtsi itself, can finally return home. Does the virtual still make sense in the face of the real, did it ever make sense? Bringing the myth home, we discover a vibrant, if still rather poor Ukrainian city. We also discover a wellpreserved city of the Habsburg Empire from 1900 as a built Gesamtkunstwerk, an integral work of art. Rossi had declared the entire old city to be just that. Collective memory evokes an epoch that died a long time ago, seemingly unrelated to the present life in its walls. But here we come to the roots of the myth.

Historic Czernowitz was then an outpost of Habsburg close to the border of Tsarist Russia, a peripheral colonial city that turned into a multicultural hub in the provinces, inhabited by Germans, Jews, Ruthenians, Romanians, Pols and Moldavians people. The cultural centre besides the theatre and the churches was above all the university. This "Western city in the East" also was an "Austrian Jerusalem", in which the educated middle classes supported a rich cultural life. After World War I this urban laboratory came under Romanian rule. As Cernauti it existed with growing tensions until its demise during the Second World War. From an initial population of 245 000 Jews, only 6000 survived the Holocaust. This catastrophe makes any retrospective idealization of the almost protopostmodern plurality of the previously existing urban culture in Czernowitz impossible. Nonetheless, it is solely this myth that contributes to the lasting appeal of old Czernowitz.

The virtual reality of the myth is located in a literary place, in the stories and poems of Paul Celan and Rose Ausländer for instance, whereas we find the Cernauti's legacy in the stories of the Romanian writer Norman Manea, who lives in the USA. The way of life behind this virtual world has thus become history. Rupture, not continuity constitutes the city's historical, cultural and social theme.

Continuity, on the other hand, can be found in the built urban fabric, which serves as an example for Rossi's theory of the permanence regarding built form. The old cityscape contrasts with the new socialist quarters built after 1945 on the city's outskirts.

Hier nun intervenieren die Teams der internationalen, genauer: der mitteleuropäischen Sommerakademie von 2006. Gedächtnis bedeutet nicht Nostalgie, nicht die Sehnsucht nach einem Ort, an dem wir alle nie waren, den wir in der Literatur noch finden. Stadt ist durch Text verstehbar, Stadt ist nicht Text. Stadt ist auch kein Themenpark, in dem die gewünschte Geschichte nachgebaut werden kann. Historisches Gedächtnis ist eine Funktion und ein Korrektiv der gelebten Gegenwart, Architektur und Städtebau soll dieser dienen, ihr eine Lebensform verleihen. Die hier präsentierten Projekte haben daher aktuelle infrastrukturelle und urbanistische Probleme von Chernivtsi zum Gegenstand, die Entwicklung der Innenstadt, die Verbindung der alten mit der neuen Stadt, ein neuer Campus, kurz: Raum für Zukunft.

Die Vision einer Wissenschaftsstadt ist ein Weg in die Zukunft. Ihre Wurzel, so gesehen auch ihr Ideal, ist immer noch das alte intellektuelle Czernowitz, aber nicht mehr als Mythos, sondern als kulturelles Kapital im neuen Europa, in der globalen Ökonomie der Aufmerksamkeit.

Jewish cemetery looking towards Chernivtsi

Reconstruction of the historical city unlike in Breslau/Wroclaw, Warsaw or Danzig/Gdansk is not an issue in Chernivtsi, nor is the critical reconstruction of Berlin of the 1990s. The collective urban shape is present, but where is the memory?

It is here, where the international – to be precise – the Central European Summer Academy starts with its well-defined interventions. Memory does not mean nostalgia or the longing for a place where none of us has ever been. The city can be interpreted through the text, for in itself it is not a text. Nor is the city a theme park in which we rebuild the past as we like. Historical memory is a function and a correction of the present we live in. Architecture and urban design serve it by providing a functional and symbolic form, a form of life. So the projects presented here address pressing infrastructural and urban development problems of the city of Chernivtsi. The enlargement of the centre, the connection of the city core with the northern suburbs, a new university campus on an abandoned industrial site, and the interaction of the River Pruth and the city - in short: space for the future. Memory needs a future, in which it can serve as orientation.

The vision of a city of knowledge is one path into that future. Its point of reference, in a way its ideal, is still the intellectual urban life in historic Czernowitz – no longer as myth, but rather as cultural capital in a new Europe and in the global economy of attention.

left: Birthplace of the poetess Rose Ausländer, born 1901 in Chernivtsi

right: Daily market on Chervonoarmijska Street

PREPARATION
VORBEREITUNG
PREGATIREA
ПІДГОТОВКА

Russland

Weißrussland

Polen

Kiev

Ukraine

L'viv Lemberg

Chernivtsi

UdSSR bis 1991

Slowakei

Bukowina

Österreich- Ungarn bis 1918

Ungarn

Rumänien bis 1945

Krim

Rumänien

ARCHITEKTUR UND STADTERNEUERUNG ALS BINDEGLIED ZWISCHEN VERGANGENHEIT UND ZUKÜNFTIGER ENTWICKLUNG OSTMITTEL-EUROPÄISCHER STÄDTE AM BEISPIEL DER STADT CHERNIVTSI, UKRAINE

ARCHITECTURE AND URBAN REGENERATION AS LINK BETWEEN PAST AND FUTURE DEVELOPMENT OF EASTERN EUROPEAN CITIES INSTANCING THE CITY OF CHERNIVTSI, UKRAINE

PROJEKTBERICHT VON *JULIA LIENEMEYER*, UDK BERLIN
PROJECT REPORT BY *JULIA LIENEMEYER*, UDK BERLIN

WARUM CHERNIVTSI?

Das Jahr 2003 stand ganz im Zeichen der Osterweiterung der Europäischen Union. Sie ratifizierte nicht nur die Beitrittsverträge mit Polen, Tschechien, der Slowakei, mit Slowenien, Ungarn und den Baltischen Staaten Estland, Lettland und Litauen, sondern stellte auch Rumänien und Bulgarien für das Jahr 2007 den Beitritt in Aussicht. Damit lenkte sie unseren Blick wieder auf Regionen, die der Eiserne Vorhang seit Ende des Zweiten Weltkrieges unserem Bewusstsein entzogen hatte. Aber nicht nur das. Sie entfachte heftige Diskussionen in der westeuropäischen Öffentlichkeit über die Frage nach Zugehörigkeit und Identität in Europa. Dies war für unser Lehrgebiet der Anlass, das Thema unter dem Schwerpunkt Architektur und Stadterneuerung zu untersuchen. Unser Interesse

WHY CHERNIVTSI?

The eastward enlargement of the European Union dominated the year 2003. Following ratification of the admission of Poland, the Czech Republic, Hungary as well as the Baltic states Estonia, Latvia, Lithuania, the admittance of Bulgaria and Romania planned for 2007 was controversially debated in the Western European media. Attention focused on a region which the Iron Curtain had previously withheld from Western European awareness. The question of whether the region formed a part of the European cultural sphere and thus a part of Europe was seen differently across Western Europe. We saw this as an opportunity to approach the question in the area of architecture and urbanism.

Map of Austria-Hungary circa 1898

richtete sich auf die südwestliche Ukraine, die Region des ehemaligen Galizien und der Bukowina mit ihren Hauptstädten Lemberg (jetzt L'viv) und Czernowitz (jetzt Chernivtsi). Die Tatsache, dass sie einst als Provinzen des Habsburger Reiches sogar Teil des deutschsprachigen Kulturraumes waren, ist weitgehend in Vergessenheit geraten. Insbesondere am Beispiel der Stadt Chernivtsi wollten wir die Vielschichtigkeit des kulturellen Erbes Europas untersuchen und die Rolle der Architektur und des Städtebaus als kulturellem Bindeglied zwischen Ost und West ausloten. Aufgrund seiner deutsch-österreichischen, seiner rumänischen, seiner sowjetischen und seiner ukrainischen Vergangenheit im Zeitraum der letzten 250 Jahre lassen sich die dafür typischen architektonischen und parallel dazu soziokulturellen Entwicklungsverläufe gleichsam modellhaft für Ostmitteleuropa sehr gut nachvollziehen.

1774 annektierten die Habsburger die Bukowina und mit ihr die Stadt Czernowitz, die bis dahin Teil des Fürstentums Moldau war. Ihr städtebauliches und kulturelles Wachstum begann 1775 mit ihrer Funktion als östlichste Garnisonsstadt von Österreich und als Sitz der Landesregierung. 1875 erhielt sie, die inzwischen Hauptstadt und Verwaltungszentrum des Kronlandes Bukowina war, zu ihrem 100 jährigen Bestehen eine Universität. Czernowitz entwickelte sich zur südöstlichsten Kulturmetropole Europas: wohlhabend, ein wenig mondän, kulturell vielfältig und tolerant, mit einer einzigartigen polyethnischer Stadtgesellschaft aus Ukrainern, Rumänen, Juden, Deutschen, Polen, Roma u.a. Um die Jahrhundertwende hatte die Stadt ihren kulturellen Höhepunkt erreicht.

Als Folge des ersten Weltkrieges kam Czernowitz/Cernauti 1918 unter rumänische Herrschaft und wurde nach Bukarest zu einer der größten Städte des Landes ausgebaut. Im Zuge des Zweiten Weltkrieges kam sie 1940 unter sowjetische Herrschaft, dann wurde sie 1941 durch die deutsche Wehrmacht und rumänischen Truppen besetzt und fiel 1944 an die Sowjetunion zurück. Strategisch unbedeutend, als Industriestadt zwar überlebensfähig, kulturell jedoch völlig dem Vergessen anheim gestellt, wurde sie zu Chernovsky, einer südwestlichen Provinzstadt der Sowjetunion. Die alte Stadtgesellschaft wurde während des 2. Weltkrieges durch eine Politik der Ausrottung, der Deportationen und Umsiedlungen fast vollständig ausgelöscht. Im Jahr 1991 löste sich die Ukraine von der Sowjetunion. Die ehemals österreichische, dann rumänische, sowjetische Stadt wurde nun ukrainisch und nannte sich Chernivtsi.

Our interest is directed towards the southwestern Ukraine, to former Galicia and the Bukovina. These European cultural regions with their respective capitals Lemberg (now L'viv) and Czernowitz (now Chernivtsi) as former provinces of the Habsburgian Empire had actually been part of the German cultural sphere, a fact that is largely forgotten. With reference to the example of the city of Chernivtsi we aim to investigate the diversity of the European cultural heritage and to study the role of architecture and urbanism as a cultural link of East and West. With its German/Austrian, its Romanian, its Soviet and its Ukrainian history the city's architectural and, in parallel its socio-cultural development over the studied time-frame of 250 years allows a representative study of the Central Eastern European region as a whole.

In 1774 the House of Habsburg annexed the Bukovina and with it the city of Czernowitz, which until then had been part of the principality of Moldova. Its urbanistic and cultural growth began in 1775 with its function as Austria's easternmost garrison town and as the seat of the provincial government. Upon its centenary in 1875, already the capital and administrative center of the crown-province Bukovina, it was bestowed with a university. Czernowitz developed into the southeasternmost European cultural metropolis: prosperous, sophisticated, culturally diverse and tolerant towards its unique polyethnic urban society formed by Ukrainians, Romanians, Jews, Germans, Poles, Roma among others. Around the turn of the century the city reached its cultural apex. As a consequence of the First World War, Czernowitz/Cernauti came under Romanian rule in 1918 and developed and expanded into one of the largest cities of Romania after Bucharest. In the course of the Second World War, the city first came under Soviet rule in 1940, was occupied by German and Romanian troops in 1941, fell back to the Soviet Union in 1944. Strategically unimportant, industrially sustainable and culturally completely irrelevant Czernowitz/Chernovsky had become one of the southwesterly provincial capitals of the Soviet Union. The old urban society was almost completely eradicated during the Second World War through a policy of extermination, deportation and relocation. In 1991 the Ukraine separated from the Soviet Union and the formerly Austrian then Romanian, Soviet city become Ukrainian and called itself Chernivtsi.

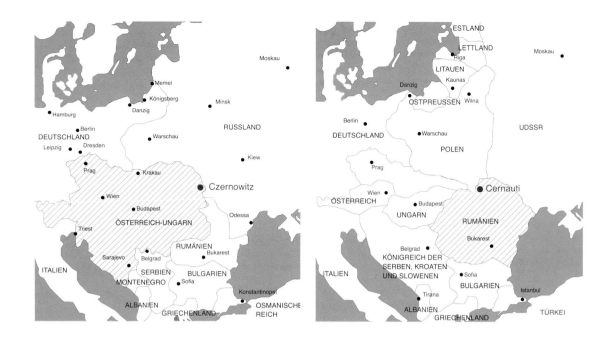

Jede Epoche hat ihre Spuren hinterlassen, die im gegenwärtigen Stadtbild deutlich ablesbar sind. Diese architektonische Vielfalt lässt den Rückschluss zu, dass die Stadtgesellschaft es trotz ihrer zahlreichen Ethnien, Konfessionen und Sprachen verstanden hat, die jeweiligen Repräsentationsansprüche zu moderieren und zu integrieren. Als Architekten interessierte uns dabei die Rolle der Architektur als Überbringer der Vergangenheit, als Hülle der Gegenwart und als Identität stiftendes Medium für die Zukunft. Über drei Jahre beschäftigten wir uns in Entwurfprojekten und begleitenden Seminaren mit der Stadt. Analog zur Chronologie der Geschichte der Stadt konzipierten wir die Themen für die Semesterprojekte: Das erste Projekt "Von Wien bis Odessa – Architektur und Identität im Aufbruch Ostmitteleuropas" beschäftigte sich über zwei Semester mit dem deutsch-österreichischen Einfluss auf Czernowitz/Chernivtsi. Das zweite Projekt "Doppelpunkt Berlin - Bukarest – The German hub of trade and culture in Bucharest" thematisierte den rumänischen Einfluss auf die Stadt und das dritte Projekt "Tomorrow in Czernowitz" setzt sich mit der sowjetischen und postsowjetischen Epoche der Stadt auseinander

left: Czernowitz/Chernivtsi 1914 - Geographical position during the Danube Monarchy

right: Cernauti/Chernivtsi 1923 - Geographical position under Romanian rule

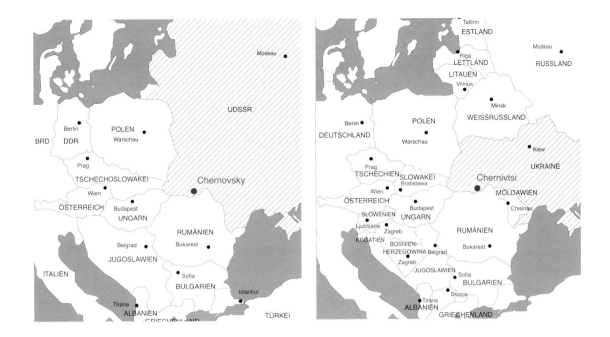

Each epoch left its traces, which can be clearly seen in the present city. This architectural diversity allows the conclusion that the urban society, despite its diverse ethnicities, confessions and languages always understood how to moderate and integrate the prevailing representational claims. As architects we were interested in the role of architecture as a messenger of the past, a mantle of the present and a source of identity for the future. Over the course of three years we worked on the city in design projects and concomitant seminars. Analogous to the chronology of the city's history we created the themes of the semester projects:

The first project over the course of a year "From Vienna to Odessa – Architecture and Identity in the Surge of Central Eastern Europe" concentrated on the German/ Austrian influence on Czernowitz/Chernivtsi. The second project over the course of a semester "Double Point Berlin – Bucharest – The German hub of trade and culture in Bucharest" focused on the Romanian influence on the city while the project "Tomorrow in Czernowitz" engaged in the study of the city's Soviet and post-Soviet periods.

left: Chernovtsy/Chernivtsi 1949 - Geographical position under Soviet Union rule

right : Chernivtsi 1992 - Geographical position within the independent state of Ukraine

View from the tower of the Town Hall towards Chernivtsi's theatre,
built 1904-1905 by the Viennese architects Helmer & Fellner

WIEN 2003
VIENNA 2003

PROJEKT: VON WIEN BIS ODESSA – ARCHI-
TEKTUR UND IDENTITÄT IM AUFBRUCH
OSTMITTELEUROPAS.
EIN OSTMITTELEUROPÄISCHES KULTUR-
UND HANDELS-
ZENTRUM AN DER DONAU.
PROJECT: FROM VIENNA TO ODESSA –
ARCHITECTURE AND IDENTITY IN THE
SURGE OF CENTRAL EASTERN EUROPE
A CENTRAL EASTERN EUROPEAN CENTER
OF CULTURE AND TRADE BY THE DANUBE

WINTERSEMESTER 2003/2004
WINTER SEMESTER 2003/2004

Das Wintersemester 2003/04 diente der Annäherung an die Region Ost-
mitteleuropa und hatte den deutsch-österreichischen Einfluss auf die Region zum
Thema. Eine Studienreise führte uns nach Wien, Hauptstadt der österreich-ungarischen
Monarchie, zu deren Gebiet große Teile der Untersuchungsregion gehörten. In
Zusammenarbeit mit Prof. Dr. Werner Sewing widmeten wir uns der Epoche der
Habsburger Monarchie und dem Einfluss der Wiener Hochkultur auf die Architektur
und Stadtkultur in Lemberg/L´viv und Czernowitz/Chernivtsi sowie der Frage, in wiefern
sich aus dem ehemaligen Vielvölkerstaat der österreich-ungarischen Doppelmonarchie
etwas übertragen lassen könnte auf das heutige multinationale Europa.

Excursion to Vienna 2003, group picture in front of the Imperial Palace

The semester was intended to further the familiarization with the Central Eastern European region and to illustrate the German/Austrian influence in the area. A study trip took us to Vienna, the capital of the Austro-Hungarian Monarchy, which controlled large parts of the studied region. In a seminar conducted by Dr. Werner Sewing the students dedicated themselves to the epoch of the Habsburgian monarchy and to the influence of the Viennese culture on architecture and urban culture in Lemberg/L'viv and Czernowitz/Chernivtsi, as well as the question, whether something could be transposed from that multiethnic state into the present multinational Europe.

Kärntner Strasse, the main pedestrian boulevard in Vienna

Wien als Hauptstadt und Sitz des Kaisers beeinflusste die städtebauliche und architektonische Entwicklung in den Kronländern der Monarchie zu großen Teilen. Viele in Wien ausgebildete Architekten gingen in die Kronländer, um dort ihr Wissen anzuwenden, und viele in Wien etablierte Architekten bauten in den Kronländern nach dem gleichen Schema wie sie es in der Hauptstadt taten. Uns interessierte die Architektur- und Stadtentwicklung Wiens, um Wiederholungen, Ähnlichkeiten oder Abwandlungen in den von uns als Schwerpunkt gewählten Städten Lemberg und Czernowitz im Rückschluss auf Wien beurteilen zu können. Was wir bisher in Literatur und Film über beide Städte erfahren hatten, so war die Verwandtschaft mit Wien unverkennbar. Das geistige und kulturelle Klima unter der Herrschaft Kaiser Franz Josefs hat beide Städte in ihrer Gestalt und ihrer Lebensform geprägt. Die Ringplätze, die Ringstrassen, die Bahnhöfe und Kaffeehäuser existieren noch heute und erinnern an ihre ursprüngliche Herkunft und Funktion. Eine Replik, die fernab der österreichischen Hauptstadt eine vergleichbare Lebensform möglich machen sollte?

previous page: Similar facade style in Chernivtsi and Vienna around the turn of the century

left: Lamppost in front of the Viennese coffeehouse on Koblyanska Street, formerly called the Herrengasse

right: Art museum, Central Square, former municipal savings bank, built in 1908

Vienna as the Austrian capital and residence of the emperor significantly influenced the town planning and architectural development in the crown-provinces. Many architects were trained in Vienna and set out into the crown-provinces to apply their knowledge while many established Viennese architects transposed the schemes developed and employed in the capital into the crownprovinces. We were interested in the architectural and urbanistic development of Vienna, in order to assess repetitions, similarities and modifications in the cities of Lemberg and Czernowitz. What we had seen until then in literature and film of the two cities rendered the relationship with Vienna undeniable. The intellectual and cultural atmosphere under the rule of Emperor Franz Josef shaped both cities in their form and way of life. The circular town squares, circular roads, the train stations or the coffee houses still exist and remind of their origins. A replica intended to allow a comparable life-style far from the Austrian capital?

Koblyanska Street, formerly the Herrengasse, the main pedestrian boulevard in Chernivtsi

Für das angebotene Entwurfsprojekt in Wien wählten wir als Standort eine unmittelbar an der Donau gelegene Fläche im Nordosten der Stadt aus. Grund dafür war zum einen die unmittelbare Lage an der Donau, die als "blauer" Faden und Verkehrsweg durch das zusammenwachsende Europa führt, zum andern suchten wir einen Ort, der möglichst viel Raum für eine freie und individuelle Gestaltung zulassen würde. Als Aufgabe sollten die Studierenden ein Kultur- und Handels-zentrum für die Länder Slowenien, Ungarn, Rumänien, Ukraine und Moldawien entwerfen, das als Plattform und Kontaktbörse zwischen den östlichen und west-lichen Teilen Europas dienen sollte. Insbesondere galt es, jedem Handelszentrum ein dem Land entsprechendes Image zu geben, welches sich in der Gebäudegestalt und dem Raumprogramm darstellen sollte. Um entscheiden zu können, womit sich das jeweilige Land repräsentieren liesse, erstellten die Studenten zunächst ein Portrait des zu repräsentierenden Landes mit seinen "typischen" Merkmalen im Bereich Geografie, Wirtschaft, Kultur, Architektur und Kunst.

Handelskai, location for the design-project next to the Danube in the north east of Vienna

For the proposed design-project in Vienna, the chosen location was an area next to the Danube in the Northeast of the city. One reason for this was the location immediately next to the Danube – as a "blue" line and transport link through an integrating Europe – and, simultaneously the objective for the site to offer as much room as possible for a free and individual concept. As an assignment, the students should design a center for culture and trade for the countries Slovenia, Hungary, Rumania, the Ukraine, and Moldova, which should act as a platform and meeting place of the western and eastern parts of Europe. It was of particular importance to give each trade center an image corresponding to the respective country, which should be represented in the form of the building and the space allocation plan. To decide how the country should be represented, the students first created a portrait of the country, embodying its "typical" geographic, economic, cultural, architectural and artistic characteristics.

Projektauswahl Wintersemester 2003/04
Selection of Projects Winter Semester 2003/04
IDENTITÄTSFRAGMENTE
IDENTITY FRAGMENTS

Gruppenarbeit von *Hans-Georg Bauer, Stephen Knuth Molloy, Beatriz Perez, Lisa Wameling*
Teamwork by *Hans-Georg Bauer, Stephen Knuth Molloy, Beatriz Perez, Lisa Wameling*

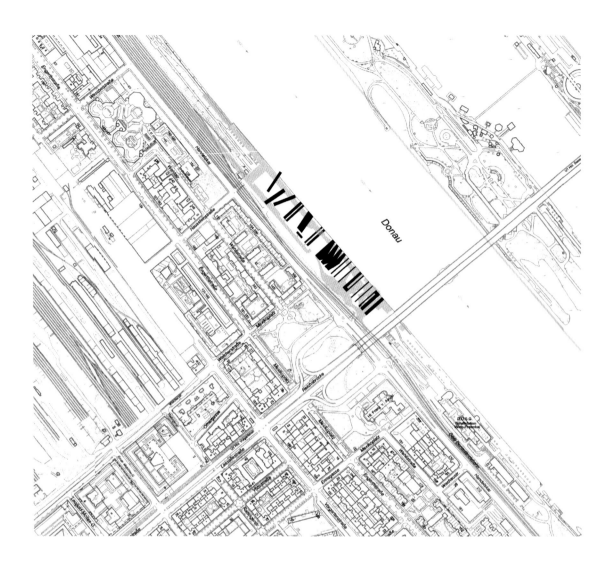

"Die osteuropäische Identität hat dank ihrer spezifischen Lebenskraft und Kreativität ihren Weg durch das Labyrinth von Imperialismus, Faschismus, Kommunismus und National-ismus gefunden. Die Intervention an der Donau am Handelskaiufer in Wien präsentiert sich als eine Serie von beliebigen Strukturen. Die überdimensionierten Betonplatten schaffen einen Rahmen für eine Reihe von kulturellen Aktivitäten, welche die Platten durchbrechen, sie umschlängeln und sich dazwischen einnisten. Die Bauten sind in einer Reihe organisiert, so dass die Platten zum Fluss hin eine offene Kolonnade formen. Dadurch bildet sich ein Verbindungsweg, der die Fußgänger zu den Funktionen führt, ohne sie vom Fluss zu trennen."

Site plan, scale 1:5000

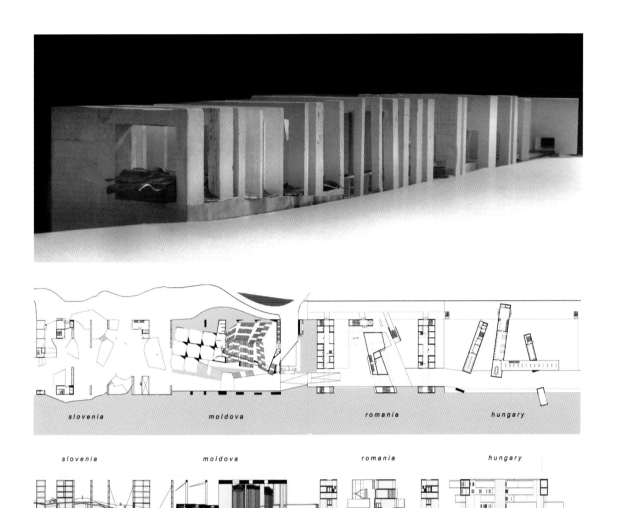

slovenia   moldova   romania   hungary

slovenia   moldova   romania   hungary

"The East European identity has, thanks to its specific life force and creativity, found its way through a labyrinth of Imperialism, Fascism, Communism and Nationalism. The intervention next to the Danube, on the Viennese "Handelskaiufer" presents itself as a series of random structures. The over-proportionate concrete slabs create a frame for a series of cultural activities, which intersect the slabs, meander around and nest in between them. The buildings are organized in a line so that the slabs form an open colonnade towards the river. This forms a connecting path which guides the visitors to the functions without separating them from the river."

Model 1:500, first floor plan and section, scale 1:500

roof plan scale 1/500

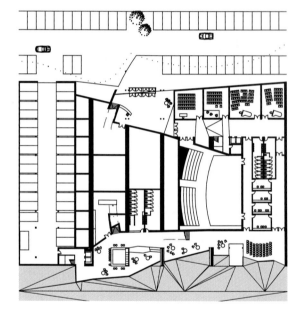

SLOVENIEN – MUSICADANUBIANA
bearbeitet von *Beatriz Perez*

"Musicadanubiana ist ein Ort für Musikevents in Wien. Junge internationale Gruppen und Musikfreunde treffen sich hier und tauschen sich aus. Die Idee kommt von dem Festival Musica Danubiana, das zum ersten Mal im Jahre 1982 als eine interessante musikalische Idee veranstaltet wurde: Das Ziel war, eine Verbindung unter den mitteleuropäischen Ländern über alte Musik zu schaffen. Musikwissenschaftler und Musikjournalisten aus der Slowakei, Rumänien, der Schweiz und Ungarn engagierten sich in Diskussionen über mittelalterliche und barocke Musik."

Interior perspective, roof plan and ground floor plan, scale 1:500

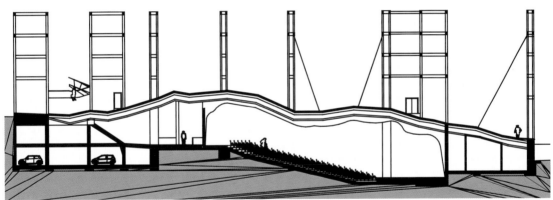

SLOVENIA – MUSICADANUBIANA
by *Beatriz Perez*

"Musicadanubiana is a location for music events in Vienna. Young international groups and music enthusiasts meet here and exchange ideas. The idea comes from the festival Musica Danubiana which was first organized in 1982 as an interesting musical idea: The objective was to create a link among the Central European countries through old music. Musicologists and music journalists from Slovakia, Romania, Switzerland and Hungary engaged in discussions on medieval and baroque music."

Interior perspective and section, scale 1:500

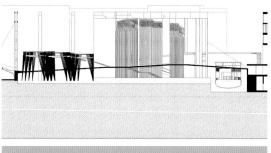

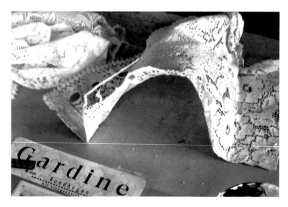

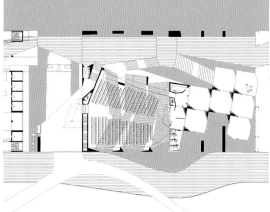

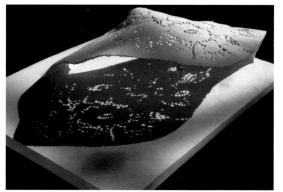

MOLDAVIEN – HOCHZEITSPAVILLION
bearbeitet von *Stephen Knuth Molloy*

"Dieses Projekt rettet das Konzept der säkularen Hochzeitszeremonie. Genau so wie Osteuropa religiöse Traditionen willkommen heißt, die vom Kommunismus abgelehnt worden sind, so sind Westeuropäer mehr und mehr daran interessiert, ihre individualistische Beziehung zu Tradition und Religionen zu definieren. Moldawien bietet seine unbeachtete Tradition dem Westen an. Das tektonische Konzept ist aus der Zweideutigkeit des Brautschleiers gewachsen, der Pavillon bietet eine spielerische Teildeckung an."

left: Section and first floor plan, scale 1:500

above right: concept formulation

middle right: dappled light

below right: ceremonial space

MOLDOVA – WEDDING PAVILION
by *Stephen Knuth Molloy*

"This project rescues the concept of the secular wedding ceremony. Just as Eastern Europe welcomes religious traditions which were rejected by the communist ideology, Western Europeans are more and more interested in defining their individualistic relation to tradition and religion. Moldova offers its unappreciated tradition to the West. The tectonic concept grew from the duality of the bridal veil, the pavilion offers a playful partial cover."

above: Departure (dinner guests)

below: Arrival (bright)

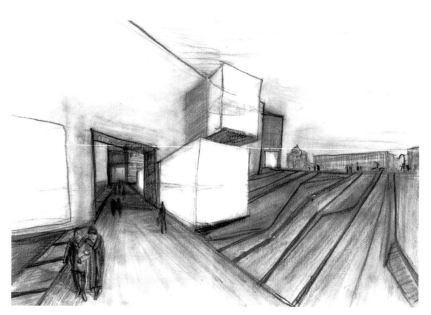

UNGARN – LITERATURLANDSCHAFT
bearbeitet von *Lisa Wameling*

"Die Ungarn überlebten die Völkerwanderung, indem sie sesshaft und national wurden und zugleich eine offene und europäische Haltung einnahmen. Dies wird durch den Städtebau meines Literaturzentrums mit nebeneinander stehenden, sich zur Donau hin auffächernden Wänden und diese durchdringenden Körpern reflektiert. Literatur und Sprache sind große Themen der Ungarn, welche ständig an ihrem Wortschatz feilten und ihn erweiterten, und in deren Reihen sich zahlreiche international herausragende Schriftsteller und Poeten befinden. Das gesamte Gebäude gleicht einem aufgeschlagenen Buch. Bilder und Geschichten spielen sich zwischen seinen Seiten ab."

above: Atmospheric perspective of the building

below left: Interior perspective of the literary landscape

below right: concept formulation

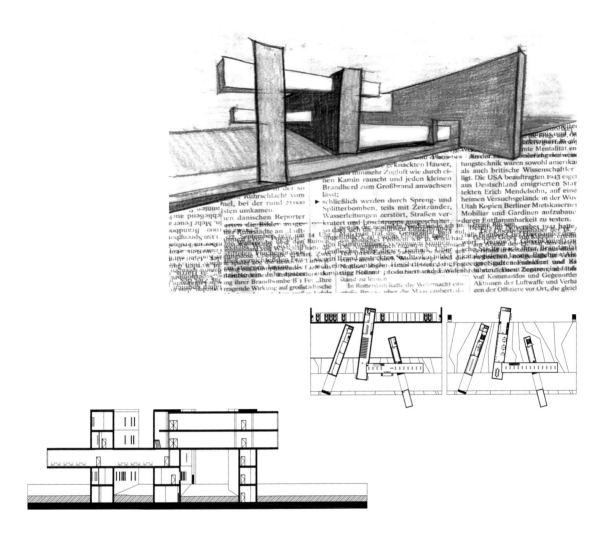

HUNGARY – LITERARY LANDSCAPE
by *Lisa Wameling*

"The Hungarians survived the migration waves by settling down and developing a national identity while adopting an open and European attitude – this is reflected in my literary center with juxtaposed walls that fan out towards the Danube and the forms that intersect them. Literature and language are important topics for the Hungarians, which permanently developed and expanded their body of language and whose ranks include numerous internationally recognized authors and poets. The entire building resembles an open book; pictures and history unfold between its pages."

above: Sketch of the building volume

middle: floor plan, scale 1:500

below: Section, scale 1:500

CZERNOWITZ 2004
CHERNIVTSI 2004

PROJEKT: VON WIEN BIS ODESSA – ARCHITEKTUR UND IDENTITÄT
IM AUFBRUCH OSTMITTELEUROPAS
IDEEN-NETZ-WERK STADT CZERNOWITZ/CHERNIVTSI
PROJECT: FROM VIENNA TO ODESSA – ARCHITECTURE AND IDENTITY
IN THE SURGE OF CENTRAL EASTERN EUROPE
IDEA-NET-WORK CITY CZERNOWITZ/CHERNIVTSI

SOMMERSEMESTER 2004
SUMMER SEMESTER 2004

Nach dem ersten Entwurfsprojekt in Wien folgte das Projekt in Czernowitz/ Chernivtsi. Begonnen haben wir mit einer durch den DAAD geförderten Studienfahrt in die Ukraine mit Besichtigung der Städte L´viv, Chernivtsi und Odessa. Ziel war es, sich ein Bild von der gegenwärtigen Situation in den Städten zu machen. Unser Schwerpunkt lag auf Czernowitz/Chernivtsi. Wir wollten aktuelle Tendenzen im Bereich Stadtplanung und Architektur herauszufinden und Kontakte zum ansässigen Stadt- planungsamt und auch zu Bewohnern der Stadt knüpfen. Aus den Gesprächen und Erfahrungen sollte sich unsere Entwurfsaufgabe ableiten lassen.

Schon im Wintersemester 2003/2004 trafen wir über den Kontakt eines Kollegen eine durch den DAAD geförderte Reisegruppe der Universität Chernivtsi zu einem Gespräch in Dresden. Wir berichteten von unseren Plänen, im Sommersemester 2004 ein Entwurfsprojekt in Chernivtsi durchführen zu wollen. Die Idee rief große Begeisterung und Zuspruch hervor. Wir bekamen die sofortige Zusage für Unterstützung vor Ort. Ihor Zhaloba, damaliger Direktor der Universitätsbibliothek in Chernivtsi und Leiter der Gruppe, wurde zu unserem ersten Ansprechpartner für die Planung und Umsetzung des Projektes. Er stellte die für uns wichtigen Kontakte zu Switlana Bilenkova im Stadtplanungsamt und Sergij Osatchuk vom Bukowina Zentrum an der Universität Chernivtsi her.

Subsequent to the first design project in Vienna, we presented the following project in Czernowitz/Chernivtsi. We started with a research trip to the Ukraine sponsored by the DAAD. This included the cities of L'viv, Chernivtsi and Odessa. The objective was to acquire, in situ, an image of the local situation, although our emphasis was on Czernowitz/Chernivtsi. We wanted to find out the current tendencies in the areas of urban development and architecture as well as to establish contact with the local urban planning office as well as inhabitants of the city. From the conversations and experiences we intended to derive our design assignment.

Already in the winter semester 2003/04 a meeting arranged by a colleague allowed us to meet a travel group of the University in Chernivtsi sponsored by the DAAD. At the meeting in Dresden we talked about our plan to do a design project in Chernivtsi. The idea sparked great enthusiasm and we received the immediate promise of local support. Ihor Zhaloba, then director of the university library in Cher-nivtsi and the head of the group became our first contact person for the planning and realization of the project. He made the important contacts for us with Switlana Bilenkova in the urban planning office and Sergij Osatchuk of the Bukowina Centre at the Czernowitz University.

Map of Ukraine

Field Study: On the roof of the former *Hotel Bristol, Plosha Filarmonij* formerly the *Rudolfsplatz*

Im April 2004 fand unsere Studienreise in die Ukraine in eine uns unbekannt bekannte Welt statt. Wir erlebten Städte, die uns im ersten Moment von ihrem Stadtbild her bekannt vorkamen. Europäische Metropolen: Boulevards, Alleen, Marktplätze, Prachtbauten in Historismus und Jugendstil, denen man den Glamour einer längst vergangenen Blütezeit noch zum Greifen nahe ansah. Und doch war etwas irritierend fremd: Die Schaufensterauslagen passten nicht zu den Gebäuden, die Gäste nicht zum pompös anmutenden Grandhotel. Heute lebt hier eine Stadtgesellschaft unter anderen Vorzeichen und spricht eine andere Sprache. Bedeutungen und Funktionen von Gebäuden und Stadträumen haben sich im Laufe der Geschichte verändert. In Chernivtsi spürten wir am stärksten den Widerspruch zwischen ursprünglicher Gebäudefunktion und heutiger Nutzung. Wenn kein Nutzungswandel stattgefunden hat, blieben die Gebäude häufig ungenutzt. So konnten wir beispielsweise das im Original erhaltene Theater und die Philharmonie der Stadt besichtigen, eine Vorstellung jedoch nicht besuchen. Beide Häuser werden kaum bespielt, es fehlt an finanziellen Mitteln. Das ehemalige Hotel Bristol ist dagegen vollständig bewohnt, es wird als Studentenwohnheim genutzt. Der ehemalige israelitische Tempel beherbergt heute ein Kino, und das ehemalige Hotel Bellevue ist Sitz der örtlichen Presse. Uns fiel auf, dass in Lemberg und Odessa der Einfluss des westlichen Kapitalismus stärker war. Es gab erste Fast-Food-Ketten, europäische Banken und westliche Produkte. Noch liegt Chernivtsi offensichtlich im Schatten der rasanten wirtschaftlichen Entwicklungen in der Ukraine, Lage und Größe der Stadt sind für Investoren bisher nicht attraktiv genug gewesen.

Regional Philharmonic Society built in 1877, *Plosha Filarmonij*

In April 2004 our research trip to the Ukraine took us into an unfamiliarly familiar world. We experienced cities, which at first sight appeared accustomed. European metropolis: boulevards, alleys, market squares, representative eclectic and Art deco buildings which still exuded the glamour of a long-gone golden age. Still something was different: the articles in the window display did not reflect of the buildings, the look of the guests did not fit in the pretentious Grand Hotel. The present urban society has different origins and speaks a different language. Relevance and functions of many buildings and urban spaces bleibt changed in the course of history. In the modern Chernivtsi we felt the strongest contrast between the former significance of the buildings and the present utilization. If there was no change of utilization, the buildings were frequently unused. For example, it was possible to visit the theatre and the philharmonic hall of city, but difficult to attend a performance. Both buildings are seldomly used as financial resources are missing. The former Hotel Bristol, however, was completely inhabited, it was used as student accommodation. The former Israelite Temple today houses a cinema and the former Hotel Bellevue functions as the seat of the local press. We noted that in Lemberg or Odessa, the influence of Western capitalism was stronger. The first fast-food chains, European banks and Western products existed. Chernivtsi still lies in the shadow of the rapid economic development of the Ukraine. Location and size apparently still are insufficiently attractive for investors.

Durch die vor Ort geführten Gespräche mit Stadtplanern, Architekten, Historikern und Literaten konnten wir uns ein Bild von der derzeitigen Situation der Stadt machen und eine Ahnung erhalten von den Problemen der Bewohner ihren Wünschen und Ideen. Oft ging es nur darum zu überleben und durch einen minimalen Einsatz von Geld und Arbeitskraft den Erhalt der Bausubstanz zu ermöglichen. Für sie war es keineswegs Konsens, dass in der Vergangenheit der Stadt auch das Potential ihrer Zukunft liegt, einem Mythos, der in unzähligen Zeitschriften, Romanen, historischen und persönlichen Überlieferungen festgehalten ist. Wir erfuhren von engen Kontakten nach Rumänien und Österreich und fanden heraus, wo eine Übereinstimmung von Notwendigem und Wünschenswertem für die zukünftige Entwicklung der Stadt liegen könnte. Wir stellten fest, dass auch Chernivtsi dabei war, sein Erbe zu sichten und anzutreten: Ein Antrag zur Aufnahme in die Liste der UNESCO zum Weltkulturerbe war bereits gestellt.

above: Theatre Square, Teatral'na Plosha, popular spot for young people

below: Chervnia Street looking south-west

The locally held conversations with urban planners, architects, historians and writers enabled us to derive a picture of the present situation in the city and to obtain an insight into the ideas and problems of its inhabitants. We noted that Chernivtsi was engaged in viewing and take up its inheritance: an application for UNESCO's world heritage list had already been issued. We learned of close contacts to Romania and Austria and found a concurrence of the desirable and the necessary for the future development of the city. To our surprise the common language was frequently German. During the conversations it became clear to us that not all of the questions we posed directly touched the pressing problems of the city and its inhabitants. It was often a question of trying to survive and to sustain the built substance with a minimum of money and effort.

It was not clear to all inhabitants that the potential for the present and the future could lie in the city's past, a myth held down in innumerable magazines, romances, historical and personal stories of events, offers a unique chance. We set ourselves the objective to reconstruct the historic development of the city and its multiethnic urban society through architecture and urbanism and to derive proposals with regard to the city's potential in development. We wanted to present our works publicly in Chernivtsi and discuss with its inhabitants to create awarenessof the city's hidden potentials.

View over the city towards Yuriy Fedkovych Chernivtsi National University, formerly the archbishop's residence, completed in 1875

Zurück in Berlin setzten wir uns zum Ziel, die historische Entwicklung der Stadt und ihrer polyethnischen Stadtgesellschaft anhand von Architektur und Städtebau zu rekonstruieren und daraus resultierend Vorschläge im Hinblick auf Entwicklungspotentiale der Stadt zu machen. Die Entwurfskonzepte sollten die folgenden Kriterien erfüllen: Sie sollten sich unter dem Aspekt der kulturellen Identität mit den Defiziten und Potentialen der Stadt auseinandersetzen und Lösungen vorschlagen. Die konzeptionellen und inhaltlichen Entwürfe sollten Impulse auf die ausgewählten Orte und deren unmittelbare Umgebung auslösen und entsprechend ihrer städtebaulichen und funktionalen Gegebenheit bespielt werden. Die Integration der inhaltlichen und gebäudeplanerischen Konzepte in das urbane Gefüge der Stadt sollte ein kulturelles Netzwerk ergeben, das der Stadt Profil und Attraktivität verleiht. Die Wahl fiel auf die folgenden Orte in der Innenstadt: Tsentral'na plosha, ehem. Ringplatz; Platz gegenüber ehem. Israelitischen Tempel; plosha Filarmoniji, ehem. Philharmonieplatz; Soborna plosha, ehem. Austriaplatz; pamjatnyk Paulyu Celanu, Paul Celan Denkmal; wulytsja Kobylyans'koji, ehem. Herrengasse; wulytsja Rus'ka, Ruskastrasse.

The former Israelite temple today houses a cinema, built 1873-1877

Back in Berlin, we presented the design assignment. Proposals were to be developed for seven chosen downtown locations, which should both confront identity and present deficits/potentials of the city in the cultural area. The designs were expected to provide impulses for their immediate surroundings and to develop the locations in accordance with their town planning and functional requirements. The thematic and conceptual integration of these design proposals into the city centre's urban structure was to give rise to a cultural network, which would bestow an individual profile and a new level of attractiveness on the city. The planned cultural network was intended to refer thematically both to the past as well as the present and future position of the city Czernowitz/Chernivtsi: as a place of understanding with the confidence for an international selfperception. The choice was between the following locations in the city centre: Tsentral'na plosha, the central square; the square opposite the former Israelite Temple; plosha Filarmonij, the square in front of the philharmonic hall; Soborna plosha, the former Austrian square; pamjatnyk Paulyu Celanu, the Paul Celan monument; wulytsja Kobylyans'koji, the former Herrengasse; wulytsja Rus'ka, Ruska street.

Impression of the city

Da die Möglichkeiten der Erneuerung in einer Stadt wie Chernivtsi vielfältig sind und einen langwierigen Prozess voraussetzen, schien es uns sinnvoll, durch die Veranstaltung einer Sommerakademie Kontakt und Dialog zwischen Bewohnern und Studenten herzustellen. Neben den gebäudeplanerischen Entwürfen entstanden Vorschläge für temporäre Installationen im historischen Gefüge der Stadt. Als eine Plattform der Begegnung und des Austausches sollten hier die Vorschläge der Studenten öffentlich gezeigt und mit den Bürgern der Stadt diskutiert werden.

Of course the possibilities of renewal in a city like Chernivtsi are numerous and require a long process. Therefore it appeared sensible to us in the first design phase to develop contact and dialogue between inhabitants and students through a summer academy. Next to the designs concerning architectural planning, this gave rise to proposals for temporary installations in the historic ensemble of the city. Locations that shape the urban space were to be engaged in differing thematic use to provide a platform for contacts and the exchange of ideas.

Central Square, Tsentral'na plosha, formerly the Ringplatz – used to be the heart of the city centre surrounded by hotels, shops and coffeehouses.

Projektauswahl Sommersemester 2004
Selection of Projects Summer Semester 2004

Radio Czernowitz
Archiv 1
Spielwiese

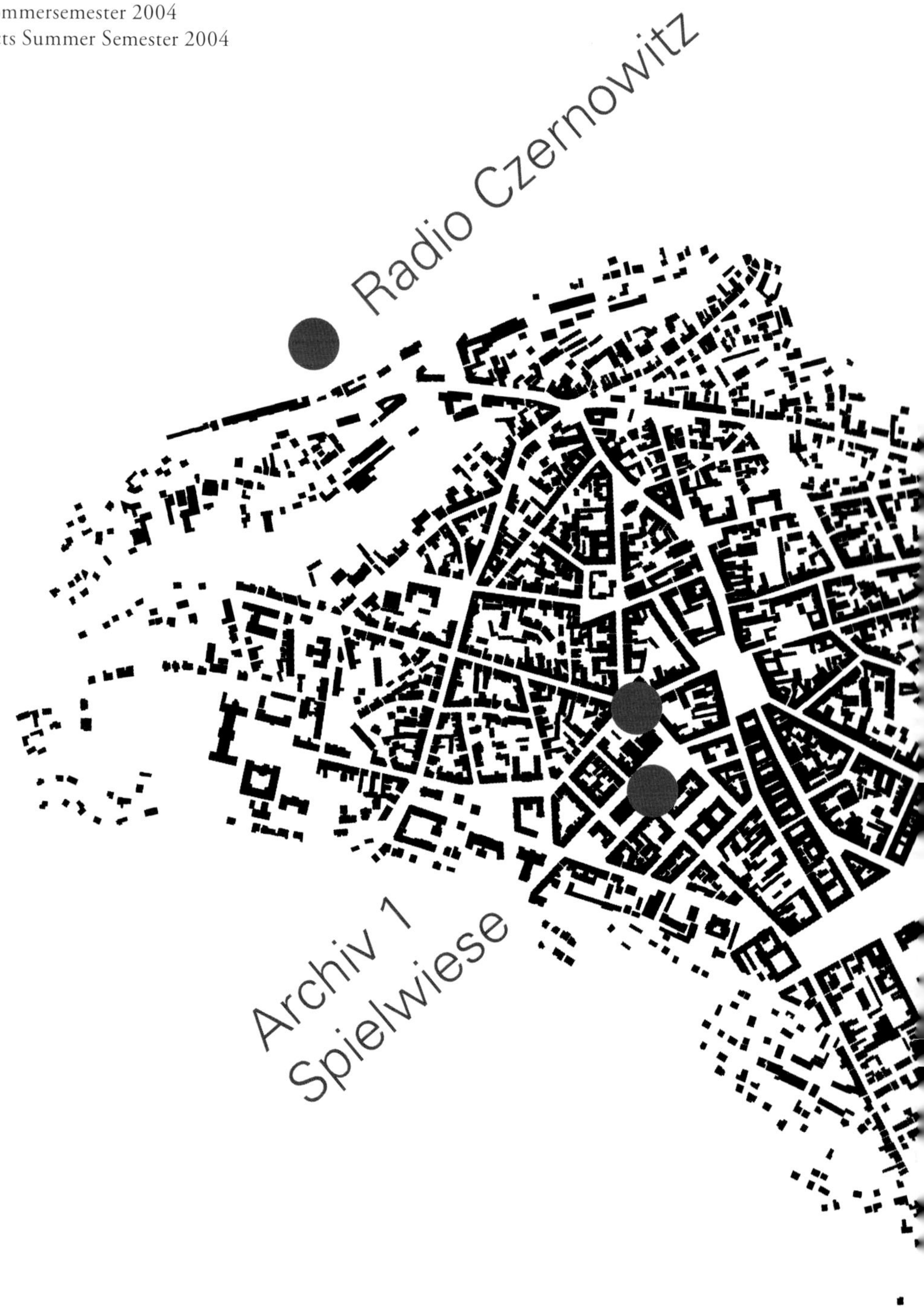

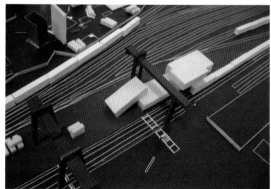

KULTURBAHNHOF - BAHNHOFSKULTUR
'RADIO CZERNOWITZ'
Entwurfsprojekt von *Christian Wentzel*

"Czernowitz ist eine Kulturstadt. Es weiß bloß keiner! "Radio Czernowitz", ist die architektonische Umnutzung des vorhandenen Güterbahnhofs in einen Kultur-Bahnhof mit Museum, Bibliothek, Bühne und Kino sowie mit einer Radiostation. Sender ist der Kultur-Bahnhof, Empfänger sind die an prägnanten Orten in Czernowitz aufgestellten Großleinwände. Das Gebäude selber dient dem Kulturaustausch, auch via Bahn. Entwurfsbestimmend für "Radio Czernowitz" waren die erhalten gebliebenen Container und russischen Schwerlastkräne. Sie sind nicht nur markantes Erscheinungsbild! Für den Kultur-Bahnhof werden sie wieder revitalisiert. Die Kultur kann also sprichwörtlich "in vollen Zügen" wieder Einzug halten. "Welcome to Radio Czernowitz".

above: Large panels set up in key city locations serve as transmitters of cultural events

below: Model of the Culture Train Station, scale 1:500

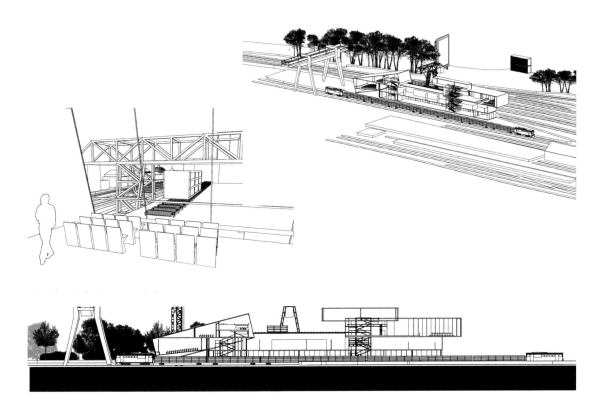

CULTURE TRAIN STATION – TRAIN STATION CULTURE
"RADIO CZERNOWITZ"
Design project by *Christian Wentzel*

     "Czernowitz is a city of culture. But nobody knows it! "Radio Czernowitz" is the architectonic reutilization of the existing freight train station in a culture train station with a museum, library, stage and cinema, as well as a radio station. The culture train station serves as a broadcasting station: large panels set up in poignant places of the city function as its receivers. The building itself serves the cultural exchange, also via rail. Determining the design for "Radio Czernowitz" are the preserved containers and Russian heavy load cranes. They are not merely impressive imagery. For the culture train station they are revitalised. Culture can also – figuratively – return "full steam". "Welcome to Radio Czernowitz".

above: Axonometric projection, scale 1:500

middle: Interior perspective of the cinema lounge

below: Section, scale 1:500

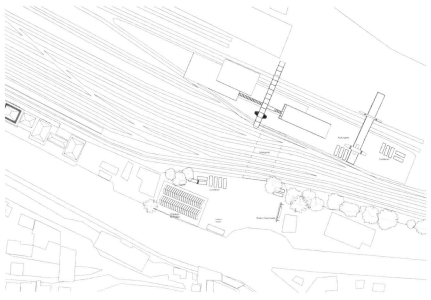

left page: : Collage of the main elevation, ground floor plan, scale 1:500

above: Arrival of the train

SPIELWIESE - INSTALLATION AM THEATERPLATZ: WORKSHOPS FÜR THEATER UND TANZ
Entwurfsprojekt von *Thomas Werner*

"Von einem Tag auf den anderen erhebt sich inmitten des Theaterplatzes ein 10m x 10m x 10m großer Kubus aus geschnürten Palettenpaketen und Schalplatten mit einem nebenstehenden 30m hohem Turmdrehkran, die als Ensemble den gewohnten Blick auf das dahinter liegende Stadttheater versperren und zu einer spontanen Irritation der Czernowitzer Sehgewohnheiten führen. Aus diesem Palettenarsenal entstehen vier permanente Installationen, welche die umliegenden funktionalen Gegebenheiten in ironischer Weise erweitern sollen: einen Busstop, das Café Quatro, die Skybox und die Lovelounges. Weiter verteilt sich nun der Palettenkubus im Laufe des Tages je nach Bedarf auf dem gesamten Theaterplatz, der somit zur Spielwiese, selbst zur Bühne wird."

left: Theatre Square, 10 a.m.: The pallet-cube is complete

right: Theatre Square, 6 p.m.: The pallet-cube transforms into an open-air theatre

PLAYING FIELDS – INSTALLATION ON THE THEATRE SQUARE: WORK
SHOPS FOR THEATRE AND DANCE
Design project by *Thomas Werner*

"From one day to another on the middle of the Theatre Square a 10m x 10m x 10m cube rises, formed of bound pallet-packets and formwork panels. As an ensemble with the juxtaposed 30m high swing crane they obstruct the view of the City Theatre, leading to a spontaneous irritation of the visual habits of Czernowitz's inhabitants. Out of this arsenal of pallets, four permanent installations develop which expand the surrounding functional enteties in an ironic fashion: A bus stop, the Café Quatro, the Skybox, and the Love Lounges. The pallet-cube spreads out over the Theatre Square in the course of the day according to the requirements. The Theatre Square thus becomes a playing field, turning into a stage itself."

Theatre Square, 4 p.m.: The pallet-cube transforms into a rehearsal stage

Theatre Square, 9 p.m.: Stage performance

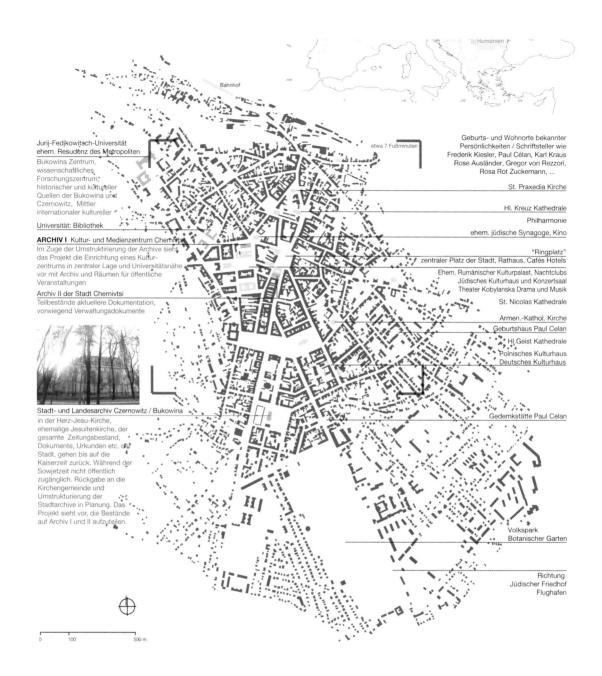

Bahnhof

Humanien

etwa 7 Fußminuten

Jurij-Fedjkowitsch-Universität
ehem. Resudenz des Metropoliten

Bukowina Zentrum,
wissenschaftliches
Forschungszentrum,
historischer und kultureller
Quellen der Bukowina und
Czernowitz, Mittler
internationaler kultureller

Universität: Bibliothek

ARCHIV I Kultur- und Medienzentrum Chernivtsi
Im Zuge der Umstruktirierung der Archive sieht
das Projekt die Einrichtung eines Kulturzentrums in zentraler Lage und Universitätsnähe
vor mit Archiv und Räumen für öffentliche
Veranstaltungen

Archiv II der Stadt Chernivtsi
Teilbestände aktuellere Dokumentation,
vorwiegend Verwaltungsdokumente

Stadt- und Landesarchiv Czernowitz / Bukowina
in der Herz-Jesu-Kirche,
ehemalige Jesuitenkirche, der
gesamte Zeitungsbestand,
Dokumente, Urkunden etc. der
Stadt, gehen bis auf die
Kaiserzeit zurück. Während der
Sowjetzeit nicht öffentlich
zugänglich. Rückgabe an die
Kirchengemeinde und
Umstrukturierung der
Stadtarchive in Planung. Das
Projekt sieht vor, die Bestände
auf Archiv I und II aufzuteilen.

Geburts- und Wohnorte bekannter
Persönlichkeiten / Schriftsteller wie
Frederik Kiesler, Paul Célan, Karl Kraus
Rose Ausländer, Gregor von Rezzori,
Rosa Rot Zuckermann, ...

St. Praxedia Kirche

Hl. Kreuz Kathedrale

Philharmonie

ehem. jüdische Synagoge, Kino

"Ringplatz"
zentraler Platz der Stadt, Rathaus, Cafés Hotels

Ehem. Rumänischer Kulturpalast, Nachtclubs
Jüdisches Kulturhaus und Konzertsaal
Theater Kobylanska Drama und Musik

St. Nicolas Kathedrale

Armen.-Kathol. Kirche

Geburtshaus Paul Celan

Hl.Geist Kathedrale

Polnisches Kulturhaus
Deutsches Kulturhaus

Gedemkstätte Paul Celan

Volkspark
Botanischer Garten

Richtung
Jüdischer Friedhof
Flughafen

0   100   500 m

ARCHIV 1 – KULTUR- UND MEDIENZENTRUM, GEDÄCHTNIS DER
STADT CHERNIVTSI/CZERNOWITZ
Diplomarbeit von *Kathrin Lind*

Memory of the cultural capital of Chernivtsi: Scientific-, historical-, and tourist sites

um 1890
Parzellierung nord-süd, Kasernengelände

um 1910
Blockrandbebauung in Planung, erster Bau
am Platz ist das Jüdische Kulturhaus mit
neobarocker Fassade, fasst den
Elisabethplatzt ein zusammen mit dem
Neubau des Theaters

1930/40
Rumänischer Kulturpalast: Kammbebauung
in Planung mit Hauptfassade zum
Theaterplatz, die Synagoge wird 1941
zerstört.

Planung
Die Blockecke wird als Platz ausgebildet,
entsprechend der üblichen Positionierung
von Kulturbauten in der Stadt. Belebung
eines zentralen Ortes durch Generieren
eines Kreuzungspunktes

ARCHIVE I – CULTURE AND MEDIA CENTRE, REMEMBRANCE OF THE CITY CHERNIVTSI/CZERNOWITZ
Diploma project by *Kathrin Lind*

Urban Development of the site

"Bei diesem Projekt mit realem Hintergrund ging es darum, eine Strategie zu entwickeln zur Neuordnung und Öffnung der städtischen Archive und zur Einbettung in das stadträumliche Wissens- und Gedächtnisnetzwerk. Das Gebäude ist ein Hybrid aus Museum, Mediathek und Archiv. Im Sinne eines ‚Schaulagers' schafft es Synergien, indem es die kulturelle Produktion, das Erlebnis derselben und die Dokumentation unter einem Dach stattfinden lässt. Das Archiv 1 und Medienzentrum ist als Kulturarchiv der Stadt geplant. Es nimmt Publikationen, Literatur, Musik und Kunst von der Stadt-gründung bis heute auf und macht sie öffentlich zugänglich. Es ist eine Trägerschaft der Stadt in Kooperation mit der Universität Chernivtsi vorgesehen. Zentral zwischen Universität und Rathausplatz gelegen ist das Archiv 1 und Medienzentrum erster

above: Interior perspective, entry hall

below: Interior perspective, exhibition space

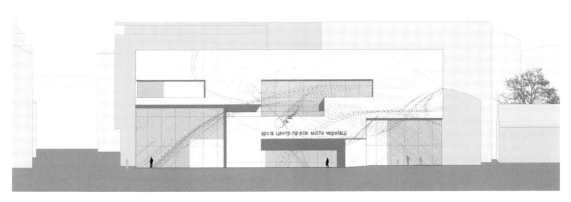

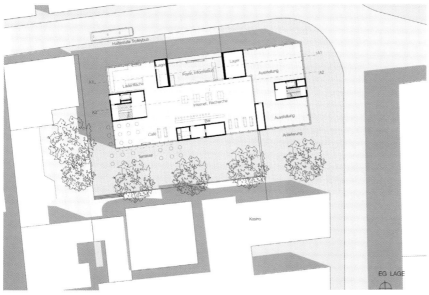

"In this project, which has a real background, the objective was to develop a strategy for the reorganization and for rendering accessible the city's archives and to embed it in the urban knowledge and remembrance-network. The building is a hybrid between a museum, a multi-media library and an archive: In the sense of a "display stor" it generates synergies by uniting cultural production, its experience and documentation under one roof. The Archive1 and Media Centre is planned as the cultural archive of the city. It takes in publications, literature, music and art from the founding of the city to this date and makes it publicly accessible. A sponsorship by the city council in cooperation with Chernivtsi University is envisaged. Located centrally between the university and Town Hall Square, Archive 1 and Media Centre is the first

above: Elevation Universytetzka Street, scale 1:200

below: Ground floor plan, scale 1:200

Anlaufpunkt für diejenigen, die sich über die Stadt informieren möchten, z.B. Bürger von Chernivtsi und Touristen aus aller Welt. Das Gebäude ist inmitten der Altstadt in wenigen Fußminuten von den wichtigsten Infrastrukturpunkten Chernivtsis aus erreichbar. Der höchste Punkt der Stadt liegt einen knappen Kilometer südlich. Durch diese Lage ist ein weiter Blick über die Stadt möglich. Das Archiv schließt den Kreuzungspunkt Universitäts- Senkovic- Ruskagasse zusammen mit der ehemaligen Synagoge und den drei Eckgebäuden. Durch diese Verdichtung und die unterschiedlichen Entstehungs-zeiten und Stile der Bauten entsteht ein Ort urbanen Charakters. Das Gebäude sitzt, wie andere Kulturbauten in der Stadt, auf der Blockecke. Das Erdgeschoß mit erhöhter lichten Höhe und von außen nach innen durchlaufendem Bodenbelag wirkt dadurch wie ein Stadtplatz, der die gesamte Fläche zwischen den angrenzenden Gebäuden einnimmt"

Picture of the urban model facing south

point of contact for all those seeking information on the city, e.g. the citizens of Chernivtsi, academics as well as tourists. The building is placed in the old town centre and within short walking distance of the core infrastructure points of Chernivtsi. The highest point of the city lies one kilometre southward; this allows a broad view over the city. The archive closes the crossing point University Street, Senkovic Street and Ruska Street together with the former synagogue and the three corner buildings. This increasing density and the varying construction dates as well as design styles a location of urban character develops. The building stands, similarly to other cultural buildings in the city on the corner of the block. The ground floor – with raised, well-lit height and floor material that runs from inside and to the outside – thus resembles a urban square which covers the entire area between the bordering buildings."

Model of the media centre facing south west, scale 1:500

BUKAREST 2005
BUCHAREST 2005

PROJEKT: DOPPELPUNKT BERLIN –
BUKAREST – THE GERMAN HUB OF TRADE
AND CULTURE IN BUCHAREST
PROJEKT: DOUBLE POINT BERLIN -
BUKAREST – THE GERMAN HUB OF TRADE
AND CULTURE IN BUCHAREST
WINTERSEMESTER 2005/2006
WINTER SEMESTER 2005/2006

Unser drittes Projekt im Wintersemester 2005/2006 haben wir in Kooperation mit Oliver Paus und dem Dozenten Stefan Ghenciulescu sowie Studierenden der Ion Mincu Universität für Architektur und Stadtplanung Bukarest durchgeführt. Zunächst sollten zwei Entwurfsprojekte mit derselben Aufgabenstellung an den beiden Standorten Berlin und Bukarest von den Studierenden bearbeitet werden. Im Anschluss daran boten wir wie bei den vorherigen Projekten eine durch den DAAD geförderte Studienreise an, die uns diesmal von Bukarest durch Rumänien nach Chernivtsi führen sollte. Entsprechend unseren Untersuchungen in Wien, wollten wir auf dieser Reise auch die architektonische und städtebauliche Entwicklung Bukarests nachvollziehen, um Rückschlüsse auf die architektonische und städtebauliche Entwicklung der "rumänischen Periode" in Cernauti/Chernivtsi ziehen zu können.

In Bukarest konzentrierten wir uns auf die Bauten der 20er und 30er Jahre. In diesem Zeitraum standen die Anhänger der Moderne in starker Konkurrenz zu dem Neo-Brâncoveanu-Stil, einer Renaissance des im 16./17. Jahrhundert nach dem Fürsten Constantin Brâncoveanu (1688-1714) benannten Baustils. Im Gegensatz zur Moderne, die einen international einheitlichen und funktionalen Bautyp anstrebte, versuchte diese Richtung einen "rumänischen Heimatstil" zu etablieren. Diese Tatsache war für uns von besonderem Interesse, da beide Baustile auch in Chernivtsi das Stadtbild der rumänischen Periode prägen. Grund hierfür war die mehr als zwanzigjährige Zugehörigkeit Chernivtsis zu Rumänien zwischen den Weltkriegen. Chernivtsi zählte in dieser Zeit zu den größten Städten des Landes und erfreute sich einer regen Bautätigkeit.

House of the architectural association in Bucharest

We completed our third project in the winter semester of 2005/2006 in cooperation with Oliver Paus and the lecturer Stefan Ghenciulescu and students of the Ion
Mincu University for Architecture and Urban Planning, Bucharest. Two design projects
based on identical assignments for differing locations – in Berlin and Bucharest –
were processed by the students. As with previous projects, we offered a study trip
sponsored by the DAAD, taking us from Bucharest in Romania to Chernivtsi. In accordance with our research in Vienna, we wanted to trace back the architectural and
urban development of Bucharest in order to draw conclusions on Cernauti / Chernivtsi. The semester was accompanied by lectures and seminars, which extended the
engagement with architecture and urban planning in Central Eastern Europe.

We focused on the buildings of the 1920s and 1930s in Bucharest. During
this period modernists rivalled with the Neo-Brâncoveanu style, a renaissance of
the building style named after the nobleman Constantin Brâncoveanu (1688-1714)
during the 16th / 17th centuries. In contrast the modernism, which aimedat a uniform
international and functional building type, this movement attempted to establish a
Romanian domestic style. This fact is of special interest for us, as both styles dominantly
shaped the urban picture of the Romanian period. The reason is the 20-year Romanian
rule between the world wars. Chernivtsi at the time was considered the second city of
the country and experienced intense building activity. In Chernivtsi we were told that
the majority of the city's multiethnic inhabitants preferred the international "neutral"
style of modernism.

Example of 1930s architecture in downtown Bucharest

Aufgabe des angebotenen Entwurfsprojektes war die Entwicklung zweier Zentren für Handel und Kultur in Berlin und Bukarest mit dem Ziel, durch die Errichtung der Zentren in den beiden Städten den kulturellen und wirtschaftlichen Austausch zwischen Deutschland und dem EU Beitrittsland Rumänien zu fördern. Es sollte ein Ort entstehen, an dem Wirtschaft und Kultur voneinander profitieren. Der Kern des Hub sollte hauptsächlich aus räumlichen Angeboten für Kulturprojekte bestehen. Finanziert werden sollte es durch die Vermietung von Büroflächen an deutsche bzw. rumänische Unternehmen, die im hub ihre Auslandsdependancen unterbringen und von den räumlichen wie inhaltlichen Angeboten des jeweiligen "Kulturzentrums" profitieren können.

Das ausgewählte Entwurfsgrundstück in Bukarest war eine dreieckige unbebaute Parzelle am Piata Baba Novac im Südosten von Bukarest. Städtebaulich interessant war dieses Grundstück, da hier drei Gebäudestrukturen aufeinander trafen: Sozialwohnungen aus den 20er Jahren, freistehende Wohnblocks aus den 60er Jahren und die für Bukarest sehr typische Randbebauung mit großen Wohnblocks aus den 70er Jahren. Ziel einer zukünftigen Bebauung sollte die Vermittlung zwischen den unterschiedlichen Strukturen sein. In Berlin fiel die Wahl des Entwurfsgrundstück auf eine unbebaute Parzelle an der südlichen Friedrichstrasse zwischen Zimmer- und Schützenstrasse, unmittelbar am Checkpoint Charlie. Das zentral gelegene Grundstück sollte den Studierenden aus Bukarest Gelegenheit geben, sich mit der städtebaulichen Entwicklung von Berlin auseinanderzusetzen. Zum Abschluss des Wintersemesters, im April 2006, war eine gemeinsame Präsentation der Ergebnisse in Bukarest als Auftakt unserer Studienreise vorgesehen. Die Reise musste aus zeitlichen Gründen verschoben werden. Kurzfristig organisierten die Bukarester Studierenden eine Reise nach Berlin und stellten ihre Arbeiten im April an der UdK vor.

left: Example of the Neo-Brancoveanu style in Bucharest

right: Example of modernism, Boulevard Magheru, Bucharest

The assignment of the proposed design project was the development of two centres for trade and culture in Berlin and Bucharest. The idea was to intensify the cultural and economic exchange between Germany and the EU-accession state Rumania through the installation of two centres in both cities. A location was to develop were economy and culture would promote one another. The core of the hub was to consist primarily of space for cultural projects. The rental of office space to foreign companies would provide finance. The companies would maintain their overseas branches in the hub, benefiting from the cultural offers at the respective "culture centre". The chosen project area in Bucharest was a triangular empty parcel on the Piata Baba Novac in the Southeast of Bucharest. The urban attraction of the space stemmed from the fact that the differing building structures meet here: Council estates from the 1920s, singular apartment blocks from the 1960s and the large perimeter block development with large apartment blocks from the 1970s that is typical for Bucharest. The objective of future constructions should be the mediation between these existing structures. The chosen project area in Berlin was an empty parcel on the southern Friedrichstraße between Zimmer- and Schützenstraße immediately next to Checkpoint Charlie. It was meant to be a centrally located plot that would give the students from Bucharest the possibility to study the urban development of Berlin. A collective presentation of the results was planned for the end of the Winter Semester, in April 2006, which should also be the prelude to our study trip to Bucharest. Due to time constraints, the trip could not take place at that point in time. The Bucharest students therefore organized a trip to Berlin and presented their work at the UdK in April.

left: Residential house in the Modernist style, Universytetzka Street, Chernivtsi

right: Residential house in the Romanian Brancoveanu style in Chernivtsi

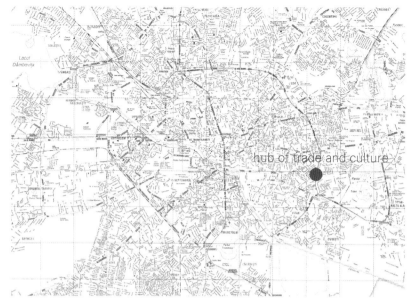

hub of trade and culture

Map of Bucharest, site of design project

Picture of the site: Piata Baba Novac, south east of Bucharest

THE GERMAN HUB OF TRADE AND CULTURE IN BUCHAREST
Entwurfsprojekt von *Mathias Wünsche, UdK Berlin*

"An einem markanten, aber auch unwirtlichem Ort in Bukarest soll ein gemeinschaftlich genutztes Kultur- und Handelszentrum entstehen. Städtebaulich ist dieser Ort für Bukarest typisch: Durch historisch gewachsene Viertel mit meist zweigeschossiger Wohnbebauung wurden in der Zeit des Sozialismus große Achsen geschlagen und mit 11-geschossiger Bebauung gerahmt - die in keiner Weise zur "dahinter" liegenden historischen Stadt vermitteln. Mein Entwurf möchte diese beiden städtebaulichen Phänomene miteinander in Bezug setzen, vermitteln und darüber hinaus einen neuen Kontext erzeugen. So werden Achsen und Höhen beider baulicher Maßstäblichkeiten aufgegriffen und transformiert. Dieses Spiel mit zwei Polen setzt sich bei der Beschäftigung mit den Funktionen des Gebäudes fort. Es existieren die zwei Komponenten Kultur und Handel. Die jeweiligen Raumprogramme werden in getrennten Gebäuden entwickelt: das Handelszentrum als orthogonale regelmäßige Struktur; das Kulturzentrum als pulsierende, sich ständig verändernde Raumfolge."

Site plan, scale 1:1000

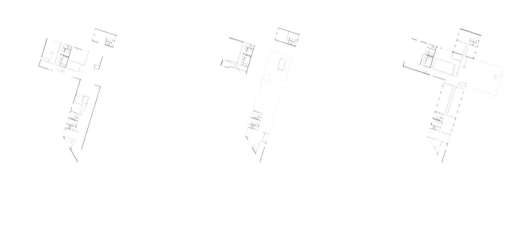

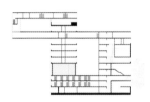

THE GERMAN HUB OF TRADE AND CULTURE IN BUCHAREST
Design Project by *Mathias Wünsche,* UdK Berlin

"On a prominent, yet inhospitable location in Bucharest, a collectively utilized culture and trade centre is to rise. In urban terms, the plot is typical for Bucharest: wide axes with 11-storey constructions have been built during socialist times through historical neighbourhoods with mostly two-storey buildings. These do not communicate with the historic town lying "behind". My concept aims to cross-reference the two urban phenomena; arbitrating while generating a new context. This way, axes and heights of both constructed frames of reference are picked up and transformed. This game with two poles continues in the engagement with the function of the building. Two component exist, culture and trade. The respective room programs are developed in separate buildings: the trade centre as an orthogonal regular structure; as well as the culture centre as a pulsating, constantly modifying room sequence."

above left: Ground floor plan, entry hall, scale 1:250

above middle: Third floor plan, lounge, scale 1:250

above right: Ninth floor plan, intersection and restaurant, scale 1:250

below: Elevation facing east and Section, scale 1:250

Perspective of the new building facing south

THE GERMAN HUB OF TRADE AND CULTURE IN BUCHAREST
Entwurfsprojekt von *Carles Serra Hartmann, Come Menage, UdK Berlin*

"Unser Gebäude präsentiert sich in Form von zwei parallel zueinander stehenden, fast transparenten Scheiben auf dem vorgegebenen Grundstück. Als Mittler zwischen der alten städtebaulichen Struktur zu Beginn des 20. Jh. und den Wohnzeilen der 70er und 80er Jahre orientiert sich unser Entwurf in Richtung Südosten dem Raster der älteren Struktur folgend. Die genaue Position beider Gebäude wird von den Blickachsen aus den angrenzenden Strassen bestimmt. Sichtbezüge und Durchgänge zu dem dahinter liegenden Stadtgebiet werden so möglich, die Kulissenmauer durchbrochen. Der Komplex besteht aus drei Baukörpern: Zwei parallelen Hochhausscheiben mit 14 und 10 Etagen und einem zweigeschossigen Gebäude als verbindender Rampenpromenade den Gebäuden entsteht ein fließender öffentlicher Raum mit Einkaufsmöglichkeiten und Veranstaltungsflächen. Die Komponente "culture" des Hub dient als innere Verbindung der verschiedenen Teile des Gebäudes und als positive und wirkungsvolle Darstellung eines Treffpunkts zwischen zwei Identitäten."

Perspective of the new building facing north

 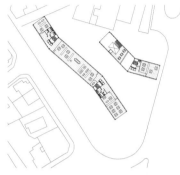 

THE GERMAN HUB OF TRADE AND CULTURE IN BUCHAREST
Design Project by *Carlos Serra Hartmann, Come Menage, UdK Berlin*

"Our building presents itself in the form of two parallel, almost transparent discs on the assigned plot. As mediator between the old urban structure from the beginning of the 20th century and the apartment blocks of the 1970s and 1980s, our design is oriented southeastward, following the grid of the older structure. The precise position of both buildings is determined by the viewing axis from the bordering streets. Sight references and passages to the urban area lying behind are thus enabled; the scenery wall is breached. The complex consists of three buildings: two parallel discs (14 and 10 storeys) and a two-storey construction as a connecting ramp promenade in the area of the ground floor and the first storey. Below and between the buildings a flowing public space is created with shopping possibilities and event spaces. The hub's component "culture" serves as an internal connection of the different segments of the building and as a positive and effective representation of a meeting point between two identities."

above: Concept formulation, view axis

below left: First floor plan, connecting ramp promenade, scale 1:200

below middle: Fourth floor plan, Trade Centre, scale 1: 200

below right: Seventh floor plan, intersection, scale 1: 200

North elevation, 1:500

above: Perspective of the new building facing south

below: Perspective ground floor, flowing public space

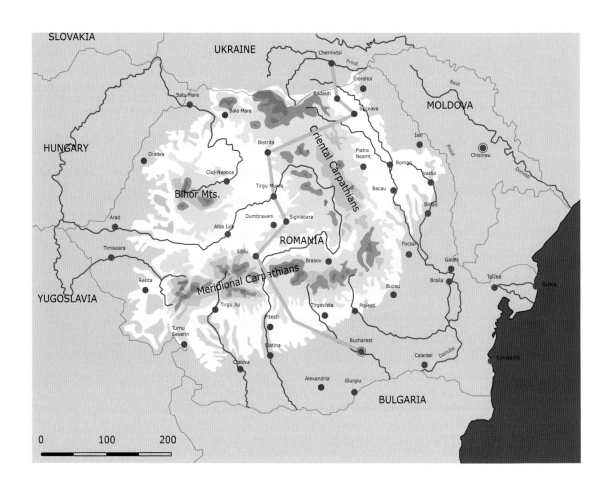

Map of Romania wit marked route of excursion, 2006

Im Juli 2006 fand die geplante Studienreise nach Rumänien und in die Ukraine mit den Stationen: Bukarest – Sibiu – Sighisoara – Suceava – Radautz – Chernivtsi statt und somit auch die Präsentation unserer Entwürfe an der Ion-Mincu Universität in Bukarest. Wir präsentierten unsere Arbeiten und besichtigten gemeinsam mit den Studierenden aus Bukarest das Entwurfsgrundstück und seine Umgebung. Nach drei Tagen in der Stadt setzten wir die Reise fort. Ziel waren die Städte Sibiu (Hermannstadt, Europäische Kulturhauptstadt 2007) und Sighisoara (Schäßburg) in Transilvanien (Siebenbürgen). Beide und weitere Städte Siebenbürgens sind von deutschen Siedlern aus der Rhein- und Moselgegend im 12ten Jahrhundert gegründet worden. Seitdem lebte hier eine deutschsprachige Minderheit, die als Siebenbürger Sachsen (Saxones=

The planned study trip took place in July 2006. From Bucharest to Chernivtsi with the stops Bucharest – Sibiu – Sighisoara – Suceava – Radautz – Chernivtsi. At the start we presented our designs at the Ion-Mincu University in Bucharest. Subsequently we visited the project area and its surroundings together with the Bucharest students. After three days in the city we continued our trip. The destinations were the cities Sibiu (Hermannstadt, European Cultural Capital 2007) and Sighisoara (Schäßburg) in Transylvania (Siebenbürgen). These and other cities in Transylvania were founded by German colonists from the Rhine and Moselle areas in the 12th century. Since then, Saxons have lived in the area as a German-speaking minority.

above: Sibiu (Hermannstadt, European Cultural Capital 2007), Romania

below: Church in Transylvania (Siebenbürgen), Romania

Deutsche) bezeichnet werden. Zwar hat sich ihre Anzahl bis heute stark reduziert, aber ihre Präsenz und ihr Einfluss in den Städten, auf dem Land und in der Sprache sind unverkennbar stark. Über Targu Mures fuhren wir weiter nach Bistrita und Vatra Dornei. Die Städte liegen im ehemaligen ungarischen Teil der österreich-ungarischen Donaumonarchie. Der architektonische Einfluss aus der damaligen Hauptstadt Budapest prägt einige wesentliche Gebäude der Jahrhundertwende, die im Jugendstil und Historismus erbaut wurden. Auf der Studienreise nach Budapest im Wintersemester 2004/05 hatten wir bereits Kenntnisse über die architektonische und städtebauliche Entwicklung Budapests gesammelt, die es uns nun ermöglichten, entsprechende Rückschlüsse zu ziehen. Wir überquerten die Karpaten und erreichten den südlichen Teil der Bukowina, der nach dem zweiten Weltkrieg mit den Städten Radautz und Suceava rumänisch blieb, während die nördliche Bukowina mit Chernivtsi unter sowjetische Herrschaft geriet. Uns interessierte die Entwicklung des Kronlandes Bukowina nach seiner Teilung bis heute. Wir besichtigten die Städte Radautz und Suceava und suchten nach Gemeinsamkeiten im Stadtbild mit dem uns bekannten Chernivtsi. Am 1. August überquerten wir die Grenze zur Ukraine und erreichten nach ca. 100 km Chernivtsi. Durch die neu gewonnenen Eindrücke auf der bisherigen Reise erlaubsten uns, die Stadt im Wechsel ihrer Epochen seit Gründung differenzierter zu beurteilen.

above: Sighisoara (Schässburg), Romania

below: scenery in the Oriental Carpathians, Romania

While their numbers have declined significantly to this day, their presence and influence in the cities, the rural areas and in the language are unmistakable. Via Targu Mures we proceeded to Bistrita and Vatra Dornei. These cities lie in the former Hungarian part of the Austro-Hungarian Monarchy. The architectural influence from the capital at the time, Budapest, marks some important Art Nouveau and historicist buildings from the turn of the century. A study trip to Budapest in the Winter Semester 2004/05 allowed us to acquire knowledge on the architectural and urban development of Budapest, which again allowed us to draw according conclusions. We then crossed the Carpathians and reached the Southern part of the Bukovina. After the Second World War, Northern Bukovina with the capital Chernivsti came under Soviet rule, the Southern half with the cities Radautz and Suceava remained Romanian. We visited the cities Radautz and Suceava and searched for common features with Chernivtsi in the urban picture. On the first of August, we crossed the border into the Ukraine and after about 100 km we reached Chernivtsi. The newly acquired impressions of the trip allowed us to make a more differentiated judgment on the development of the city from the Habsburg Epoch through the Romanian period until the present. New historic and regional links became clear to us; the understanding of what renders the city Chernivtsi unique has thus becomes far more detailed and broadens the existing image.

Municipal Building in Targu Mures, Romania

Public Fountain in the park of Vatra Dornei, Romania

Moldovita Monastery, Bucovina, Romania

CZERNOWITZ 2006
CHERNIVTSI 2006

PROJEKT: TOMORROW IN CZERNOWITZ
PROJECT: TOMORROW IN CZERNOWITZ
SOMMERSEMESTER 2006
SUMMER SEMESTER 2006

In Vorbereitung auf die Sommerakademie 2006 kehrten wir zurück nach Chernivtsi als unserem Entwurfsstandort. Unser Projekt 2006 nahm sich die sowjetisch bzw. sozialistisch geprägte Stadt und ihre Entwicklung ab 1991 bis zur Gegenwart vor. Nach der nationalsozialistischen Katastrophe fand in Chernivtsi 1945 der Neubeginn unter sowjetischer Herrschaft statt. Die Stadt wurde bevölkert, hauptsächlich mit besitzlosen Schichten aus dem Osten der Ukraine. Sie wuchs bis zu ihren heutigen Ausmaßen. Gleich vielen anderen sowjetisch bzw. sozialistisch geprägten Städten entstanden gleichförmige Plattenbausiedlungen am Rande der Stadt, ohne kulturelles Leben oder eigener Identität. Die Innenstadt Chernivtsis hingegen blieb fast gänzlich unangetastet, nur einzelne Gebäude im stalinistischen Baustil wurden in den fünfziger Jahren errichtet.

Dank des großen Engagements vor Ort durch unsere Partner Pavlo Kolyadinsky und Oksana Matiychuk, beide Mitarbeiter der Universität von Chernivtsi, lag uns zu Jahresbeginn 2006 endlich ein digitaler Schwarzplan der gesamten Stadt vor. Seit Beginn unseres Vorhabens im Wintersemester 2003/2004 hatten wir uns um aktuelles Planmaterial bemüht. Dieser digitale Schwarzplan ermöglichte es uns endlich, topografische und infrastrukturelle Zusammenhänge herzustellen und wesentlich tiefer in die stadtplanerischen Zusammenhänge einzusteigen. Jetzt konnten wir die um die Innenstadt liegenden Bezirke stadträumlich analysieren und ihre Nahtstellen zur Innenstadt untersuchen, Defizite und Potentiale herausarbeiten und die gesamte Stadt in ihrer gegenwärtigen und zukünftigen Entwicklung betrachten.

Jewish cemetery gravestones

In preparation for the Summer Academy, we returned to Chernivtsi as the location for our design work, this time in cooperation with the Ion Mincu University for Architecture and Urban Planning Bucharest, the Technical University Graz, and the Polytechnical College Chernivtsi. The projects were worked on in the respective universities and were presented in Chernivtsi at the beginning of August as a prelude to the Summer Academy. We focused on the town's Soviet / Socialist shape and its development from 1991 onwards to the present and towards the future.

Following the Nationalist Socialist catastrophe came the restart under Soviet rule. The town was repopulated, mainly with poor and landless people from the East of the Ukraine. The town expanded to its present extent. Similar to many other cities under Soviet / Socialist influence, Socialist high-rise residential areas were developed near chernivtsi's outskirts, lacking cultural life or an individual identity. The town center remained untouched, individual buildings in the Stalinist style were added in the 1950s.

Since the beginning of our plans in the Winter Semester 2003/04, we tried to acquire the most recent maps. Through the intense engagement of our partners in Chernivtsi, Pavlo Kolyadinsky and Oksana Matiychuk, both employed at the University of Chernivtsi, we received a complete digital ground plan of the town at the beginning of 2006. This plan enabled us to establish topographical and infrastructural contexts and to dive more intensely into the urban planning contexts. Our goal lay in analyzing the parts of the city centre, investigating the transitions towards the town center, the deficits and potentials, and to observe the town as a whole in it's present and future development.

Public spaces: Monument of T.Shevchenko

Über den eigenen Tellerrand hinaus schauen hieß für uns auch, die Denkansätze der anderen eng mit der Geschichte Chernivtsis verbundenen Länder Österreich und Rumänien einzubeziehen. So konnten wir für unser Projekt 2006 die Zusammenarbeit mit der Ion Mincu Universität für Architektur und Stadtplanung Bucharest weiterführen, mit Oxana Boyko von dem Polytechnical College die Kooperation in Chernivsti ausbauen; mit Grigor Doytchinov von der Technischen Universität Graz einen neuen Kooperationspartner gewinnen. Mit diesen Kooperationspartnern und ihren Studierenden war es uns gelungen, die polyethnische Stadtgesellschaft von damals für einen kurzen Zeitraum und in ganz kleinem Rahmen wieder herzustellen. Die Zusammenarbeit nutzten wir zum einen fachlich, um gemeinsam regionale und überregionale Entwicklungspotentiale zu definieren. Zum anderen ging es uns auch darum, der jüngeren Generation Gelegenheit zu geben, sich über ihre unterschiedlichen Erfahrungen in Europa auszutauschen und gemeinsame Visionen eines zusammenwachsenden Europa am Beispiel der Stadt Chernivtsi zu entwickeln.

left: Stalinist buildings were added in the fifties, Universytetzka Street
right: Unpaved street at the edge of the historical city centre close to Sorbona Square

Looking further than the end of one's nose also implied for us including other countries in our research which were closely linked to Chernivtsi's history, such as Austria and Rumania. In addition to our existing contacts to Bucharest and Chernivtsi, we were able to find as a partner Grigor Doytchinov from the Technical University Graz as well as Oxana Boyko who worked at the Polytechnical College in Chernivtsi. Through this cooperation between the universities from Graz, Bucharest, Chernivtsi, and Berlin we succeeded in reestablishing the town's polyethnic society from past times in a short time frame and on a small scale. On one hand we profited from the team work on the professional level as we attempted to commonly define potentials for development on a regional and supraregional basis. On the other hand, we hoped to give the younger generation a possibility to exchange their differing experiences regarding Europe and to amplify common visions regarding an expanding Europe with the example of the town Chernivtsi.

Public spaces: The square opposite the former Israelite temple

Auf unsere Anfrage hin haben unsere Partner vor Ort mit Hilfe von Architekten und dem Stadtplanungsamt mehr als 30 aktuelle städtebauliche und stadtplanerische Themen zusammengetragen, für die es galt, kurzfristige und längerfristige Lösungsansätze zu entwickeln.

Dies war unsere Grundlage für die Entwicklung der Aufgabenstellung sowohl für die Sommerakademie als auch bei dem vorbereitenden Projekt. Wir fassten die Themen in vier Bereiche zusammen und ließen jeden Bereich von einer Universität bearbeiten. Unsere Studenten in Berlin hatten die Aufgabe, sich mit dem geografischen Zentrum von Chernivtsi zu beschäftigen, dem "weißen Fleck" zwischen historischem Stadtkern und dem auf der anderen Flussseite gelegenen Stadtteil Sadagura. Durch unterschiedliche städtebauliche Vorschläge sollten Möglichkeiten aufgezeigt werden, wie die Gebiete um den Fluss definiert und aufgewertet werden könnten. Programmatische Schwerpunkte hierbei waren: Naherholung, Tourismus, Kultur und Wissenschaft.

Industrial zone - Chernivtsi's geographical centre, a 'white stain' between the historic centre and Sadagura

Responding to our query, our partners in Chernivtsi accumulated over 30 currently relevant urban and town planning themes with the help of architects and the office for town planning. These themes demand short-term and long-term solutions.

This served as a foundation for the further expansion of the undertaking, both for the Summer Academy as well as the preparatory project. We combined the various topics into four thematic groups, each of which was taken on by one university. Our students received the task to work on Chernivtsi's geographical center, a "white stain" between the historic center and Sadagura, the part of town located on the other side of the river. Based on the differing town planning schemes presented, we attempted to sketch new possibilities to redefine and upgrade the areas near the river. The programmatic emphases were as follows: local recreation, tourism, culture, and science.

River Pruth - Inner-city recreation area

Projektgebiet am Pruth

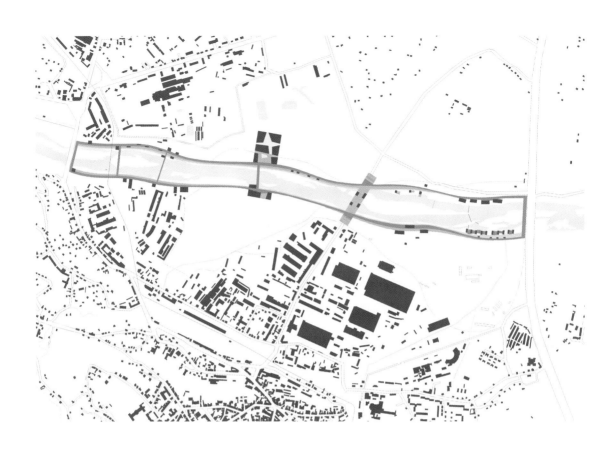

CZERNOWITZ AM PRUTHUFER
Entwurfsprojekt von *Maeva Baudoin, Filip Steins, Sven Marx*

"Der Pruth hat die Gestalt eines Flusses, der soeben aus den Bergen entlassen worden ist. Niedrige Wasserstände über das Jahr wechseln sich ab mit kurzem Hochwasser in Herbst und Frühling, zum Ende der Hitzeperiode und zur Schneeschmelze. Der Fluss transportiert viel Kies und Geröll, da er trotz seiner niedrigen Wasserstände von 80 Zentimeter über das Jahr eine hohe Strömungsgeschwindigkeit hat. Das natürliche Bild des bebauten Dammes, der gleichzeitig der Stadt Schutz gewährleistet, schafft eine Stadt am Wasser. Der Damm kanalisiert den Fluss nicht. Die Dammlinien sind in einem solchen Abstand zum Fluss, dass Kiesbänke im und am Wasser weiter ihren Veränderungen unterliegen können. Die Gebäude am Damm haben immer ein Gegenüber und stehen so in Kommunikation miteinander über den Fluss hinweg. Der Damm soll die verschiedenen Zustände der Stadt zeigen: So soll die Büro -, Arbeits - und Kulturzone am oberen Teil des Dammes eine lebendige Stadt ans Wasser führen, während im weiteren Verlauf des Dammes der Fluss an der lebendigen Stadt, dem öffentlichen Raum, an der Universität, am Markt, am Park und an der Natur vorbeifließt."

Site plan, scale 1:2000

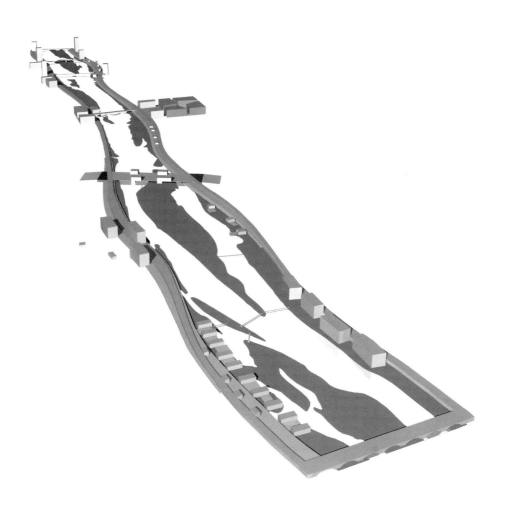

CZERNOWITZ BY THE BANKS OF THE RIVER PRUTH
Design Projcet by *Maeva Baudoin, Filip Steins, Sven Marx*

"The Pruth holds the shape of a river, which has just been released from the mountains. Low water levels throughout the year alternate with short, temporary floodings in autumn and springtime and towards the end of the hot season and when the snow melts. The river transports a lot of gravel and stone debris, since it has a high water velocity regardless of its low water level of 80 centimetres during the year. The natural appearance of the dam lined with edifices creates a town by the water and simultaneously offers protection for the town. The dam does not canalise the river. These artificial lines lie at such a distance from the river that gravel banks in and by the water may remain subject to their modifications. The buildings by the dam have a continuous opposing form and thus communicate with each other across the river. The dam is meant to reflect various conditions of the city: the office, work and cultural zone by the upper part of the dam lead a vivacious town to the water. In the further reaches of the dam, the river flows by the public areas formed by university, market square, park and the nature."

Axonometric projection: The natural appearance of the dam lined with edifices creates a town by the water

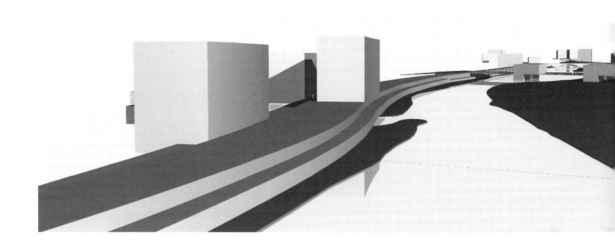

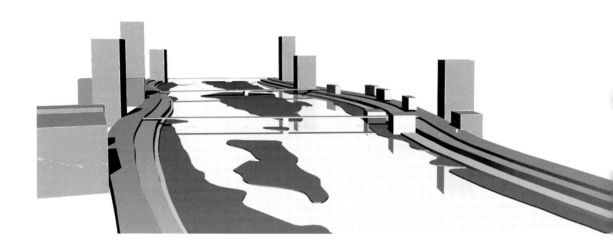

above: Exhibition- and cultural buildings flank the dam

below: Perspective of solitary towers along the waterfront

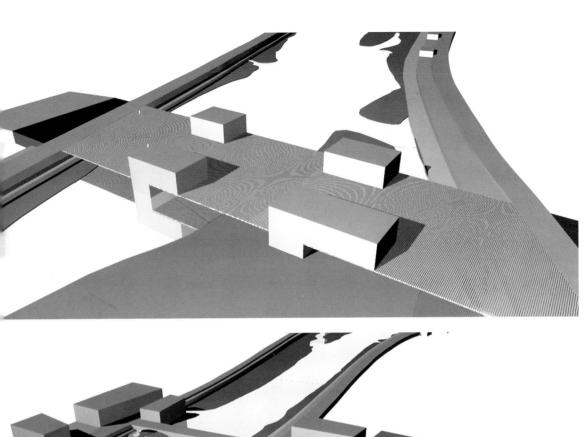

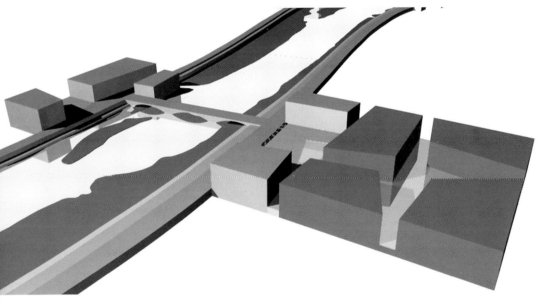

above: Market place shaped as a bridge over the river

below: University buildings surround the water like blocks of stone

Durchgang Snop

Durchgang unter der Brücke

Ansicht M_1:1000

Uni-Shops
Band 4

Fakultat Musik
Band 1.2

Studentenwohnheime
Band 4

Fakultät bildende Kur
Band 1.2

TOMORROW IN CZERNOWITZ
Entwurfsprojekt von *Kasia Braun, Elena Fischmann, Paula Konga*

"Das von uns geplante Gebiet liegt am Fluss Pruth zwischen den Stadtgebieten Czernowitz und Sadagura. Es ist geprägt durch Industriebauten aus der Sowjetzeit. Die Gebäude und Technologien sind alt und überholt nach heutigen Maßstäben, viele Bereiche sind ungenutzt. Lange Zeit kam es in dieser Gegend durch unregelmäßige Pegelstände des Pruth zu Überschwemmungen. Das Resultat ist ein Vakuum, das zwischen Czernowitz und Sadagura entstanden ist und die Stadtgebiete voneinander trennt. Die Trennung wird durch den Fluss zusätzlich verstärkt. Es führen lediglich zwei stark frequentierte Verkehrsbrücken herüber. Unser Ziel: Das Gebiet zwischen Czernowitz und Sadagura aufzuwerten und beide Stadthälften zu vereinen. Es soll eine Universität auf dem Gelände entstehen, die ein junges internationales Publikum anzieht. Auf dem Gebiet sind zwei Wohnbrücken geplant, die das wesentliche Gestaltungselement der ganzen Anlage darstellen. Die Achsen der Brücken ziehen sich bis in die Innenstadt hinein (Czernowitzer Grünflächenpfad). Auf der befahrbaren Hauptbrücke befindet sich der Uni-Campus mit 4 Fakultäten: Gestaltung, Bildende Kunst, Darstellende Kunst und Musik. Untergebracht sind weiterhin Bibliotheken, Mensa, Verwaltung, Ateliers, Arbeitsräume, Einkaufsmöglichkeiten und studentische Wohnheime. Die zweite Brücke ist lediglich zu Fuß begehbar. Auf ihr befindet sich ein breites Freizeitangebot: Cafés, Restaurants, Biergarten etc.. Über das ganze Gebiet von der Autobahnbrücke am Kalinovskij- Markt im Osten bis zur bestehenden Autobahnbrücke im Westen erstreckt sich eine Gondelseilbahn. Auf dem übrigen Gelände entsteht ein Park, unterteilt in parallel zum Fluß verlaufende Streifen mit unterschiedlicher Vegetation und Nutzung."

Elevation, scale 1:1000

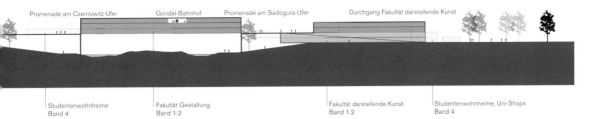

Promenade am Czernowitz-Ufer   Gondel-Bahnhof   Promenade am Sadogura-Ufer   Durchgang Fakultät darstellende Kunst

Studentenwohnheime
Band 4

Fakultät Gestaltung
Band 1.2

Fakultät darstellende Kunst
Band 1.2

Studentenwohnheime, Uni-Shops
Band 4

TOMORROW IN CZERNOWITZ

Design Project by *Kasia Braun, Elena Fischmann, Paula Konga*

"The area mapped out by us lies by the River Pruth between the urban zones Czernowitz and Sadagura; industrial buildings from Soviet times shape it. Buildings and technologies are old and overcome by contemporary standards; numerous parts are unused. For a long time, irregular water levels of the Pruth led to floodings in this region. The result is a vacuum, that has developed between Czernowitz and Sadagura and separates the urban zones. This disconnection is underlined by the river; only two heavily-used traffic bridges span it. Our objective, was to re-evaluate the area between Czernowitz and Sadagura and to reunify both halves of the city. A university is to be built on the area, to attract a young, international public. Two residential bridges are planned in the area. They form the defining elements of the compound. The bridges' axes extend into the city center (Czernowitz Green Zone Path). The university campus with its four faculties – design, fine arts, drama, and music – is located on the main, road-traffic bridge. A library, canteen, office administration, studios, working spaces, shopping possibilities, and student accommodations are located here as well. The second bridge is only accessible by foot. It offers a broad leisure program: cafés, restaurants, beer gardens, etc. A cableway over the entire area from the highway bridge by the Kalinovskij Market in the East to the existing highway bridge to the West. A park, partaged into strips running parallel to the river and holds various kinds of vegetation and functions, unfolds on the remaining land."

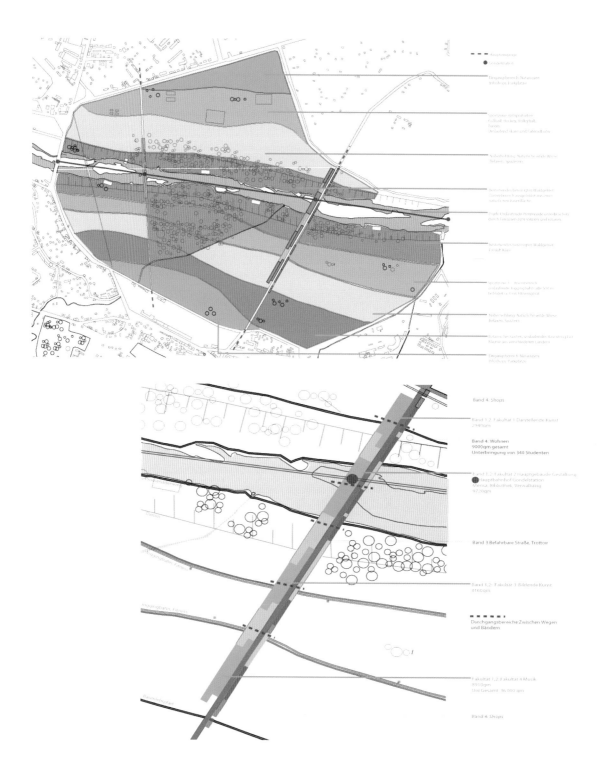

above: Site plan, scale 1:2000

below: Living bridge - University building, scale 1:1000

above: Perspective of the living bridge with cable cars stretching over the area

below: Cable car station at the highway bridge by Kalinivskij Market

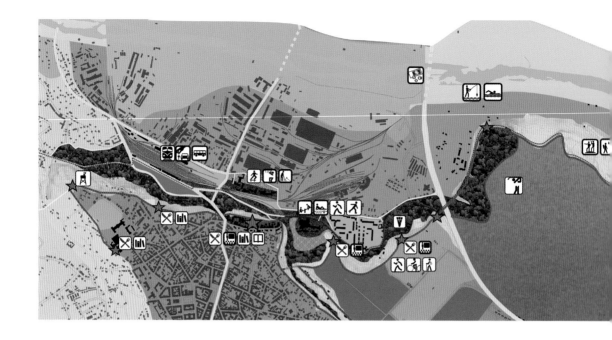

PROMENADE CZERNOWITZ - DIE WIEDERENTDECKUNG DES PANORAMAS
Entwurfsprojekt von *Felix Forthmeijer, Matthias Tscheuschler*

"Der für Czernowitz charakteristische Geländesprung markiert als Beginn und Grenze der historischen Stadtentwicklung die Oberstadt und stellt dennoch die geographische Mitte des gesamten Stadtgebietes dar. Damit einher geht eine Vielzahl weiterer naturgegebener und künstlicher Besonderheiten, die sich auf die Geländekante beziehen lassen und so die Bedeutung dieses Gebietes betonen: Mit der Topographie herausgebildet hat sich eine besondere Vegetation, Wege- und Gewässerverlauf reagieren ebenso auf die Höhenentwicklung wie die funktionale Zonierung des Stadtgebietes. Die Anlage von Industrie und Friedhöfen verstärkt den Eindruck der Kante als der eigentlichen Grenze der Stadt. Die Verbindung zur Unterstadt erfolgt nur durch einige wenige Straßen, das strukturelle und gesellschaftliche Zentrum der Stadt, der Rathausplatz, befindet sich in unmittelbarer Nähe zur Kante. Bisher existieren jedoch nur wenige Punkte, an denen sich ein Eindruck von der besonderen topographischen Situation erhalten läßt. Wir schlagen eine Promenade entlang des Geländesprungs vor, sie integriert diese Punkte in ein Gesamtbild der Oberstadt, schafft die Verbindung zur Unterstadt und zum gegenüberliegenden Pruthufer samt der Zwillings-stadt Sadagura. Die Promenade beschreibt nicht nur die topographische sondern auch die historische und gesellschaftliche Ebene der Stadt. Zwischen der Habsburghöhe im Westen, dem Jüdischen Viertel und den Auen im Nordosten lassen sich rund 300 Jahre Czernowitzer Stadt- und Kulturgeschichte nachvollziehen.

Program, scale 1:10000

CZERNOWITZ PROMENADE – THE REDISCOVERY OF THE PANORAMA
Design Project by *Felix Forthmeijer, Matthias Tscheuschler*

"The elevation alterations characteristic for Czernowitz marks the upper town as a beginning and border of the historic town development and nonetheless represents the geographic center of the entire urban area. This coincides with a number of naturally given and artificial peculiarities, which relate to the edge of the terrain and therefore underline the importance of this area: along with the topography, a special vegetation has developed; the courses of paths and of the stream react to the change in altitude coinciding to the functional partitioning of the town's area. The planning of industrial plants and cemeteries augments the appearance of this edge as the city's actual borderline. The connection to the Lower Town only is possible through very few streets; the structural and social town centre, the town square, is located in direct proximity to the edge. But up to this point, only few points exist, at which an impression of the extraordinary topographical situation may be obtained. We build a promenade along the topographic height elevation, which integrates these points into an overall picture of the upper town, creating the connection to the lower town and the other margin of the river Pruth as well as its twin city Sadagura. The promenade describes not only the topographic but also the historic and sociological levels of the city. Between the Habsburg Height in the West, the Jewish neighbourhood and the "Auen" in the Northeast, one can trace back 300 years of Czernowitz urban and cultural history.

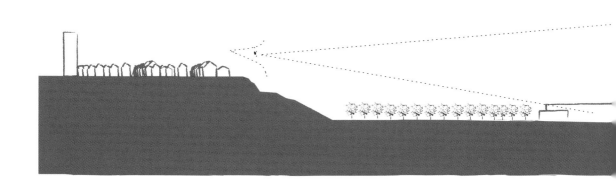

Damit ist die Promenade nicht nur für die Einwohner der Stadt von Interesse, sondern ebenso für Touristen. Die authentischen Orte entlang der Promenade wie Universität, Goebels- und Habsburghöhe, Synagogengasse, Jüdischer Friedhof werden ergänzt um weitere Angebote der Kultur sowie der sportlichen Betätigung. Die Geländekante begrenzt jedoch nicht nur die Oberstadt, sondern auch das unmittelbar ihr zu Fuße liegende Gebiet des Bahnhofes. Entlang des Gleisverlaufs nach Osten ist die Talebene in ihrer Entwicklung bisher sich selbst überlassen geblieben. Wir schlagen hier die Einrichtung der Czernowitzer Botanischen Gärten vor, die den idealen Hintergrund zu den weiteren Programmpunkten bilden würde.

Section through the city showing the change in altitude

Programm

neues Programm
Kulturzentrum ....

bestehendes Programm
Industrieverlagerung ....

Stadtkante
Promenade & temporäre ....
Nutzungen

die Region
Europa-Radweg ....

Freiraum
Botanische Gärten & Raum für ....
Aktivitäten

Stadtlandschaft:
Oberfläche und Artefakte ....

Topographie:
Talebene des Pruth ....

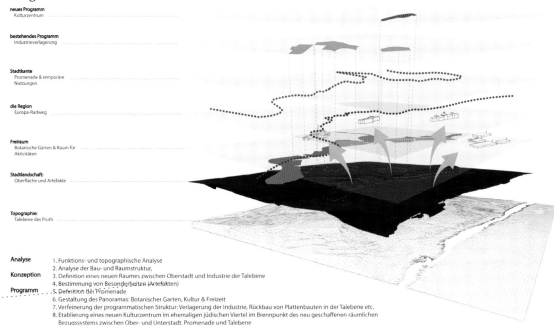

Analyse
1. Funktions- und topographische Analyse
2. Analyse der Bau- und Raumstruktur,
Konzeption
3. Definition eines neuen Raumes zwischen Oberstadt und Industrie der Talebene
4. Bestimmung von Besonderheiten (Artefakten)
Programm
5. Definition der Promenade
6. Gestaltung des Panoramas: Botanischer Garten, Kultur & Freizeit
7. Verfeinerung der programmatischen Struktur: Verlagerung der Industrie, Rückbau von Plattenbauten in der Talebene etc.
8. Etablierung eines neuen Kulturzentrum im ehemaligen jüdischen Viertel im Brennpunkt des neu geschaffenen räumlichen Bezugssystems zwischen Ober- und Unterstadt. Promenade und Talebene

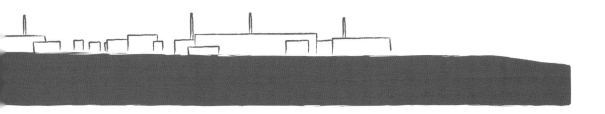

    With this, the promenade is of interest not only for inhabitants of the city but also to tourists. The most authentic locations along the promenade such as the university, Goebels- and Habsburg Heights, Synagogue Lane, Jewish Cemetery are complemented by further cultural offers as well as athletic activity. The corner of the area borders not only the upper town, but the area around the railway station in its immediate vicinity. Along the tracks to the East, the valley's development has been largely left to itself. We propose the establishment of the Czernowitz botanical gardens, which offer the ideal background to the other program points."

Diagram of the programmatic layers

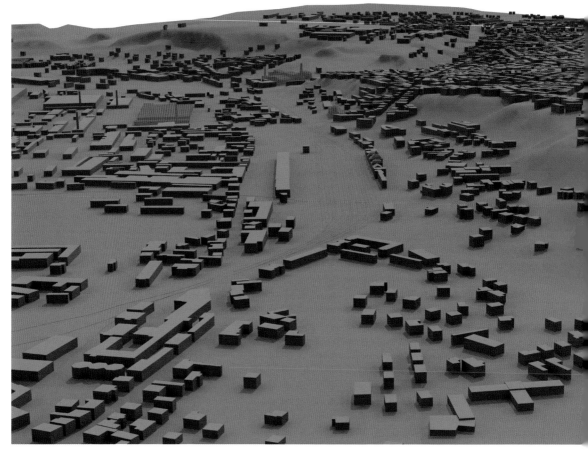

above: Digital model showing the area around the railway station

below: Promenade along the topographic height elevation

Conversion of the disused industrial plants

THE SITE
DER ORT
LOCATIA
РОЗТАШУВАННЯ

ARCHITEKTURGESCHICHTE VON CERNĂUTI IN 10 MINUTEN
CHERNAUTI'S ARCHITECTURAL HISTORY IN 10 MINUTES

SPAZIERGANG VON DER STEINZEIT BIS ZUR GEGENWART (1938)
VON *ING. ARCHITEKT JOSEPH LEHNER, PROFESSOR*
ARTIKEL AUS DER DEUTSCHEN TAGESPOST, 24./25. DEZEMBER 1938,
SEITE 9
A STROLL FROM THE STONE AGE TO THE PRESENT
BY *ING. ARCHITECT JOSEPH LEHNER, PROFESSOR*
ARTICLE FROM THE "DEUTSCHE TAGESPOST" (GERMAN DAILY NEWS),
24TH/25TH DECEMBER 1938, PAGE 9

Gerade hier, wo sich zwischen dem Karpatenvorland und dem so genannten Bukowiner-Wald der Pruth durchzwängt, musste eine von der Natur begünstigte Niederlassung entstehen, die allem Menschenstrom Sperre und Kontrollort wurde. Gewiss war es der Cecina in der Nähe von Cernăuti, der, als erhabener Punkt die Landschaft beherrschend, zur Anlage eines festeren Bauwerkes reizte.

Ein Wachtturm wird es wohl gewesen sein, der als erstes stabileres Bauwerk hier errichtet wurde. (...) Die hohe Kultur der ländlichen profanen und sakralen Holzbaukunst bei uns zu Lande lässt darauf schließen, dass sie sehr alt ist und uns somit die Kenntnis von der Bauart menschlicher Niederlassungen weit zurückliegender Zeiten vermitteln kann. Zwei Holzkirchen in unserer Stadt erinnern noch an diese, dem Boden entwachsene Holzbauperiode. Die Nikolauskirche in der Str. Gen. Averescu und die Caliceaneakirche in der Nähe der Friedhöfe lassen uns ungefähr ahnen, wie es einmal bei uns ausgesehen haben dürfte. Wie diese Holzkirchen, standen im alten Cernăuti die hölzernen Wohnhäuser in reizvoll idyllischen Gärten und lassen uns in der Fantasie ein romantisch versponnenes Stadtdasein schauen. Das Zentrum dieses Alt-Cernăuti befand sich in der Gegend des Türkenbrunnens.

Im Laufe der Jahrhunderte entwickelte sich Alt-Cernăuti zu einer bedeutenderen Zollstation und einem im Hinblick auf die hier sich bildenden Landesgrenzen von Fremden oft besuchten Markt- und Warenumschlagsort. Das Einlagern der Waren aber erforderte feste, gemauerte Magazine und Keller. In Verbindung und im Anschluss an diese entstanden wohl die ersten gemauerten Wohnhäuser der Kaufleute und Zöllner.

Um diese Zeit dürfte auch die Cecinaburg zum Schutze des Grenzhandels in Stein wehrhaft aufgebaut worden sein. Die Bauformen dieser Steinbauten sind uns leider nicht erhalten, doch können wir ruhig annehmen, dass ihr baukünstlerischer Wert bei weitem nicht an die traditionsgebundenen Holzbauten heranreichen konnte. Wir sehen hier sozusagen zum ersten Mal aus der Notwendigkeit menschlichen Lebens zwei gleichzeitige Baustile entstehen: den volkhaften Holzbaustil und den zweckhaften Steinbaustil. Dieses wäre ungefähr das spärliche Entwicklungsbild der Baukultur von Cernăuti bis zur Okkupation der Bucovina durch Österreich. Der Aufschwung, den Czernowitz als Landeshauptstadt unter der österreichischen Verwaltung nahm, war ein den gegebenen Umständen entsprechender.

Some hatchets and shards from the stone age excavated in Chernauti's municipal area as well as near the village Sipenit, which could be ascertained as a stone Age settlement due to the more plentiful findings, allow the presumtion, that our home town Cernauti already existed as a human settlement in prehistoric times. (...)

Of all places, the area between the Carpathian foreland and the so-called Bukovina Forest, where the Pruth squeezes through, a settlement developed, favoured by its surroundings and functioning as a barrier and control point for all streams of people. Surely the Cecina, an exalting and dominating point of the landscape around Cernauti stimulated the growth of a firmer edifice.

Most probably, a watchtower functioned as the first stable building here. Wood presumably functioned as the original material for the cretion of this structure. Naturally, building types from this early period were not preserved, and even the historically founded Bastarnen and Gothic settlements in our region did not leave behind any persisting remnants. The high culture belonging to secular and sacral wooden architecture in our countries' rural areas awakens the suspicion, that this art is very old, and that it can therefore communicate the knowledge concerning the nature of human settlements from the past. Two wooden churches in our town still remind of this organic timber construction period. The Nicholas Church on Gen. Averescu Str. and the Caliceanea Church near the cemetery allow us to more or less presume what it might have looked like around here in past times. Similar to these churches, the old wooden residential buildings in Cernauti stood appealingly in idyllic gardens, enabling to fantasize about the town's romantically dreamy existence. The center belonging to this old Cernauti was located in the area surrounding the Turkish Well.

Map of Chernivtsi and surrounding area in 1774

Die Stadt vergrößerte sich innerhalb weniger Jahrzehnte um ein Vielfaches. Dem Baumaterialienmangel, der einer solchen forcierten Vergrößerung folgen musste, steuerte man auf mancherlei Weise: Vorstadthäuser baute man weiter aus Holz, mit den so charakteristischen Eingangslauben, die Bürger-, Geschäfts-, und Kanzleihäuser wurden aber in Stein und Ziegel errichtet. Da musste selbst die Burgruine Cecina herhalten, um dem damaligen starken Bauwillen mit der Lieferung von Steinmaterial zu genügen. Den Stil dieser Bauwerke können wir als einen "ärarischen Kolonialstil" bezeichnen. Es wurde einfach, aber gediegen dem Josefinischen Zopfstil Rechnung getragen. Aus dieser Zeit datieren das alte Generalsgebäude, das Haus Ecke Str. Romana-Unireaplatz und andere in ihrer äußeren Form nicht mehr erhaltene Stadthäuser. Wie gesagt, zeichneten sich die ärarischen Bauten dieser Periode durch größte Einfachheit aus, während die Bürgerhäuser wohl etwas mehr Schmuck anlegten, wie auch das Beispiel am Unireaplatz es uns beweisen kann.

Die Stabilisierung der Verhältnisse in dieser neu erworbenen Provinz Österreichs führte auch dazu, dass das Ärar sich mit zunehmendem Wohlstand der Provinz auch eines reicheren künstlerischen Ausdrucks in baulichen Belangen befleißigte. Die ärarischen Bauten aus der ersten Hälfte des 19. Jahrhunderts lassen auf eine einheitliche künstlerische Bauaufsicht schließen. Noch erhaltene Beispiele dieser Zeit sind die Gendarmeriekaserne, das Garnisonsgericht und die Hauptwache. Ja, selbst die sakrale Baukunst scheint damals unter ärarischer Aufsicht gestanden zu haben. Die alte katholische Kirche in der Str. Reg. Ferdinand, die griechisch-katholische Kirche in der Str. Romana, die Kathedrale und viele Landkirchen ähnlicher Art verraten die gleiche streng geführte Hand. Im ärarischen Biedermeier wirkte der strenge Zopf noch stark nach. Das bürgerliche Biedermeier konnte sich selbstverständlich viel freier und reicher entwickeln.

Ein treffendes Beispiel dieses bürgerlichen Biedermeiers ist das Haus der "Dacia-Romania" in der Str. Iancu Flondor 27. Einige Durchgangshöfe zwischen der Str. Regele Ferdinand und der Str. Bucurestilor in ihrer biedermeierlich-wienerischen Art lassen darauf schließen, dass hier in Cernăuti noch so manch schönes Biedermeierhaus gestanden hat.

left: Turkish well, one of the eldest public facilities

right: Area of Old Cernauti today

In the course of many years, Old-Cernauti developed into a more significant customs point and a site for markets and the turnover of stock, highly frequented by foreigners from beyond the regional borders, which had begun to crystallize. The stowing away of goods required solid, brick-layed storage rooms and cellars. In connection with, and following these buildings, the first brick-layed residential houses belonging to merchants and customs officers evolved. Around this time, the Cecina Fortress must have been built in a well-fortified manner to secure trans-border trade. These stone structures' original shape is unfortunately not preserved.

However we can presume, that their architectural value could in no way reach that of the traditional wooden constructions. We can distinguish more or less two building types evolving simultaneously due to human necessities for the first time : the traditional style of timber constructions and the functional style belonging to stone structures. This basically reflects the scarce developmental picture regarding Cernauti's building culture until Austria's occupation of the Bukovina. The boom which Czernowitz experienced as a provincial capital under Austrian administration was strongly linked to the given circumstances. The town experienced a manifold growth within only a few decades. One tried to control a shortage in building materials which inevitably had to follow this forced growth in several ways : suburban houses were built from wood as before, equipped with alcoves ; the residential houses, stores, and barristers' chambers were erected with stone and brick. Even the ruin formerly constituting the Cecina castle complex had to give way by delivering stone material to becalm the strong need to build at the time. The style defining these buildings may be categorized as a state-run colonial style. It simply but soundly ac-comodates the Josephinian rococo style. The old Generals' Building, the building at the corner of Romana Str. and Unirea Square, as well as several other town houses not preserved in their original outward appearance date back to this time. As mentioned, the state-run buildings of this period can be distinguished by their simplistic appearance, whereas the middle-class houses were designed in a more decorative fashion, as can be proven by the example of Unirea Square.

left : The old Generals' Building (1780) today

right : The old main guard-house today

Die Gründerjahre der zweiten Hälfte des 19. Jahrhunderts brachten unserer Heimatstadt wohl eine reiche Bautätigkeit, aber verhältnismäßig arme Kunst. Mit besonderer Feststellung aber wollen wir die Kunstwerke Hlavkas die Erzbischöfliche Residenz und die Armenische Kirche, von dieser Einordnung ausschließen. Diese beiden Kunstwerke, die in den Sechziger Jahren des vergangenen Jahrhunderts entstanden sind, geben unserer Stadt ein so ausgesprochenes Baugepräge, dass wir diesem eigenwilligen Künstler ganz besonderen Dank schulden. Er hat das Verdienst, unsere Stadt vor dem restlosen Versinken in die wertlose erborgte Baukultur der Gründerjahre bewahrt zu haben. Ein einziges Türmchen der erzbischöflichen Residenz wiegt sämtliche Pseudo-Renaissance-Palastfassaden in unseren Straßen auf. Gewiss verleugnet auch Hlavka nicht den Geist seiner Zeit, er schwelgt in historischen Reminiszenzen, aber sein Eklektizismus ist der eines ganz großen Künstlers. Wir Einwohner von Cernăuti können stolz sein, dass wir gerade in dieser, an architektonischen Schöpfungen armen Zeit ein für Jahrhunderte unserer Stadt charakteristisches Bauwerk erhalten haben.

Yuriy Fedkovych Chernivtsi National University, former archbishop's residence, finished in 1875

The stabilization of circumstances in this newly acquired province also resulted in an increase in the province's prosperity. This again caused a more elaborate artistic expression regarding building concerns within the state. The state-run buildings from the first half of the 19th century appear to developed under a uniform building supervision. Examples preserved to this day include the gendarmerie barracks, the garrison court, and the main guard-house. Even the ecclesiastical architecture seems to have been under state-run control. The Catholic church in the Reg. Ferdinand Str., the Greek-Catholic churches in Romana Street, the cathedral, as well as many established regional churches of similar appearance bespeak a similarly strong lead. The stern late rococo style continued to have an effect lived on within municipal Biedermeier style. The Biedermeier style originating from the middle class could naturally develop much more freely.

The "Dacia-Romania" in the Iancu Flondor Str. 27 is an accurate example for this middle-class Biedermeier style. Several connecting courts between the Regele Ferdinand Str. and the Bucurestilor Str. with their Viennese-Biedermeier style suggest that there used to be many a beautiful Biedermeier-style house in Cernauti.

left: Villa, 20th century

right: Interior of the town's theatre

Das beginnende 20. Jahrhundert brachte uns einen Bauimpuls und mit ihm manches Schöne. Das Sparkassengebäude, die Handelskammer, der Innenraum des Stadttheaters und einige Wohn- und Villenbauten geben uns Zeugnis von einem großzügigen Bauwille, der um eine entsprechende Form rang. Diesem Suchen und Versuchen machte der Weltkrieg ein Ende. Nach dem Kriege steht die wieder nach Norden hin wirkende Grenzstadt Cernäuti vor der Aufgabe, ihrer Vereinigung mit dem Mutterlande auch in baulichen Belangen gerecht zu werden. Vor allem baute die Industrie. Sie baute zweckmäßig, schmucklos, oftmals zu zweckmäßig und schmucklos – und deswegen hässlich! Langsam rang sich in der Welt der Stil der "neuen Sachlichkeit" durch. Der allzu wilde Expressionismus der Inflationszeit, der in der Baukunst nur spärliche Früchte trug, wurde von einem sogenannten Kubismus abgelöst, einem Baustil, der aus dem Bedürfnis entsprang, die Bauaufgaben nach innen und außen wahrhaft zu gestalten, sich nicht von überalterten Formen verführen zu lassen, sondern neue Wege in der Beherrschung der Baumassen zu finden. Auch unsere Stadt suchte diesen modernen Strömungen gerecht zu werden, ja sie versucht es heute noch.

Noch kann man sich kein rechtes Bild vom neuen Bauschaffen unserer Stadt machen, es fehlt die notwendige Distanz! Die Fehler, die bei fast allen Spekulationswohnhäusern gemacht wurden, werden hoffentlich durch die neue Bauordnung in Zukunft verhindert werden können. Der Wille, Cernäuti zu einer modernen Stadt zu auszubauen, ist nur zu begrüßen. Allerdings liegt die künstlerische Situation des Tages nicht so günstig, wie in den von einheitlicheren Anschauungen beherrschten Zeiten. Der Baukünstler der Gegenwart muss eigentlich drei Stile beherrschen: den traditionellen Volksbaustil, der in Villen, Kleinwohnhäusern u.ä. zu Worte kommen will; den sachlichen Zweckbaustil, dem Industriebauten, Wohnhäuser größeren Ausmaßes, Spitäler u.ä. folgen müssen, und den repräsentativen Nationalstil, der kulturellen, administrativen und sakralen Bauten entsprechend erscheint. Wir wollen hoffen, dass die in Angriff genommenen und geplanten Großbauten unserer Stadt eine glückliche Hand zur Planung und Ausführung erhalten; eine Hand, die von einem tiefer schauenden Geist geführt wird. Möge zum Heile unserer Stadt sich eine Baukultur in diesen Tagen gestalten, deren wir vor unseren Enkeln nicht werden zu schämen brauchen.

The years of the Wilhelminian Style during the second half of the 19th century brought a great amount of building activity, but only a comparatively poor development in the fine arts. However, we have to exclude Hlavka's works of art – namely the archbishop's residence and the Armenian church – from this classification with special emphasis. Both works of art, which originate from the 1860's of the past century, give our town such a characteristic architectural imprint, that we owe special thanks to this headstrong artist. He is accredited with saving our town from entirely sinking into the worthless and borrowed building culture of the Wilhelminian years. A single small tower belonging to the archbishop's residence outweighs the great number of pseudo-renaissance-palace facades in our streets. Certainly Hlavka does not negate the spirit of his time, he revels in historic reminiscences, but his eclecticism is that of a great artist. We, Cernauti's inhabitants, can be proud, that our town received such an extraordinarily characteristic example of architecture precisely at this time depleted of architectonic creations.

The commencing 20th century brought us a building impulse and many beautiful buildings. The savings bank building, the chamber of commerce, the interior of the town's theatre, as well as several residential buildings and villas verify the generous will to build, which strived to create an appropriate form. The first World War put an end to this trial and error search. Following the War, Cernauti once again functioned as a border town towards the north and stood before the challenge to complete the reunification with its motherland on the architectural level as well. Especially the industry began to construct buildings. It built in a functional, non-ornamentel fashion, often too functionally and plainty – and therefore in an unsightly manner. Slowly, the style of the "New Objectivity" established itself throughout the world. The much too wild Expressionism of the period of inflation which only yielded few fruits in architecture was replaced by the so-called Cubism, a style in architecture. This style sprang from the need to truly design architectural assignments from the inside to the outside, not to be compromised by antiquated forms, but to detect new ways in restraining the built masses. Our town tried to live up to these new expectations as well, yes, it is still attempting to do so today. Up to this point it is still difficult to create a contemporary wellrounded picture of this town for oneself, one is still lacking the necessary distance! The mistakes which occurred with nearly every new speculative residential building project will hopefully avoided in the future thanks to the new building regulations. The attempt to expand Cernauti as a modern town can only be welcomed. However, the artistic situation nowadays is not as beneficial as in times formed by more unitary views. The contemporary architect actually has to master three styles: the traditional folklorist architectural style, which wishes to have a say in mansions, small-scale private houses, and others; the objective functionalist style, which industrial buildings, residential buildings of greater dimensions, hospitals etc. yield to, and the representative national style, which accordingly appears in connection with cultural, administrative, and sacred buildings. We hope that the large-scale projects in planning which persons responsible are attempting to tackle will find a gifted hand for the planning and realization process; a hand that is guided by a profound spirit. Let us hope that a building culture may develop for the well-being of our town which we do not have to lower our heads for in front of our grandchildren.

Theatre Square, Jewish National house, built 1907-1908 and Romanian National house, built in 1937

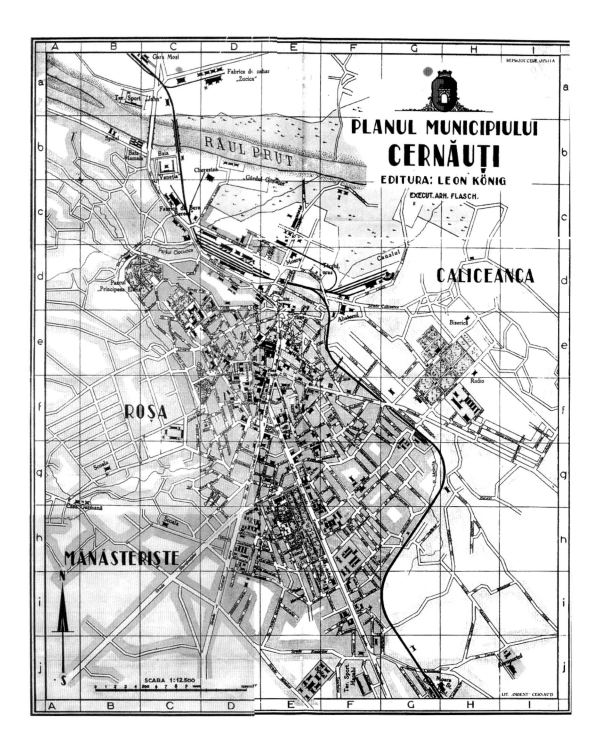

Map of Cernauti, Romanian era

DAS HAUS AN DER BARLEONGASSE
THE HOUSE ON BARLEON LANE

VON *PETER A. LEHNER*, GEB. AM 10. OKTOBER 1925 IN CERNAUTI,
RUMÄNIEN GEKÜRZTE FASSUNG MIT FREUNDLICHER GENEHMIGUNG
DES AUTORS
BY *PETER A. LEHNER*, BORN ON THE 10TH OF OCTOBER 1925 IN
CHERNOWITZ ROM. CERNAUTI ABRIDGED VERSION WITH THE
AUTHOR'S KIND PERMISSION.

Das Haus an der Barleongasse – es war für mich von meinem fünften bis zu meinem vierzehnten Lebensjahr der Nabel der Welt.

Als mein Vater, Dr. Ing. Josef Lehner, in den Jahren 1930/31 dieses Haus an der Barleongasse baute, hieß dieselbe seit zwölf Jahren bereits "Strada Zimbrului", also Strasse des Auerochsen, nach dem Wappentier der Bukowina. Das Haus war das erste im Sinne moderner Architektur errichtete Gebäude in Czernowitz und deshalb verschiedenerseits nicht unumstritten.

Die Strasse selbst war ein Paradies für uns Kinder, ungepflastert und ungeteert. Das einzige Auto in der Strasse besaß unser Nachbar Dr. Liborius Zelinka, ein junger Jurist, welcher mit der Tochter des Besitzers des Nachbarhauses verheiratet war. Dieses Nachbarhaus war eine schöne Villa, errichtet im Jugendstil.

Die Barleongasse begann unweit der Tramwaystation "Volksgarten" als Parallel-strasse zur Siebenbürgerstrasse (rumänisch: Strada Transsilvaniei). Für mich begann sie jedoch mit der kleinen Greislerei, die der Familie Goldberg gehörte. Der Geruch von Terpentin überdeckte fast den von eingelegten Heringen und bildete mit diesem eine unglaublich intensive Mischung, ab und zu verstärkt durch den Geruch von frisch mit Öl imprägnierten Fussbodendielen.

From the age of five to fourteen, the house on Barleon Lane served as the centre of my universe.

When my father, Josef Lehner, PhD of engineering, built this house in Barleon Lane in 1930/31, it had been called 'Strada Zumbrului' – street of the aurochs after the coat of arms carried by the Bokowina family – for the past twelve years. This house was among the first to be built in the style of modern architecture in Chernowitz. Therefore it inevitably encouraged lively discussions.

The street itself, in its unpaved and untarred state, was heavenly for us children. The street's only resident who owned a car was our neighbour, Dr. Liborius Zelinka. The young jurist was married to the daughter of the neighbouring house. This house was a beautiful mansion, which had been erected in the art nouveau style.

Barleon Lane commenced in the vicinity of the tram stop 'Public Park' and ran as a parallel road to the Transylvania Lane (in Romanian: Strada Transsilvaniei). For me, however, the lane began with the small corner shop, which belonged to the Goldberg family. The smell of turpentine almost covered the pickled herring. The unbelievably pungent smell resulting from this mixture was occasionally intensified by the oil from the freshly impregnated floor boards.

The house on Barleon Lane, 1932 – Architect Prof. Joseph Lehner

Die rechte Seite der Strasse begrenzte ein orangefarben gestrichener Bretterzaun, der den großen Garten der "Maternitate" (Gebäranstalt) abschloss – der einzige Zaun in der Nachbarschaft, den ich nie überklettert habe. Die linke Strassenseite begann mit zwei kleinen Häusern, gefolgt von fünf Reihenhäusern mit den Nummern 5 bis 13. Fast am Ende der Strasse war das Haus von Hedy Mathias, einer Cousine meiner Mutter, ein Haus, konservativ und niedlich, erbaut nach ihren Wünschen von meinem Vater. Nicht weit davon entfernt endete dann die Barleongasse.

Den rumänischen Namen dieser Strasse haben wir nie verwendet wie auch den vieler anderer Strassen und Plätze nicht. Wie zum Beispiel den Austriaplatz, Habsburgerhöhe, Russische Gasse etc. – so beharrlich können sich gewisse Bezeichnungen halten. Dies auch, wenn Weltreiche untergehen und die Obrigkeit eine andere wird, vor allem, wenn die gesellschaftliche Struktur erhalten bleibt, und die ethnischen Gruppe deren es bekanntlich viele gab, ihre Identität nicht aufgeben mussten.

Diese in der K. u. K. Monarchie gepflegte Toleranz wurde weitgehend erhalten, und wenn übereifrige und chauvinistische Kreise behaupteten, der wirtschaftliche und kulturelle Aufschwung in den wenigen Jahren der Zugehörigkeit zu Rumänien sei größer gewesen als in den 137 Jahren der Österreichischen "Okkupation", so wusste man, was davon zu halten war. Zum Glück waren solche Übernationalisten die Ausnahme und rekrutierten sich meist aus Zuzüglern aus dem Regat oder waren frisch gebackene Rumänen wie mein Klassenlehrer im "Aron Pumnul", welcher sich von Maximiuc in Maximescu gewandelt hatte und uns "Minoritari" schikanierte.

Mich hatte er besonders aufs Korn genommen, und wenn ich auf seinen Anruf "Hei Franz!" konterte: "Domnule Professor, eu nu mã chem Franz!" (...ich heiße nicht Franz!), brüllte er los: "Taci din gurã, toti nemti se chem Franz!" (...halt den Mund, alle Deutschen heißen Franz!).

Falsch wäre es jedoch zu vermuten, dass die ethnischen Gruppen planmäßig unterdrückt wurden. Und wenn ich mit Lederhosen und weißen Stutzen (Kniestrümpfe) herumlief, wurde ich keineswegs verlacht oder gar angerempelt. Der viel besungene Geist der Toleranz in der Bukowina und speziell in Czernowitz lebte auch während der rumänischen Zeit weiter und kaum jemand war daran interessiert, diesen zu zerstören. Das kulturelle und gesellschaftliche Zusammenleben der verschiedenen Nationalitäten, Konfessionen und Gesellschaftsschichten war so eingespielt, das auch die eingesessene rumänische Bevölkerung – nunmehr Staatsvolk – sich weiterhin an die seit langem herrschenden Spielregeln gegenseitiger Toleranz hielt.

Czernowitz war 1775 keine rumänische und keine ukrainische – konnte aber naturgemäß auch keine deutsche Stadt werden. Sie wuchs, dank der wesentlich verbesserten Lebensbedingungen unter der Schirmherrschaft des Doppeladlers und wurde so die wahrscheinlich kosmopolitischste Stadt Europas.

An orange wooden fence, enclosing the gardens of the maternity ward, lined the right side of the street. This was the only fence in the neighbourhood over which I never climbed. The left side of the street commenced with two small houses, followed by five terraced houses with the numbers 5 through 13. Towards the end of the street stood Hedy Mathias' house, one of my mother's cousins.

This house was conservative, charming, and had been built by my father according to all her wishes. Not far beyond this house, Barleon Lane came to an end.

We never pronounced the Romanian name of this street, similar to many other local streets and squares. Such places included the Austria Square, the Habsburg Heights, the Russian Lane, etc. – that's how strongly such terminology can persevere. This is even the case when empires demise and the authoritive command alters, especially when the social structure prevails, and ethnic groups, which exist in large numbers, may uphold their cultural identity.

This tolerance, as practiced under the K & K Monarchy, was largely maintained. If overly eager and chauvinistic individuals claimed that the economic and cultural upswing was greater during the few years of Romanian affiliation than during the 137 years of Austrian "occupation", one knew what to think of that. Luckily such extreme nationalists were an exception and usually recruited from followers of the Regat. Others were "new" Romanians such as my teacher in the "Aron Pumnu" who had transformed from a "Maximiuc" to a "Maximescu" and consequently harassed us adolescents

His remarks were primarily aimed at me, and when I answered to him calling me "Hei Franz!" with: "Domnule Professor, eu nu ma chem. Franz!" (…I am not called Franz!), he would shout: "Taci din gura, toti nemti se chem. Franz!" (…shut up, all Germans are called Franz!). However, it would be wrong to assume that ethnic groups were systematically oppressed. When I walked around wearing leather pants and white knee socks, I was not mocked or jostled at all. The much praised tolerant spirit in the Bukovina and especially in Chernowitz continued to exist during the Romanian time and barely anyone intended to destroy it. The mutual lives of the diverse nationalities, confessions and social classes – both culturally and socially – functioned so harmoniously that the immigrated, yet merged Romanians – now the native population – continued to uphold the long-established code of conduct, which ensured cultural tolerance.

In 1775, Chernowitz was neither a Romanian nor a Ukrainian town – simultaneously it could not become a German town either. Due to the fundamentally improved living standards, Chernowitz grew. Under the double-eagle it perchance emerged as Europe's most cosmopolitan town.

Warum aber hatte Czernowitz und nicht Radautz oder Suczava, das größer und zeitweise Hauptstadt des Fürstentums Moldau war, den Sitz des orthodoxen Bischofs für das Land? Es kann die geografische Lage gewesen sein, Suczava lag nicht am geplanten Verbindungsweg Siebenbürgen-Galizien. Man darf aber vermuten, dass da auch eine politische Überlegung ausschlaggebend war, die man auch als Gespür werten könnte, nämlich: Suczava war eine durchaus rumänische Stadt, Czernowitz hingegen ein ethnisch nicht erfassbares Konglomerat von Rumänen, Ukrainern, Juden, einigen türkischen Kaufleuten und angeblich sogar drei deutschen Familien, von denen keine nationalen Widerstände zu erwarten waren. Dieses Nichtüberwiegen einer ethnischen Gruppe scheint ein sehr gutes Fundament gewesen zu sein für die daraus sich entwickelnde Mentalität der Toleranz.

Als ich 1990 – fünfzig Jahre nach verlassen der Heimat und noch zu sowjetischer Zeit – Czernowitz besuchte, bot mein Elternhaus in der Barleongasse einen traurigen Anblick: von großen Bäumen umwuchert, mit abbröckelndem Verputz und diversen Glasschäden. Am Betreten des Grundstückes wurde ich durch den sehr abweisenden Blick eines Bewohners gehindert, sodass mir das Interieur des Hauses nicht zugänglich war, was mir wahrscheinlich einen Schock ersparte.

Groß war daher mein Erstaunen, als ich vor knapp drei Jahre, im Juni 2003, wieder vor dem "Haus an der Barleongasse" stand – es sah so aus, als ob die Bauleute erst gestern abgezogen wären. Es war wunderbar renoviert, in Form und Farben wie kurz nach der Fertigstellung vor 73 Jahren. Die einzige Veränderung war die das Grundstück umgebende Gartenmauer, sonst hätte ich das Gefühl gehabt, eine Zeitmaschine betätigt zu haben.

The house on Barleon Lane, 1990

Despite these merits, why did Chernowitz accommodate the orthodox Episcopal seat instead of Radautz or Suczave? The latter was larger and had at times even functioned as the capital of the dukedom Moldova. Its geographical location may have been the reason. For Suczava was not located on the planned transit route Transylvania-Galicia. In addition, it is safe to assume that a political deliberation played a decisive role, which can only be grasped by a certain delicacy of feeling. For Suczava was a thoroughly Romanian town. Conversely, Chernowitz offered an ethnic conglomeration, which is difficult to fully grasp. The town consisted of Romanians, Ukrainians, Jews, several Turkish merchants and supposedly even three German families. Despite this diversity, no nationalist resistance was anticipated from any of these ethnicities.

During my visit to Chernowitz in 1990 – fifty years after leaving my home town and still during Soviet times – my parental home offered a devastating sight: large proliferous trees surrounded the house, plaster was gradually crumbling away from the exterior walls and there were several broken panes of glass. The tenant's rejecting stare hindered me from setting foot on the premises. The interior of the house was thus inaccessible to me, which probably spared me from a severe shock.

My astonishment was therefore all the greater when I stood in front of the "House on Barleon Lane" once again nearly three years ago, in June 2003. In seemed as though the construction workers had just left the day before. It had been marvellously renovated with its shape and colours almost as they had been after its completion 73 years earlier. The only variation consisted of the garden wall surrounding the property, otherwise I would have felt as though I had made use of a time machine.

The house on Barleon Lane, 2003

URBANITATEA EST-EUROPEANĂ DUPĂ 1989.
O COLIZIUNE DE IDENTITĂȚI ȘI UN ARHIPELAG
DE SPAȚII PRIVATE
EASTERN EUROPEAN URBANISM AFTER 1989
COLLIDING IDENTITIES AND AN ARCHIPELAGO
OF PRIVATE SPACES

BY *ȘTEFAN GHENCIULESCU*

Pare destul de riscant să vorbești despre caracteristici generale ale dezvoltării arhitecturale și urbanistice de după 1989 în fostele țări din est. Diferențele economice, politice și, mai ales, cele culturale, înainte vreme atenuate și ascunse de un regim comun, au explodat după căderea comunismului. Greu de găsit astăzi similarități între Slovenia și Turkmenistan, de pildă, chiar dacă atât de tipicele cartiere de blocuri socialiste se regăsesc încă în peisajul ambelor țări.

Totuși, poate că putem defini un număr de trăsături comune, care împreună diferențiază regiunea atât în raport cu țările dezvoltate, cât și cu cele în curs de dezvoltare. Cea mai importantă dintre acestea ar fi colapsul spațiului public într-un spațiu al nimănui, înconjurând un arhipeleag de insule private : o individualitate extremă a acțiunilor urbane și arhitecturale. O alta ar fi recuperarea abruptă a identităților și coliziunea dintre aceste identități – socialism și post-socialism, naționalismul opus deschiderii etc.

Regimurile totalitare transformă spațiul public al orașelor în domeniul puterii absolute. Ca atare, acesta este intens supravegheat și transformat într-un loc al propagandei și al expresiei autorității, o scenă pentru sloganuri, parăzi și operații monumentale. În cazul regimurilor comuniste, acest tip de dominare a fost mai accentuat și generalizat. Inițiativa privată era practic inexistentă, statul reprezentând practic singurul proiectant, investitor și executant. De aceea, relațiile sociale normale și-au găsit refugiu aproape exclusiv în spațiul privat. Acasă puteai să scapi de supraveghere (în principiu), să vorbești liber, să asculți Radio Europa Liberă sau să organizezi petreceri cu prietenii, dat fiind că nu prea mai aveai unde să ieși în oraș. Doar în interior puteai individualiza unitatea standard de locuit.

Neașteptata dispariție a controlului totalitar a dus pe de o parte la înghețarea operațiilor statului (reluate apoi timid și într-un cu totul alt context) și, pe de cealaltă, la o erupție a inițiativei private : o frenezie de activități, de eforturi de apropriere a spațiilor individuale, și, ca sumă a acestor milioane de acțiuni, o dezvoltare generală aproape imposibil de controlat.

Această explozie a vitalității urbane a dus în mod paradoxal mai departe fenomenele de închidere și de refugiu în spațiul privat. Articularea și negocierea dintre lumea publică și cea privată sunt extrem de slabe și asistăm la formarea unei colecții de spații individuale disparate plutind într-un mare spațiu al nimănui. Nu este vorba despre o abandonare propriu-zisă a spațiului public – dimpotrivă, acesta este folosit, consumat intens și în moduri ce se schimbă cu rapiditate, din el sunt extrase permanent fragmente, devenind un câmp de bătălie pentru interese și expresii individuale. O urbanitate sub forma unui arhipelag de locuri disjuncte.

It is quite risky to try defining a common character in urban and architectural development within the former states of the Warsaw Pact after 1989. Economic, political, and above all, cultural differences, moderated and concealed before this break, literally exploded after the demise of Communism. One could hardly find any similarities now between Slovenia and Turkmenistan, for instance, even if typical socialist apartment neighbourhoods keep popping up in both nations' landscapes.

Nevertheless, we could perhaps define a few common features that collectively set the region apart both from more developed and developing countries. The most significant one would be the subsiding of public space into an archipelago of private spheres – the extreme individualization of urban and architectural actions; the second one – the abrupt recovery of identities and the clashes between them – socialism and post-socialism, nationalism vs. openness etc.

Totalitarian regimes use the towns' public space as a domain for their absolute power. Thus, it is closely surveilled and converted into space for propaganda and the authority's image cultivation, for slogans, parades, and impressive manoeuvres. With communist regimes, this dominance was as intense and extensive as can be. Private initiative was barred, since the state functioned as the sole planner, investor, and executive. Therefore, social connections, naturally implying a relative amount of autonomy, took refuge within private space almost entirely. Private homes principally became safe havens from state surveillance, where individuals could talk more un-reservedly, listen to Radio Free Europe or throw parties for friends, as there were no real places to go out to anymore. One could only alter or bestow a personal touch to the inside of the standardized habitation units. The unexpected departure of totali-tarianism firstly led to a freeze of state operations, revived slowly and in a different context, and secondly to a boom of private initiative. The former unpredictability of a centrally controlled system was replaced by a frenzy of private activities, steady efforts to adequately furnish private space, and an almost uncontrollable development. This boom of urban vitality forms a continuity or even intensification of the previously bred mentality regarding a lack of involvement and an escape into the private sphere. The dialogue between the public and private sphere has diminished. We see a collection of individual spaces grouped on a common ground. This ground – the public space of the city - is not abandoned : it is used, consumed intensely and in rapidly changing ways, while bits of it are continuously snatched. It becomes a battleground of interests. It is not empty, but it doesn't shape into a coherent whole anymore. An extreme social and spatial fragmentation has caused urbanism to become a disjointed archipelago of places.

Bucharest 2007

Ne putem întreba în ce măsură aceste fenomene sunt specifice doar zonei în cauză şi inevitabile pentru o perioadă de tranziţie sălbatică către o societate normală sau reprezintă un nou tip de atitudine faţă de spaţiul public. Cum ar putea arhitecţii şi urbaniştii să răspundă acestor tendinţe? Să se supună, acceptând situaţia, să propună modele ideale fără nici o şansă de a fi puse în practică, să aştepte" normalizarea "sau să încerce să re-inventeze, împreună cu comunităţile, moduri de a coagula spaţiul public?

În ceea ce priveşte coliziunea identităţilor urbane, aceasta nu reprezintă cu siguranţă o trăsătură exclusiv est-europeană. Ce pare însă destul de specific este schimbarea abruptă a politicilor şi percepţiilor. Pasiunea şi nerăbdarea de a reînvia trecutul de aur de dinaintea perioadei totalitare se alătură sau se luptă cu visul modernizării sau cu nostalgia după liniştea controlată a socialismului. Dialectica reinventării trecutului şi modernizarea frenetică sunt vizibile peste tot, de la" reconstrucţia (nu întotdeauna) critică "a Berlinului la zgârie-norii" cu specific naţional "din Moscova.

Situaţia devine cu atât mai complicată în ariile multiculturale, sau în cele ce aveau demult un astfel de caracter. Cui să aparţină azi aceste oraşe, din punct de vedere identitar şi al aproprierii? Putem spera ca distrugeri înfiorătoare cum au fost cele din războiul civil din fosta Iugoslavie (bombardarea podului din Mostar ce leaga partea musulmană de cea creştină a oraşului este extrem de simbolică) să rămână de domeniul trecutului. Însă se pare că învăţăm cu toţii teribil de încet să acceptăm o istorie plurală şi faptul că un trecut comun nu este o ameninţare, ci un potenţial uriaş. Văd asta în Transilvania, provincia central-europeană a propriei mele ţări, România, unde într-un oraş cum e Clujul, odinioară principalul oraş maghiar al provinciei, construcţia de monumente sau chiar şantierele arheologice au fost folosite în anii '90 pentru a exprima prezenţa actuală majoritară a populaţiei româneşti. Ce-i drept, lucrurile au evoluat considerabil. În aceeaşi mare regiune, oraşul Sibiu (Hermannstadt) fondat de comunitatea săsească este în 2007 Oraşul European al Anului, promovând multiculturalitatea.

În perioadea de dinaintea Şcolii de vară, îmi amintesc cercetările pe care studenţii mei le făceau pe site-uri web despre Cernăuţi. În mod ciudat, în funcţie de originea lor – germană sau austriacă, românească, ucraineană sau israelită – majoritatea acestor surse par să vorbească de oraşe complet diferite, datorită accentuării aspectelor legate de comunitatea proprie în detrimentul celorlalte. Situaţia la faţa locului mi s-a părut puţin diferită – mai bună – şi aceasta ar putea fi motiv de optimism. Deschiderea şi toleranţa, acceptarea unei moşteniri comune, şi ceva mai multă încredere în modernitate nu vor aduce cu siguranţă înapoi Cernăuţiul mitic, dar ar putea fi chiar mai importante pentru dezvoltarea oraşului decât multe dintre proiectele strict economice. Cred că Şcoala de vară din 2007 a fost un eveniment în acest spirit şi că ar trebui repetată şi dezvoltată.

The main question is to what extent such phenomena are specific and inevitable for this erratic period of transition towards a "normal" society or whether they present a new way of interaction with public space. How can architects and planners respond to these tendencies? Surrender, accept, or propose ideal models that have no realistic chance, wait for "normalization", or re-invent methods to coalesce the public in combination with the communities?

The phenomenon of a clash of different urban identities is certainly no exclusively Eastern European one. Perhaps the specific attribute consists of the abrupt change in policies and the perception involved in it. An urge to recover the golden past previous to totalitarian times goes along or fights with the dream of modernization or the nostalgic reminiscence of the tranquillity during socialist control. The dialectic of reinvention of the past and frenetic modernization are apparent everywhere, from the not always "critical reconstruction" in Berlin to Moscow's "national" skyscrapers.

This situation becomes particularly complicated in presently or formerly multi-cultural regions. Where do cities belong to in terms of identity and affiliation? We can hope that terrifying destructions as in the Yugoslavian Civil War – the destruction of the Mostar Bridge between the Christian and the Muslim parts of the city is symbolic – will not occur again. But it seems that we only gradually learn to accept a pluralist history and to understand that a shared past is not a threat, but a great potential. I can see this in Transylvania, the Central European province of my country, Rumania. In a town like Cluj, an important Hungarian city of the province, the erection of monuments or even archaeological sites was used to express the now prevailing presence of the Romanians. In the same region, however, the formerly German city Sibiu (Hermannstadt), became European City of the Year in 2007, promoting its multicultural presence.

I remember researching in books and on websites with my students for facts on Czernowitz. Oddly enough, according to their origin – German or Austrian, Romanian, Jewish, Ukrainian – many of these sources seem to talk about different cities, emphasizing their own aspects above the others. The real setting seems somewhat different – and better – and this should give reason for optimism. Openness and tolerance, the acceptance of a common heritage and more trust in modernity will certainly not bring a mythical Czernowitz back, but may be more important for the city's future development than many of the strictly economic projects. I believe that the summer Academy of 2006 functioned in such a manner and that it should therefore be repeated and developed further.

БУДІВНИЦТВО В ЧЕРНІВЦЯХ: ОСНОВНІ НАПРЯМКИ ТА ПЕРСПЕКТИВИ РОЗВИТКУ (ПОГЛЯД ЧЕРНІВЧАНИНА)
CONSTRUCTION WORK IN CHERNIVTSI: MAIN DIRECTIONS AND DEVELOPMENT PERSPECTIVES (AN INHABITANT'S VIEW)

ВОЛОДИМИР ГИНДИЧ
BY *VOLODYMYR HYNDYCH*

З часу здобуття незалежності та початку розбудови Української держави і до сьогоднішнього дня таке соціально-економічне явище як будівництво в місті Чернівцях, можна умовно розділити на декілька найбільш знакових періодів розвитку та становлення.

Розглянемо, як усе це відбувалося. Треба зазначити, що, крім бажання щось будувати, реконструювати чи реставрувати, має великий вплив економічна спроможність держави та її громадян, наявність накопичення достатньої кількості вільних ресурсів для інвестування в будівництво. Потрібні також висококваліфіковані фахівці, починаючи від архітекторів та інженерів і закінчуючи виконавцями, на яких покладена реалізація проектів. На якість робіт, безумовно, впливає наявність сучасної будівельної техніки, матеріалів та технологій у даній галузі.

На початку 1990-х років, одразу після розпаду Радянського Союзу, будівництво, як і інші напрямки діяльності суспільства, перебувало в глибокій кризі. В цей час практично не велося будівельних робіт, за винятком закінчення розпочатого раніше будівництва багатоповерхових житлових будинків. Багато об'єктів соціальної інфраструктури як державних, так і відомчих були призупинені (заморожені) та покинуті, оскільки на їх добудову не вистачало коштів.

Потрібно зазначити, що Чернівці мають притаманну небагатьом містам України специфіку, а саме – в архітектурному та будівельному сенсі це, по суті, два різних міста. Старе місто, з його доволі щільною поквартальною забудовою та повністю сформованим компактним історичним центром та квартали новобудов, так звані"спальні райони". У Старому місті з післявоєнного часу і до початку 1990-х років велося дуже незначне будівництво з урахуванням історичного середовища, а також статусу заповідної території. Тому ми маємо зовсім небагато прикладів будівництва на території центру міста в цей період. Окрім декількох будинків на вулиці Ватутіна та будинку на вулиці Худякова (Поштовій), будинку на розі вулиць Університетської та Ватутіна, а також будівлі телецентру по вулиці Братів Руснаків у проміжку 1950-1960 років жодних масштабних будівельних робіт в центрі міста не велося.

Починаючи з середини 1990-х років, з покращенням економічної ситуації в країні, накопиченням обігового капіталу як фірмами, так і окремими особами, спостерігається стрімке зростання попиту на технічні та

When observing the time span from the Ukraine's declaration of independence to the present, the socio-economic phenomenon related to building construction in Chernivtsi developed in several significant stages.

Let us observe this conversion in the following. In order to realize the desire to construct, reconstruct, or restore, it is imperative that the state and its citizens possess the possibility to do so economically or that they receive all available free resources in order to do so. They demand qualified specialists, from architects and structural engineers to project and building site supervisors. Modern construction machinery, materials, and technologies available in the area undoubtedly influence the quality of work.

In the early 1990s, immediately superseding the demise of the Soviet Union, building construction projects experienced a deep crisis, subsequent to the development in other fields. No construction work took place in Chernivtsi at the time apart from the completion of a few high-rise apartment buildings begun earlier. Many infra-structural projects, both on state and communal level, came to a halt due to a lack of fiscal resources for their completion.

Chernivtsi possesses a special structural peculiarity, as do only few Ukrainian cities; this quality is formed by the combination of two architecturally and structurally different parts of town. The compact historic center with its dense block structure adjoins the parts of town characterized by new building projects, the so-called "sleeping suburbs". From the post-war years until the early 1990s, the old town center was barely altered due to the existing historic building substance and the thereof resulting preservation orders. Due to the prevailing protection of historical monuments in the city center, very few new buildings were erected here, leaving the historic part of Chernivtsi with very few examples dating from the era from the 1940s to the 1990s.

Socialist era apartment blocks in the south of the city

житлові приміщення. Це призвело до початку так званого будівельного буму. Розпочинаються ремонтні роботи з реконструкції та благоустрою великої кількості приміщень різного типу - від підвалів, напівпідвалів до перших поверхів та мансард. У цей час відбуваються перші спроби масштабних реконструкцій та окремих будівництв, посилюється тиск капіталу на суспільні права та інтереси з вимогою реалізації масштабних проектів будівництва. Але, незважаючи на окремі помилки та невдачі, на сьогоднішній день в центральній частині міста здійснено набагато більше капітальних ремонтних робіт і реконструкцій, ніж будівництва нових будинків. Те, що було збудовано та реконструйовано завдяки спільним зусиллям міської адміністрації та громадськості в контролі над проектами та виконання робіт з будівництва, органічно вписалось у навколишній міський ландшафт. Для прикладу – реконструкція зруйнованого будинку по вулиці О. Кобилянської, 19, що був відбудований відповідно до початкового авторського проекту австрійського архітектора Шрутека часів Габсбурзької монархії, новобудова на площі Соборній (Торговельний дім "Соборний"), що гарно завершила кутовий злам кварталу. В Старому місті також ведуться та плануються кілька амбітних проектів з здійсненню реконструкції та будівництва. Наприклад, масштабна реконструкція та добудова універмагу "Рязань" на вулиці Червоноармійській, ідея підземного паркінгу та готелю на площі Соборній.

У центральній частині міста існує ряд складних проблем, зокрема проблема ґрунтів та високого залягання ґрунтових вод є чи не найголовнішою, що робить актуальною програму створення мережі дренажних комунікацій для збереження старих будівель. Не менш вагомими викликами в Старому місті, заповідній його частині є, насамперед, збереження, реставрація, а також високопрофесійна реконструкція архітектурних споруд, пам'ятників, металодекору, елементів оздоблення та неповторних міських ландшафтів. Надзвичайно важливим, не тільки з огляду на естетичну цінність, є збереження та планування нових зелених насаджень. Пам'ятаймо, що Чернівці впродовж усієї своєї історії мали славу не тільки архітектурного, торговельного та мистецько-культурного центру, але й надзвичайно мальовничого міста, яке буквально потопало в зелені різноманітних, часто дуже екзотичних дерев. Його околиці, і не тільки вони, весняної пори перетворювались на суцільний квітучий сад.

Говорячи про забудову в Старому місті, не можна не згадати про квартали індивідуального будівництва як в центрі, так і на міських околицях. Будівельні та ремонтні роботи велися тут, незважаючи на економічну кризу, практично безперервно. У місцях віллової забудови в районі вулиць Фрунзе, Чапаєва, Стеценка, Боброва уже в наш час будівлям завдано непоправної шкоди, окремі з них повністю перебудовані так, що від первісного вигляду не залишилось і сліду. Те, що з'явилось на їх місці, дуже далеке від архітектурної досконалості та повністю випадає з колись цілісного та гармонійного ансамблю. Новобудови індивідуальних житлових будинків у районах "Роші", "Клокучки", заводу "Кварц" за незначними винятками можуть слугувати зразками нічим невиправданої "помпезності", гігантоманії та показушності, як зразки поганих смаків та людської гордині.

From the mid 1990s onward, a rapid increase in the demand for technical premises and living estates evolved due to the improvement of the country's economic situation, in addition to an accumulation of capital both by companies and by individuals. This initiated a construction boom. Large-scale reconstruction, refurbishment, and both private and public building projects were launched. Unfortunately, the investors' views did not coincide with the community's needs at all times. However, much of the necessary major refurbishments and reconstructions took place in the town center as opposed to the slow development regarding the newer parts of town. Through the joint effort of the town's administration and the community, the newly erected and refurbished buildings smoothly fit into the town center's already existing scenery. In the old town center, ambitious reconstruction and construction projects continue to this day.

In the town center, the composition of the soil and the high ground water level call for a complex drainage system in order to preserve old building substances. The preservation, restoration, and professional reconstruction within the town center pose as an important challenge. The preservation and rearrangement of public parks are similarly essential not only regarding esthetic value. One should remember that Chernivtsi has always been renowned as not merely an architectural, trading, artistic, and cultural center, but appeared simultaneously as a picturesque town overspread with plants and exotic trees and accentuated by parks. Its suburbs turn into a blossoming garden during springtime.

left: Refurbishment in the historical city centre
right: Newly-erected building in Chernivtsi

Ситуація з будівництвом до середини 1990-х років була такою: в східному та південному напрямках міських околиць, а також в районах Садгори та Старої Жучки велося масштабне житлове та промислове будівництво – зводились комплекси заводів "Кварц", "Гравітон", "Електронмаш", "Радіоламповий" та інші, будувались мікрорайони Проспекту Незалежності, вулиць Стасюка, Комарова, Південно-Кільцевої, Руської, Хотинської.

У наш час велике будівництво здійснюється в кварталах нового міста, що, за задумом міської влади та проектантів, повинно буде зняти ділову та господарську напругу зі Старого міста і забезпечити поступове переміщення бізнес-центру в район Проспекту Незалежності. Для прикладу, тут проведено велику реконструкцію та завершено "довгобуд" на розі вулиці Червоноармійської та Проспекту Незалежності, що перетворило останній в сучасний супермаркет "Майдан". Новою, не зовсім вдалою з естетичної точки зору, є споруда торговельного центру "Формаркет" на розі вулиць Стасюка та Проспекту Незалежності, що виникла на місці тимчасових торговельних ларків. Ця доволі велика споруда, яка збудована за кошти підприємців тимчасового ринку, повинна була покращити умови праці людей, підняти рівень обслуговування покупців та допомогти ліквідувати гострий дефіцит торговельних площ в місті. Але, на жаль, на сьогоднішній день, будівельні роботи ще не завершені.

Також активно реконструюються перші поверхи житлової забудови 1970-1980-х років, перетворюючись у магазини, салони, перукарні, офісні приміщення. Спостерігаються численні спроби не завжди вдалої житлової забудови мікрорайонів, яка ведеться на вільних площах в уже існуючих житлових кварталах міста. Проте тут потрібне високопрофесійне проектування, оскільки будівництво посеред житлових масивів хоч і є привабливим з огляду на економію при проведенні комунікацій та адаптацію в уже готову інфраструктуру, однак значно погіршує санітарну та екологічну ситуацію в місті. Дуже часто така забудова призводить до зникнення дитячих майданчиків, садових насаджень, скверів, місць відпочинку. Непоправної шкоди завдається зеленим насадженням, а також призводить до масової вирубки дерев та кущів, що рано чи пізно при великій щільності спільного проживання людей на невеликій за площею території, а також стрімкого збільшення кількості автотранспорту, призведе до дуже негативних наслідків.

Щодо перспективних планів будівництва та реконструкції, відомо, що п иких житлових комплексів зі своїми інфраструктурами, автономними опалювальними системами, покращеним плануванням квартир. Відрадним є той факт, що, окрім житлових, торговельних та офісних будинків, планується побудова об'єктів для дозвілля та відпочинку городян. Це, зокрема, проекти критого льодового майданчика, аквапарку тощо.

Впевнено можна зазначити, що майбутній стрімкий розвиток будівництва, його естетична складова, місця реалізації проектів будуть значною мірою залежати від рішень міської адміністрації, професійності проектувальників та будівельників, активності та небайдужості міської громади до долі історичної та культурної спадщини, свого сьогодення та майбутнього своїх нащадків.

Until the mid-1990s, large-scale residential and industrial complexes were conceived in the eastern and southern suburbs, as well as in Sadgora and Stara Zhuchka. "Quartz", "Hraviton", "Elektronmash", Radiolamp", and other industrial plants were erected.

Presently, the authorities attempt to relieve the old town center by developing the suburb surrounding Prospekt Nezalezhnosti and in consequence gradually moving Chernivtsi's industrial cluster from the old town center into this suburb.

The ground floors in residential buildings erected in the 1970s and 1980s are being refurbished and subsequently turned into stores, hair salons, and offices. New private residential housing is spreading throughout already existing residential areas dominated by apartment buildings erected with precast concrete slabs. This new development still requires town planning, since the new construction within residential areas makes sanitary and ecological concepts mandatory; the indispensable new service lines integrated into the existing sewer system upgrade the town's infrastructure. Nevertheless, such new building projects result in the disappearance of playgrounds, open spaces, public parks, and other recreational areas. Public parks suffer irreparable harm; many trees and bushes disappear, inevitably resulting in negative consequences for such densely populated areas when observing the rapid increase in cars.

Regarding future plans for construction, redevelopment, and sanitation measures in Chernivtsi, large residential estates and improved apartment building systems will be realized. Additionally to this, several recreational facilities will also be realized in the near future, namely a covered ice-skating rink, an "aqua park", etc.

The esthetic component in future rapid building development will fortunately depend on the decisions made by Chernivtsi's administrative body and approaching projects will be realized with the skill of professional designers. The interest of Chernivtsi's community regarding the fate of their historic and cultural heritage, their own present and their children's future takes a stand regarding the new projects' appearance.

МІСТОБУДІВНІ ПЕРСПЕКТИВИ. ГЕНЕРАЛЬНИЙ ПЛАН МІСТА ЧЕРНІВЦІ. TOWN PLANNING PERSPECTIVES – THE GENERAL PLANNING SCHEME FOR CHERNIVTSI

ЦВИЛЬОВ В.Н., КОРОТУН І.В.
KOROTUN I.V., TSVYLYOV V.N.

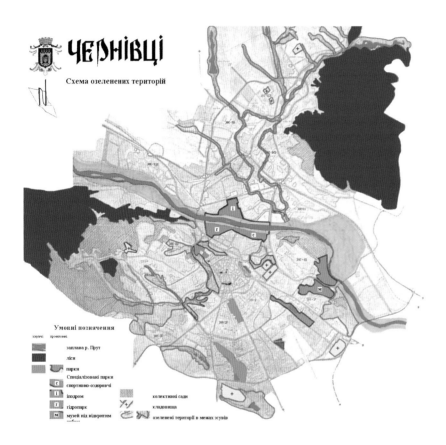

Територія міста Чернівців дорівнює 15340 га. Територія цінної історичної забудови – 226 гектарів. Загальна кількість населення 254 тис. Морфорельєф – заплава ріки Прут та пагорбистий правий берег. Під всі види будівництва можна використати біля 40% загальної площі. У 2003 році завершено коригування генерального плану міста Чернівців. Замовником на виконання проектних робіт виступила Чернівецька міська рада. Попередній генеральний план був затверджений у 1993 році, а розроблений у 1990 році (у радянський період), термін його дії первісно був запланований до 2010 року.

Previous general planning scheme, green spaces

The territory of Chernivtsi covers an area of 15,340 hectares. The parts of town comprising of historic edifices amount to a total of 226 hectares and hold 254,000 residents. The topography is formed by a level, easily flooded riverbank on the left side of the River Pruth and a hilly right bank. About 40% of the total town area may be built on. In 2003, the revision of the general planning scheme for Chernivtsi, requested by the Chernivtsi City Council, was completed. The previous general planning scheme was developed in 1990 and approved in 1993, during Soviet times, the original duration for its realization being estimated until 2010.

Previous general planning scheme, master plan

Але прогнозований цим генеральним планом розвиток міста у зв`язку зі змінами соціально-політичних умов, що відбулись в українському суспільстві, став нереальним. Аналіз розвитку генерального плану (також і в інших містах України) показує, що прогнози розвитку чисельності населення і обсягів будівництва були значно завищені. 10-15 років назад ніхто не прогнозував зменшення народжуваності, потужних еміграційних потоків, зміну суспільного ладу і розвитку ринкових відносин у суспільстві [1]. Радикальних змін зазнали сфери прикладання праці. З`ясувалось, що спосіб впровадження виробничої діяльності, який існував на західноукраїнських землях з кінця другої світової війни, не є конкурентноздатним. Це викликало появу нової для нашого суспільства проблеми – безробіття. Це у свою чергу спричинило появу приватного малого та середнього бізнесу, який частково вирішує проблему зайнятості населення, але потребує підтримки з боку державних структур. З боку розвитку ГП, це вимагало утворення нових територій, зайнятих ринковими територіями, закладами торгівлі та громадського обслуговування невеликих будівельних об`ємів. Суспільство отримало демократичні свободи, що викликало появу нових суспільних інституцій: релігійних громад різного віросповідання, громадських установ. З`явилось соціальне замовлення на будівництво культових споруд, що практично було відсутнє у радянські часи. Ці та інші обставини зробили попередньо розроблену у радянські часи містобудівну документацію генерального плану розвитку міста непридатною до використання.

Міська адміністрація зрозуміла необхідність коригування та адаптації генерального плану розвитку міста з метою більш ефективного керування містобудівними процесами. Діючий генеральний план міста Чернівці виконаний проектним інститутом"Містопроект", м. Львів, головний архітектор проекту Віталій Дубина. Проект пройшов громадське обговорення, експертизу Держбуду України та затверджений сесією Чернівецької міської ради у відповідності із чинним законодавством.

Новим генеральним планом передбачено розвиток транзитно-торгових та туристичних напрямків господарювання.

2. Головним елементом каркасу міської структури є потужна транспортна артерія – вулиця Головна. Вона перетинає місто у напрямку з півночі на південь. Ділянки вулиці в межах території історичного центру на сьогодні є проблемними для загальної транспортної структури міста.

3. Генеральним планом передбачена низка заходів, спрямованих на покращення існуючої ситуації: створення об`їзної та кільцевої магістралей, створення ділянок паралельного руху в місцях концентрації транспортних потоків. Наприклад, по вул. Нікітіна – паралельна вул. Гагаріна і розвантажує від транспорту привокзальний майдан.

Due to changes regarding social and political conditions within the Ukrainian society, the town's predicted development became illusory. An analysis of the town planning schemes of that time in other Ukrainian cities indicates that the forecasts for population growth and for the quantum of necessary construction work were set too high. A decrease in the birth rate, strong emigration flows, and a change in the social order in addition to changing conditions on the market were not expected 10 to 15 years ago. Labour relations experienced radical changes. The industrial activity as existing in the Western Ukraine since WW II could not remain competitive. This situation caused another new problem for society – unemployment. It led to the establishment of private businesses on a small to medium-sized scale, partially solving the problem of unemployment but requiring the support of state authorities. On behalf of this structural change, the general planning scheme was adapted in order to reorganize parts of town in a structure appropriate for applying small building dimensions. This concerned commercial areas such as market spaces, public services, etc. The Ukrainian society gained a free democracy, resulting in the appearance of new social institutions – various religious communities and other public establishments. This stimulated a demand for ecclesiastical premises, which had been virtually non-existent during Soviet times. The abovementioned circumstances, among others, rendered the previously developed town planning prospects outdated.

Chernivtsi's administrative body realized the necessity to correct and adjust the general planning scheme to the town's new developmental process, contriving a more effective management. The present general planning scheme for Chernivtsi was developed by "Mistoproekt" Design Institute, Lviv, the leading architect being Vitaliy Dubyna. The project passed public discussion boards and expert panels by the State Construction and Architecture Committee of the Ukraine; it was approved at a session of the Chernivtsi City Council according to the acting legislation.

The new general planning scheme implies a development of transit trade and the stimulation of the tourism branch.

2. Galovna Street, an arterial road, forms the vital element in the town's traffic system. It crosses the city from north to south. At present, several parts on Galovna Street lying within the boundaries of the historic centre are ill-fitted regarding their role within the city's traffic system.

3. The general planning scheme implies a number of measures aimed at improving the present situation, namely the construction of a bypass and a ring road, creating sections with parallel traffic flows in congested parts of Chernivtsi. For instance, Nikitin Street, running parallel to Gagarin Street, takes part of the traffic load off the market place near the railway station.

4. Промисловий комплекс м. Чернівців виник та розвивався на березі ріки Прут, відрізаючи місто від річки і позбавляючи його рекреаційних територій. Генпланом міста ріка Прут розглядається як основна композиційна та рекреаційна вісь. Підприємства, що розташовані в заплаві ріки, передбачено ліквідувати і поступово провести конверсійні перетворення функції території. Передбачається також подальше використання міського пляжу, створення гідропарків, спорудження культурно-відпочинкових об`єктів.

5. Матеріальне виробництво, зберігаючи на ближню перспективу свою провідну роль, поволі поступається іншим супутним містоутворюючим галузям: транспорту, зв`язку, інформаційним технологіям. Сфера обслуговування поглинає 22 % загальної чисельності населення, або 42 % від зайнятих у всіх сферах суспільної діяльності. Ця тенденція зумовлює перетворення функції виробничих приміщень під обслуговуючі, зокрема, під заклади торгівлі. Прикладом є торговельний комплекс"Боянівка", загальною торговою площею 40 тис. м2, місто Чернівці, вул. Хотинська, 43 (адміністративний район Садгора). Це реконструкція зі зміною функцій (конверсія) недобудованого заводу медичного обладнання.

6. Великі підприємства, які працювали на військово-промисловий комплекс колишнього СРСР, нині збанкрутували. Калинівський ринок – міське комунальне підприємство, на сьогодні є основним джерелом надходження податків до місцевого бюджету. Підприємство розміщене на лівому березі ріки Прут і є потужним стимулятором зростання економічної активності у місті, а також забезпечує місто додатковими робочими місцями.

7. З будівництвом об`їзної дороги пов`язаний подальший економічний розвиток південних міських територій, покращення транспортної інфраструктури та збереження забудови та покращення екологічної ситуації історичної частини міста. У зв`язку з цим її будівництво є для міста актуальною задачею.

8. Об`їзна дорога, крім вище викладеного, покращить транспортний зв`язок з житловим мікрорайоном"Руський" з заселенням у 3 тисячі мешканців. Мікрорайон"Руський"потребує структурного доформування, функціонального насичення об`єктами обслуговування, що відбувається у даний період.

left: Golovna Street, south of the city

right: Gagarin Street, towards the historical city centre

4. Chernivtsi's industrial area developed on the bank of the Pruth River, disconnecting the town from the river and depriving it of recreational zones. The general planning scheme sees the Pruth River as an important recreational axis. Enterprises currently located in the realm of the river's flood lands will be removed and the buildings' functions dominating in this stretch will be gradually converted. In the future, the city's beach will be reused and recreational facilities constructed.

5. While maintaining its leading role in the near future, heavy industry gradually makes way for other industrial sectors, mainly focusing on transport, communication, and information technologies. The services sector employs 22 % of Chernivtsi's labour force. This trend determines a functional transformation regarding commercial facilities from industrial to service-oriented ones. The "Boyanivka" Shopping Centre with a total shopping area of 40,000m^2, located at 43 Khotynska Street, stands as a good example. It was converted from an unfinished medical equipment plant to a shopping center.

6. Large enterprises, formerly thriving through their work for the USSR's military industry, have presently gone bankrupt. Presently, the Kalynivskyy Market depicts the enterprise in Chernivtsi that serves as the main source of local tax revenue. activity in the city and provides jobs.

7. The construction of the bypass triggers further economic development in the southern parts of town through the improvement of the transport infrastructure and the creation and improvement of the ecological situation within the historic part of town. Due to the mentioned motivations, its construction poses as an urgent task for Chernivtsi.

8. On top of the above said, the bypass will improve the accessibility of the "Ruskyy" Housing Estate, counting 3,000 residents, by motorized traffic. Furthermore, in order for the "Ryskyy" Housing Estate to function fully, it is imperative that a complete structural organization and a functional satiation with convenience services takes place ; this is currently initiated.

9. "Chernivtsi Airport" creates a number of serious problems for town planners.

Chernivtsi's industrial area developed on the bank of the Pruth River

9. Аеропорт "Чернівці" ставить перед містобудівниками ряд серйозних проблем. Сьогодні він майже не функціонує (1-2 рейси на тиждень, у радянські часи – 12 -14 рейсів на день). З одного боку є розуміння того, що аеропорт є важливим фактором майбутнього розвитку міста. З другого боку, на сьогодні він фактично стримує розвиток значних територій, оскільки посадочна смуга перешкоджає будівництву кільцевої магістралі. Уникнути цієї перешкоди можливо за допомогою тунелю, будівництво якого є надзвичайно вартісним проектом для міського бюджету.

10. Не функціонуюче сьогодні підприємство – завод "Кварц" – один з рубежів південної межі міста. У цьому напрямку виникає новий конгломерат : житлова забудова панельними 9-ти поверховими будинками та приміська забудова індивідуальними житловими будинками – адміністративні території села Остриця.

11. Район не функціонуючого підприємства Електронмаш, автовокзалу та проспекту Незалежності – перспективна реконструкція та конверсія територій, майбутня структуризація територій житлової забудови.

12. Гора Цецино, висота 535 метрів над рівнем моря (Балтійська система координат) природна домінанта. Вона надає міському рельєфу привабливості та динамічної активності. Лісовий масив гори Цецино – природний заказник, на території гори розміщені пам`ятки археології.

13. Чоловічий монастир Різдва Пресвятої Богородиці "Гореча" розташований на правому березі ріки Прут. Тут знаходиться найстаріша кам`яна споруда, яка датується 1767 роком. Її будівництво пов`язане з подіями російсько - шведської війни і Прутським походом російського царя Петра I 1711 року. Чернівці – місто з цікавим історичним минулим, зі значним економічним і містобудівним потенціалом. Інтеграційні процеси, що інтенсивно відбуваються на території Європи, а також економічний розвиток України, безумовно, сприяють розвитку Чернівців – столиці колишнього герцогства, а нині – краю Буковини.

Література :

1. Дубина В. Генеральний план міста Чернівці.// Архітектурний вісник, 4 ; Львівська політехніка, Львів, 2003. С.9.

2. Завалецький О. Майбутнє Чернівців – транзитно-торговий і туристичний центр.// Архітектурний вісник, 4, Львівська політехніка, Львів, 2003. С.6.

3. Коротун І.В. Етапи розвитку та забудови міста Чернівці. Формування історико-культурної заповідної території. // Матеріали Міжнародної наукової конференції 1-4 жовтня 2001р. Архітектурна спадщина Чернівців австрійської доби. Чернівці МПіНУ, ЧНУ. Чернівці.Золоті літаври- 2003. С. 9 - 15.

It is hardly utilized; there are only 1 to 2 flights a week compared to 12 to 14 flights per day during Soviet times. On one hand, it is mutually understood that an airport poses as an essential factor for future development. On the other hand, the airport presently limits the development in important areas since the runway hinders the construction of a ring road. This obstacle may be circumvented with a tunnel. Nevertheless, the construction of a tunnel would be a costly undertaking for Chernivtsi.

10. The remnants of a failed business endeavour regarding the "Quartz Plant" on Golowna Str. partially form Chernivtsi's southern boundary. A new housing estate with nine-story apartment buildings and a suburban development area consisting of single houses is starting to shape towards this direction.

11. The environs surrounding the unsuccessful venture "Elektronmash Enterprise" located on Golowna Str., namely the bus station and Prospekt Nezalezhnosti, will be converted, initiating the growth of a residential development area.

12. Mount Tsetsyno, reaching 535 meters above sea level, stands as a natural dominant point. It adds appeal and a dynamic appearance to Chernivtsi's relief. The forest covering Mount Tsetsyno is part of a natural reserve; archaeological monuments are spread over the stretch of the mountain.

13. "Horecha Monastery" of the Blessed Virgin is located on the right bank of the Pruth River. One can find Chernivtsi's oldest stone building here, dated back to 1767. Its erection is connected with the Russian-Swedish War and the Pruth Campaign launched by the Russian Tsar Peter I in 1711. Chernivtsi possesses an intriguing history and holds a significant economic and town planning potential. The integration processes taking place throughout Europe, as well as the economic development of the Ukraine both work as factors undoubtedly contributing to the positive development of Chernivtsi, the capital city of the former duchy and present region of Bukovina.

Literature:

1.Dubyna V. General Planning Scheme for Chernivtsi City.// Architectural Bulletin, 4 ; Lviv Polytechnic University, Lviv, 2003. P.9.

2.Zavaletskyy O. Future of Chernivtsi – Transit, Trade and Tourist Centre.// Architectural Bulletin, 4, Lviv Polytechnic University, Lviv, 2003. P.6.

3.Korotun I.V. Stages of Chernivtsi City Development. Formation of Historical and Cultural Reserve Territory. // Materials of the International Scientific Conference October 1-4, 2001. Architectural Heritage of Austrian-Time Chernivtsi. Chernivtsi, Ministry of Education and Science of Ukraine, Chernivtsi National University. Chernivtsi.Golden Drums-2003. P. 9 - 15.

left: Kalynivskyy Market, main source of local tax revenue

right: Pruth River as an important recreational axis

THE EVENT
DAS EREIGNISS
EVENIMENTUL
ЗАХІД

Group picture of the participants of the Summer academy

International Summer Academy of Architecture in Chernivtsi 2006
Czernowitz Tomorrow - Ideas for the City of Chernivtsi

Art Museum, Central Square 10, Chernivtsi
Sunday, 13. August 2006, 18:00 pm
Exhibition from the 14. - 23. August

Participating the University of Technology Graz
the Polytechnical College Chernivtsi
the Ion Mincu University Bucharest
the University of Arts Berlin

Students:

Bastian Bechtloff
Irina Bogdan
David Bürger
Kostya Chebriy
Sasha Chebriy
Jenica Craiu
Raluca Davidel
Lisa Dietersdorf
Olga Dundich
Konrad Edlinger
Elena Fischmann
Natasha Galyshka
Elisa Hernando Vilar
Konstantyn Komarovskyy
Dirk Krutke
Sebastian Lupea
Joachim Maier
Sven Marx
Palka Inna
Patraboy Nataly
Sigrun Rottensteiner
Vanessa Sartori
Nina Sleska
Dina Sokur
Elena Stoian
Adrian Timaru
Stefan Tuchila
Veronica Tudor
Matthias Tscheuschler
Tanja Vakoliuk
Michael Wierdak

Tutors:

Oxana Boyko
Grigor Doytchinov
Stefan Ghenciulescu
Emil Ivanescu
Julia Lienemeyer
Günter ZampKelp

Sponsored by
University of Arts Berlin, German-Ukrainian Forum e.V., DAAD, Region Administration Kaernten, Robert Bosch Foundation, Modulor, German Embassy Kyiv

Posters of the participants of the Summer Academy English/Ukrainian

Міжнародна літня академія архітектури в Чернівцях 2006
Chernovitz Tomorrow – ідеї для Чернівців

Художній музей, Центральна площа 10, Чернівці
Відкриття у неділю, 13 серпня 2006 о 18.00
Виставка працюватиме 14-23 серпня 2006

За участю:
Технічного університету м. Граца, Австрія
Політехнічного технікуму м. Чернівців, Україна
Іон Мінку університету м. Бухарест, Румунія
Університету мистецтв м. Берлін, Німеччина

Студенти:

Бастіан Бештлофф
Ірина Богдан
Давід Бергер
Костянтин Чебрій
Олександр Чеврій
Дженіка Краю
Ралюка Давідел
Ліза Дітерсдорф
Ольга Дундич
Конрад Едлінгер
Елена Фішман
Наталія Галушка
Еліза Хернандо Вілар
Костянтин Комаровський
Тетяна Ваколюк
Дірк Крутке
Себастьян Люпея
Юахім Мая
Свен Маркс
Інна Палка
Наталія Патрабой
Сігрун Ротенштайнер
Ванесса Сартурі
Ніна Слеска
Діна Сокур
Елена Стоян
Адріан Тімару
Стефан Тучіла
Вероніка Тудор
Матіас Чойшлеар
Міхаель Вірдак

Викладачі:

Оксана Бойко
Грігор Дойчінов
Штефан Генчулеску
Еміль Іванеску
Юлія Лінемаер
Гентер ЦампКельп

Sponsored by
University of Arts Berlin, German-Ukrainian Forum e.V., DAAD, Region Administration Kaernten, Robert Bosch Foundation, Modulor, German Embassy Kyiv

Чого потребує місто?
WHAT DOES CHERNIVTSI NEED?

Павло Колядинський
By *Pavlo Kolyadinsky*

Міжнародна літня архітектурна академія була організована Університетом мистецтв Берліна, Технічним університетом міста Ґраца, Університетом Іон Мінку міста Бухареста, Чернівецьким національним університетом та Центром Буковинознавства. Більш як п'ятдесят архітекторів – молоді фахівці та їхні керівники-професори з чотирьох країн працювали спільно впродовж двох тижнів у Чернівцях над розробкою нових архітектурних проектів для міста. Завдяки своїй історії та сучасній містобудівній структурі Чернівці виглядають як чудова робоча лабораторія для студентів-архітекторів, які приїхали сюди, щоб дізнатися більше про це місто, вдосконалити свої професійні навички, а також обмінятися досвідом. Утворивши робочі групи з представників різних країн, студенти поставили перед собою мету запропонувати нові творчі рішення для існуючих містобудівних проблем міста.

The International Summer Academy of Architecture and Urbanism 2006 was organized by the University of the Arts Berlin in cooperation with the Technical University Graz, the Ion Mincu University in Bucharest, and the Chernivtsi National University and Bukovina Center. Over 50 architects – students and their professors from four countries – worked together for two weeks in Chernivtsi, developing new architectural projects for the town. Due to its history in combination with its modern town-planning structure, Chernivtsi appeared as the perfect working-laboratory for the architecture students who came here to learn more about the area, improve their skills, and exchange

above left: Appointment at the City planning department - Mr. Tsvylyov explains the general planning scheme of Chernivtsi

above right: Workspace of the Summer Academy - Presentation of design projects from the Ukrainian students

below: Drozdowski hall, German National House - Lecture in the context of the Summer Academy

Слід зауважити, що йшлося не про розробку абстрактних проектів, а про концепції, що мали б дуже конкретну прив'язку до реальних потреб міста. Очікувалося, що кожною робочою групою буде запропоновано оригінальну концепцію перепланування одного з міських районів, які особливо важливі для життєдіяльності Чернівців.

Спочатку існувала загальна ідея проведення заходу, яка була розроблена за межами міста і навіть країни, і це вимагало, в першу чергу, дослідити наявну містобудівну ситуацію в місті.

Отож, чого потребує місто ?

Для того, щоби це з'ясувати, потрібно було провести попередні польові дослідження - зустрічі із архітекторами, які працюють в місті Чернівцях – виконують приватні замовлення, беруть участь у містобудівних радах та конкурсах, компетентними посадовцями із Департаменту архітектури і містобудівного комплексу, які розробляють і реалізують концепцію архітектурного розвитку міста, начальником історико-архітектурного заповідника міста. Вони вказали на ділянки міста, які знаходяться в особливому полі зору міських органів влади і над якими реально проводиться робота або принаймні теоретично визначено недоліки у плануванні даної території чи обговорюються нові приховані потенціали. В результаті було окреслено певні більші та менші райони міста, кожен з яких утворював актуальну, прикладну тему для детальнішої роботи і пропонував більш як один можливий розв'язок. Було складено перелік таких тем, їх виявилось понад 30. Така кількість тем повинна була забезпечити вільний вибір задачі для вирішення. Межі районів-тем було чітко окреслено на плані міста, що полегшувало їхню подальшу конкретизацію, збір матеріалів та роботу над темою. Фотофіксація, історична довідка про територію, картосхеми повинні були уможливити попередню роботу над темою навіть на відстані, без особистого знайомства із даною територією і не мали на меті однозначно регламентувати постановку проблеми, а швидше слугували орієнтиром для роботи, оскільки межі районів і звучання тем могли вільно змінюватися відповідно до конкретного індивідуального бачення автора майбутнього проекту.

Міжнародна архітектурна академія спробувала на високому професійному рівні продемонструвати місцевій владі, архітекторам та громадськості міста ті нові потенціали Чернівців, про які вони, можливо, і не здогадуються, спровокувати публічні обговорення. Чи цікаво для мешканців міста дізнатися більше про особливості того місця, де вони живуть ? Завданням Академії було, окрім іншого, привернути увагу до нагальних потреб міста.

Це особливо стосується Чернівців, оскільки місто швидко розвивається і велика кількість нових об'єктів проектується і споруджується. Містобудівні помилки можуть дуже дорого коштувати, тому кілька нових свіжих поглядів могли би стати надзвичайно цінними для майбутньої картини міста.

Під час підготовки та проведення Академії було поставлено ще одну мету – дати імпульс до відкриття архітектурного факультету при Чернівецькому національному університеті.

their knowledge. Grouped in international working teams, the students were expected to offer new creative solutions for the existing town-planning problems in chernivtsi.

In addition to this, the completed projects should not remain abstract, but should display a very distinct connection to the practical needs of the town. Each group should develop an original concept to re-plan a part of town vital for the development of new activity within Chernivtsi.

The development of a general concept, derived from the town itself and even from the entire country, primarily demanded an investigation into the current town planning situation of Chernivtsi.

So what does this town need?

In order to find an answer to this question, a field research was initiated: firstly, meetings consisting of lectures and discussion rounds were arranged with architects working in Chernivtsi. These included architects working for private clients, others that participate in town-planning councils and competitions, competent officials from the Department of Architecture and Town Planning who develop concepts for the town's architectural conversions, and of course the director for historical architectural edifices and areas in Chernivtsi standing under a preservation order. They delineated the town districts which either receive a certain amount of awareness at present from the local administrative body, which are currently thoroughly restructured, which reveal weak points resulting from earlier plannings, or which indicate new potentials to be discussed. As a result, several bigger and smaller parts of Chernivtsi were outlined. Each chosen area offered prevalent relevant issues demanding more detailed thought and suggested more than one possible solution. A list consisting of 30 such topics was drafted. Such a quantity of possible topics provided a free choice of theme and area on which to concentrate. The boundaries for each district's topic were clearly defined on the map in order to facilitate the students' further concise definition of the theme, their collection of materials, and the resulting project work with their topic. The preparatory work on the chosen project was made possible – even at a distance and without personal knowledge concerning the area – by providing the students with photographic materials, historical references about the area, and maps. However, the project themes were not created in an attempt to state the problem unambiguously; they rather served as an orientation in the students' working process, since the areas' boundaries and themes could mutate freely, depending on specific personal ideas held by the project's designer.

The International Summer Academy of Architecture and Urbanism attempted to demonstrate the new potential regarding Chernivtsi's future development to local authorities, architects, and the town community, and to provoke debates. Is it interesting for Chernivtsi's inhabitants to discover the particular qualities and potentials of their surroundings. The academy also strove to draw attention to issues of current importance in Chernivtsi.

This is especially relevant to Chernivtsi, as it is developing rapidly and various new objects are being designed and built. Town planning mistakes may be very expensive; therefore a new vision holds great value for the future outlook of the city.

During the preparation and the subsequent conducting of the Summer Academy, one more aim was upheld – to give a powerful impulse for founding a department of architecture at the Chernivtsi National University.

THE LOCATION DEVELOPMENTS

BY *PROF. GRIGOR DOYTCHINOV*

The city of Chernivtsi presents itself nowadays with a centralized structure. The existing radial network of streets and zones has been laid down during the Austrian period and has determined since than the future extension of the city. Instead of replacing the city centre and the city extension down the slope, which is typical for European cities, the center has been moved up to the hill. The unique situation of the city centre on the top of the topographic saddle in the Austrian period and the restrictions for a development in the plain area north and east of the historic part floated periodically by the river Pruth are giving the framework for the clearly expressed monocentric structure. The monocentrism leads to an overcrowding of the historic city centre, where the most exclusive cultural heritage and the characteristic public spaces are to be found. Some steps in decentralizing have been done in the socialist period by locating supermarkets and other facilities in the zones of housing development, mainly south of the historic city centre. These planning steps have not been able to change the monocentric image of the city. The arising of the number of cars since the 1990s which pass the centre has increased the problem.

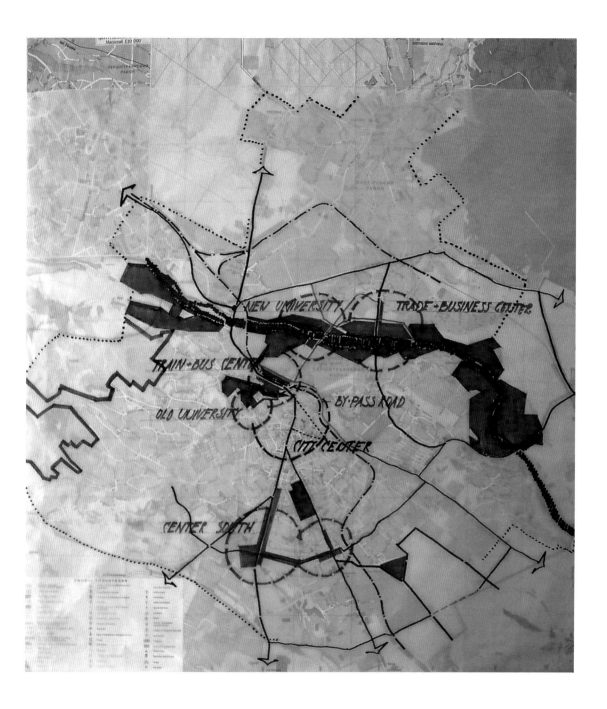

Concept scheme of the four design-project sites

At the same time the historic centre has turned his back to the area of the river Pruth which is characterized by belts of green accompanying the river banks. The green strip is crossing the urban area offering a lot of locations for leisure and recreation used actively by the citizens of Chernivtsi. The most of these locations are not designed and not adapted for public use. It can be concluded in generally that the river does not correspond actively with the composition of the city. The whole strip is on the other side of great importance for the ecology of the city and a great potential for future development. This potential can be used by creating a better connection between the historic centre and the river strip, by establishing of important city functions on the river bank, especially on the north one and turning back the face of the railroad station into the north direction. The river strip has to be threaten as the background of a secondary modern centre of the city.

Some existing public facilities in the south of the historic centre should be completed and extended. On this way the mass of housing development in the southern part of Chernivtsi will improve its city composition and receive the image of a modern city centre with an own identification. Not at least an upgrading of the housing milieu is needed to reflect the needs and expectations of the inhabitants.

The Summer Academy of Architecture in Chernivtsi 2006 has faced the above defined problems. The four teams of students have dealt with four locations, which have been recognized as potentials for the city development offering concepts and images. The first location is that of the existing railroad station and the surrounding area. The aim of the concept is to extend the functions of the station to a modern transportation center with train and bus stations, shopping activities and to establish a new and more actively used network of connections to the historic core of the city. The second location on the north bank of the river is proposed to be the New University centre of the city with direct connections with the river front. A third location is the Chernivtsi Trade and Business Centre founded on the existing Kalinivsky market and extended with functions of commerce, business and recreation. The fourth location reflects on the need to maintain the housing development from socialist period south of the centre creating a new image of the area.

The development of the four locations is based on a restructuring of the network of streets: The Rus´ka street is being prolonged on the north side of the railway road leading directly to the northern, "second" face of the railroad station and is connected by a new bridge to the territories north of the river. The transformed direction of the Rus´ka street will lead to a reducing of the transit transport through the historic centre and on the south side of the station. The new connection crossing the river is creating a short link between the historic part of the city and the "new territories" on the river Pruth banks.

Map of Chernivtsi 2006, showing the four design-project sites

Projektgebiet am Pruth

Kalinivski Market

University

Center

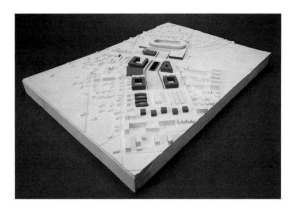

CENTRE SOUTH: STITCHING
A Social and Architectural Section through the City

Our team's project circumscribes an area with a roughly triangular shape. Two historic axes – Holovna Street and Chervonoarmiys'ka Street, as well as a fragment of a large boulevard from the Socialist time – Prospekt Nezhaleznosti, define the three sides. Differently from other areas that are more or less undeveloped and require local area planning, these extensive grounds contain several densely constructed areas that alternate with vacant or underdeveloped plots.

On the other hand, this part of town is extremely rich in terms of urban diversity. At one end of Chernivtsi lies the preserved historic town, which is compact and possesses a clear structure: streets, squares, rows of buildings with courtyards, and recognizable landmarks; in the south, its dialectical counterpart is located - the uncompleted socialist city, with an oversized boulevard that ends abruptly and prefabricated buildings, which stand freely on public space. The two straight axes previously mentioned connect these extremes, with the stretch in between composed of an eclectic structure ranging from fin-de-siècle buildings – mainly barracks – to hospitals, 1920 garden cities, detached houses and public buildings from the socialist era. Additionally to these fragments, the entire area displays signs of the dynamic and chaotic development during the past 17 years: new apartment buildings, temporary shops, commercial centers, advertising panels, glazed-in balconies on socialist apartment blocks, as well as the reshaped space in between.

Picture of the models, scale 1:1000

Pictures of the site: Chervonoarmijska Street, Holovna Street and the Nezhaleznosti Prospect

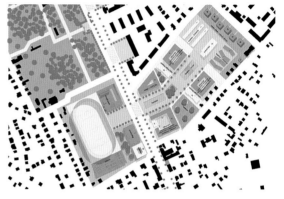

While the new developments are anything but beautiful, they show the population's needs and the creation of a singular character defined by a dynamic of its own, not requiring formal urban planning. A natural expansion of the center, connecting the old core and the densely built areas of the 1960s seems possible here. Moreover, this would not require an operation to start from scratch, eliminating the need for an expansive plan, allowing instead a more selective way of development: small-scale, delicate measures are applied in the right places according to general underlying principles, which the team defined together. These concentrate on creating new openings and connections while focusing on regeneration rather than demolition. Walking along boulevards and exploring the urban structures serves to clarify how at times a small gesture, like tearing down a concrete garden wall and replacing it with a transparent enclosure, suffices to dramatically change the character of neighborhood.

Such projects can teach students to design insertions and connections rather than homogenous structures. They learn to explore tendencies and learn how to control, emphasize, or reduce them instead of ignoring them and simply trying to impose "good" rules and forms. This seemed particularly relevant for the former socialist estates, where the guiding of individual activities can be an alternative both to chaotic change and fragmentation of space occurring at present, and to central planning now become impossible.

Team: Konstiantyn Komarovsky, Chernivtsi; Dirk Krutke, Berlin; Sebastian Lupea, Bucharest; Sigrun Rottenstein, Graz; Nina Sleska, Graz; Stefan Tuchilá, Bucharest; Tanja Vakoliuk, Chernivtsi; Unit Adviser: Stefan Ghenciulescu, Bucharest

above: Pictures of the site

below: Site plan, scale 1:100

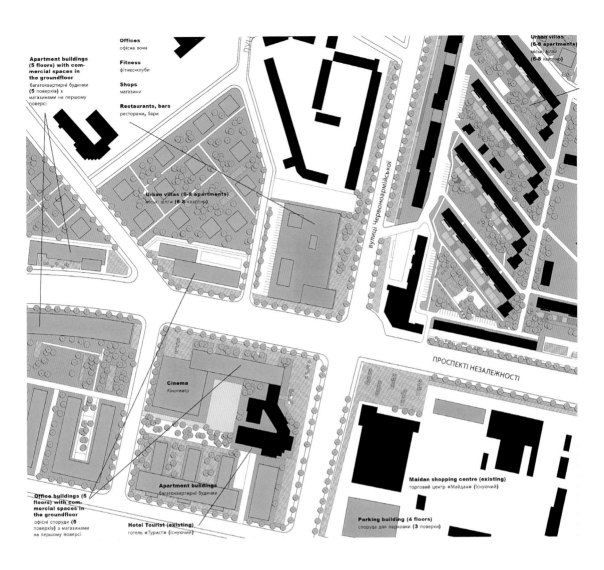

Apartment buildings (5 floors) with commercial spaces in the groundfloor
багатоквартирні будинки (5 поверхів) з магазинами на першому поверсі

Offices
офісна зона

Fitness
фітнес-клуби

Shops
магазини

Restaurants, bars
ресторани, бари

Urban villas (6-8 apartments)
міські вілли (6-8 квартир)

Urban villas (6-8 apartments)
міські вілли (6-8 квартир)

вулиці Червоноармійської

ПРОСПЕКТІ НЕЗАЛЕЖНОСТІ

Cinema
Кінотеатр

Maidan shopping centre (existing)
торговий центр «Майдан» (Існуючий)

Office buildings (5 floors) with commercial spaces in the groundfloor
офісні споруди (5 поверхів) з магазинами на першому поверсі

Apartment buildings
багатоквартирні будинки

Hotel Tourist (existing)
готель «Турист» (Існуючий)

Parking building (4 floors)
споруда для парковки (3 поверхи)

Site plan, scale 1:1000

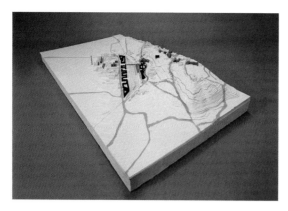
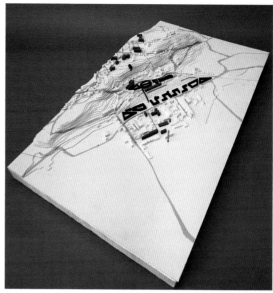

BORDERLINE
Overcoming topographic and man-made borderlines

Chernivtsi's central station, built 1907 during the Danube Monarchy, constitutes the focal point of our project. Located between the border of the historical city center in the south, marked by a steep und wooded hill, and the area of the River Pruth's former flood plains in the north, it is connected by only one road, Gargarin Street, leading into the city center.

Our team's undertaking consisted in detecting the deficits and potentials inherent in the areas surrounding the central station and proposing solutions for a future development. We defined three main zones: Gargarin Street as the entrance to the city in front of the central station and the area on the opposite side of the street as its counterpart. Secondly, The wooded hill connecting the city center with the central station as a recreational zone. And, last but not least, the Pruth area, north of the main station and south of the River Pruth.

After analyzing the various zones we defined one major goal: to overcome the topographic and man-made borderlines and to create new connections.

Picture of the model, scale 1:2000

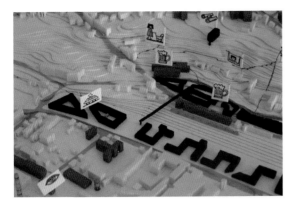
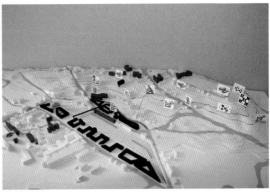

All areas are more or less surrounded by railroad tracks, differences in altitude, or the River Pruth, which function as borderlines. In consequence, these areas are secluded from the rest of the city and develop in an isolated fashion. While walking through the areas we discovered many informal routes, tracks which are officially non-existent but which have been worn in over time through the continuous use by the city's inhabitants. We used these informal walks to determine the correct positioning of new connections proposed in our project: A skywalk, used also as a city terrace, over the railroad tracks, which should connect the train station with the area around the Pruth. Furthermore the proposal incorporated an elevator as a direct connection between the city center and the main station, which should be erected in combination with a newly planned public building on top of the hill on Boguna Street. Additionally, this elevator would function as a sign for the enhancement of Chernivtsi's silhouette for visitors entering from the north.

We also formulated interventions to stimulate a development for the newly opened areas in the following directions: The area across the main station on Gagarin Street is an undefined plot combining parking, kiosks, and brushwood. As the main entrance into the city, this area holds a high potential for development into an urban space defined by public buildings and squares. It could bring the historic city center and the main station into accord. Functions such as hotels, restaurants, shops, and various smaller enterprises could be located here.

The Pruth area is largely covered with industry nowadays, partly in use, partly vacant and, sporadically, some private housing. The proximity to the city center and the riverbank offers an ideal prerequisite for a living area with local commerce and recreation. The vacant clinker factories could be used as locations with cultural programs. The train station opens only to the south side, to the city center; the north side at Sevastopol´ska Street is almost entirely closed off by a wall, which marks the edge of the former industrial railroad depot. This should be moved to the existing connecting train station. Consequently, the area could be used for the new international bus station, for offices, restaurants, cafés, terraces and squares bestowing an urban character upon the area.

The model showing pictograms with suggested activities

The wooded hill disconnects the city center and the main station; the hill is abandoned and difficult to reach. In former times it was a pleasant recreational area connected to Fed'kovychy Park, the former "Habsburghöhe". Breweries such as Göbels Bierbrauerei offered refreshments in their beer garden Göbels Höhe, located on a public walk connecting the city center with the train station. We propose to reactivate this beautiful area in the midst of the city by placing a new beer garden in the forest in combination with a public walk and a fitness parcours.

Team: Irina Bogdan, Bucharest; David Buerger, Graz; Kostya Chebriy, Chernivtsi; Sasha Chebriy, Chernivtsi; Raluca Davidel, Bucharest; Joachim Maier, Graz; Matthias Tscheuschler, Berlin; Unit Adviser: Julia Lienemeyer, Berlin; Emil Ivanescu, Bucharest

left: The railway station facing the tracks; The frontage of the railway station facing Gagarin Street

right: Area between the railway station and the Pruth River; Vis à vis the railway station

right page:

left: Nikitin Street; Informal pathways connecting the railway station with the city centre, Searching for remains of the former beer garden Göbelshöhe

right: Entrance to the wooded hill; Proposal for a museum located on top of the wooded hill on Boguna Street

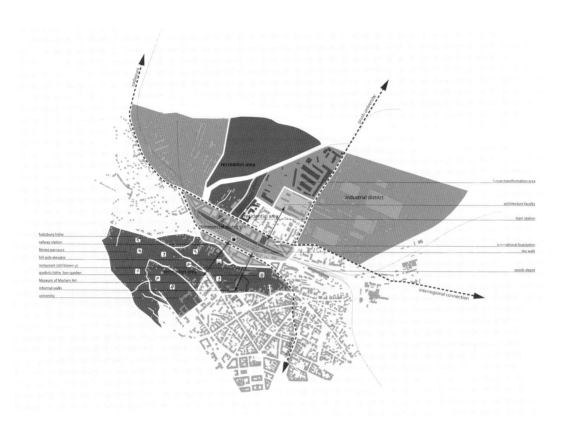

Labels in upper site plan:
recreation area
industrial district
future transformation area
architecture faculty
tram station
residential area
commercial district
international busstation
sky walk
goods depot
interregional connection
habsburg höhe
railway station
fitness parcours
hill-side elevator
restaurant (old brewery)
goebels höhe_beergarden
Museum of Modern Art
informal walk
university
recreation area

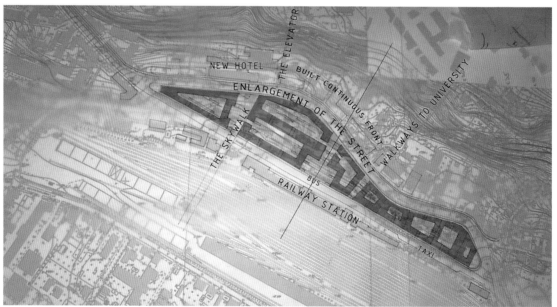

Labels in lower plan:
THE ELEVATOR
NEW HOTEL
BUILT CONTINUOUS FRONT
WALKWAYS TO UNIVERSITY
ENLARGEMENT OF THE STREET
THE SKYWALK
BUS
RAILWAY STATION
TAXI

above: Site plan, scale 1:2000

below: Plan, scale 1:1000, of the proposal between Gargarin- and Nikitin Street

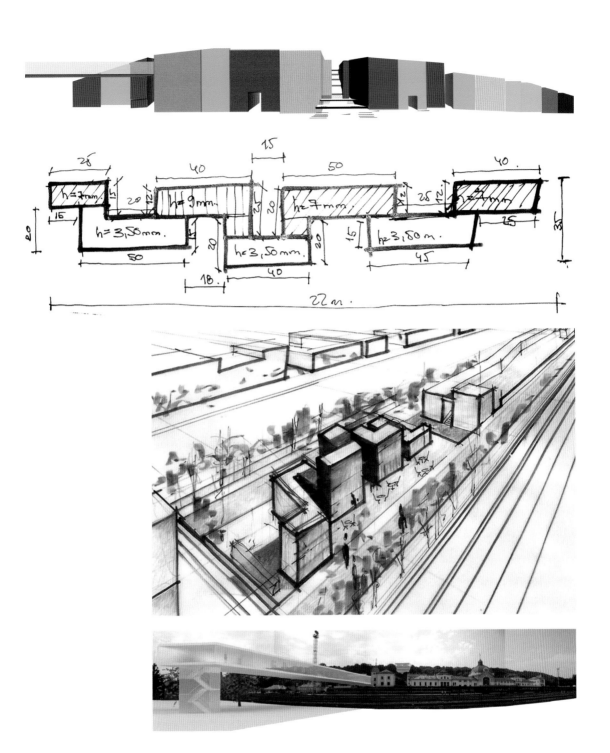

above: Conceptual image of the proposal

middle: Revitalisation of the former industrial railroad depot on Sevastopolska Street

below: A skywalk over tracks and street proposed in the project

THE EUROPE UNIVERSITY BY THE PRUTH

The Pruth assumes the moody temperament of a mountain river, displaying its inviting gravel banks to swimmers in the summer, but transmutes into a fierce stream only hours later, not seldomly rising high above its initial water level. This caused Chernowitz to retreat onto a nearby hilltop. The town has therefore not seized the chance to become a town by the river. Especially the callow northern riverbank holds potentials in urban development that will prove its importance for the town's future expansion.

This notion finds support in the already planned third bridge across the river in this area. It will connect the shut down industrial zone between the town center and the southern riverside with the northern riverbank. Simultaneously, the bridge will initiate future urbanizations along both sides of the river.

The notion to found an International Europe University rests upon the conceptual proposal to revive the town's multiethnic past.

The positioning of such an institution by the northern toehold of the planned bridge originated from the proposal to generate a site with a strong radiance power. From this point, new town parts can develop in the direction of Sadagura and the eastwardly located Kalinivski Market.

This effect is amplified by the close relation of the university's facilities towards the planned commercial center, located within catchment area of the mentioned market places.

left: Picture of the model, scale 1:2000

right: Picture of the model, scale 1:1000

During the Summer Academy, the university facilities located north of the bridge were improved with two alternative results in mind.

One alternative positions the university complexes on a dam erected to regulate the water. Public squares develop, which are oriented towards the river and which incorporate the Pruth's fluctuating water surface. These squares, which are found in the town itself, underline the river's integration into the city. This project envisions a bridge with two lanes and a moderate flow of traffic. The second alternative places constructional measures at a certain distance from the embankment, leaving it untouched. The mentioned bridge should acquire four lanes in this project work.

Previous to the Summer Academy 2006, in consideration of the industrial waste, the measures of modernization sparked the deliberation to pronounce the factory chimneys in this area as buildings of national heritage.

This resulted in the integration of multistorey buildings with mixed functions in both alternatives, creating a correlation to the factory chimneys.

Team: Elisa Hernando Vilar, Graz; Sven Marx, Berlin; Inna Palka, Chernivtsi; Nataly Patraboy, Chernivtsi; Vanessa Satori, Graz; Dina Sokur, Chernivtsi; Elena Stoian, Bucharest; Adrian Timaru, Bucharest; Michael Wierdak, Berlin; Unit Adviser: Prof. Günter Zamp Kelp, Berlin.

left: Dam on the northern side on the river; Green spaces along the river

right: Southern riverside; Gravel banks

left page

above: International European University

below: View towards the University
Library tower

this page

above: Site plan, scale 1:1000

below: Bird's-eye view facing west

UNIVERSITY CENTER

Sketch of the system of connections

above: Visual and physical link between the two sides of the river

below: Collage showing the possible impact of the university tower

THE KALINIVSKI MARKET IN CHERNIVCI
Decay of a formal order and omnipotence

The renaissance of urban life in the Ukraine during the 1990s appeared contradictory to the changes in urban shape. Following political changes and the renewal of the historic centre, various para-architectonic ventures have evolved in Chernivci. The inherited monotone and ascetic urban milieu seemed to explode into fragments. Garages turned into boutiques, department stores split up into smaller shops, and market places have sprouted on formerly fallow lands. In psychological terms, the speedy transformation concerning the urban milieu had a cathartic function – it enabled to forget the hierarchy of values in the vertical and put its messages solely horizontally, directly in reach for the people. The socialist urban culture organised space in the vertical and implemented a clear hierarchy. The para-architectonic activities destroyed this historic utopia and replaced it with a geopolitical one. The "urban parterre" was packed with symbols of a strange reality.

The Kalinivski Market in Chernivci symbolizes this period of transition. The market covers formerly fallow land on the north-eastern periphery of Chernivci. The area was made accessible by building the River Prut Bridge connected to the town's tangential road. The booming market has not been disturbed by unclear real estate situations or by missing infrastructure. The potentials embedded in Chernivtsi's remaining open spaces revealed possibilities for a development that had not been thought of before for this area. The market originally operated as a black market and gave impulses to the free market economy in the crisis-ridden city, ensuring freedom of movement for persons, merchandise, and capital. In the first years following the political changes, Kalinskyy Market served as the only location for the free exchange of goods and services. The market area has multiplied rapidly. It developed a vast dynamic of its own and reached a regional importance.

Picture of the models, scale 1:1000

The market puts special challenges today. It is on one hand an auto-generated structure, the result of a self-organised adaptation by those involved. The lack of a sustainable planning made the rapid development possible, which lead to the creation of new building phenomena. The creative potential is manifested in the diversity and improvisation of the organisation of public and private spaces. On the other hand the market has presently reached a size, which becomes problematic if continued with the original concept and which makes it imperative to search for a new order. Even the social and political framework has been converted to match a stabilized democratic system. To continue the uncontrolled growth would lead to a self-destruction. The market has established itself without any doubt as an important location for the regional economy and as an urban centre. To consider it as a temporary phenomenon would pose as an unused chance for urban development and a mistake from the economic point of view.

Team: Bastian Bechtloff, Berlin; Jenica Craiu, Bucharest; Olga Dundich, Chernivtsi; Konrad Edlinger, Graz; Elena Fischmann, Berlin; Natasha Galshka, Chernivtsi; Veronika Tudor, Bucharest; Unit Adviser: Prof. Grigor Doytchinov, Graz

above: Collage of the site: Highway bridge over the River Pruth in imediate proximity to the market

middle: Collage of the site: Existing Kalinivski Market

below: Top view of the model

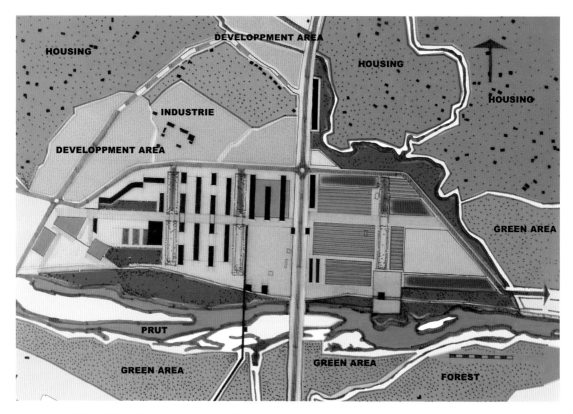

above: site plan, scale 1:1000

below: Pictures of Kalinivski Market

following page: Sketch of the new market

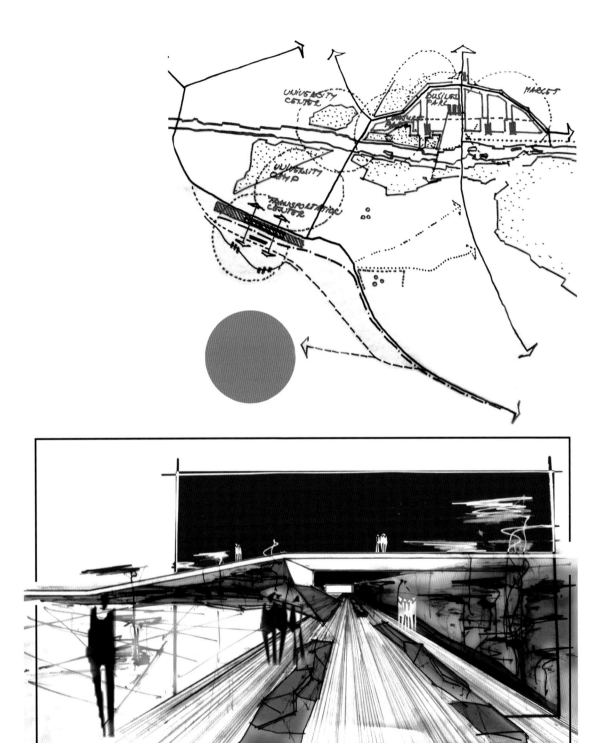

above: Scheme of connections and traffic system

below: Sketch of the river shore

PRESS
PRESSE
PRESA
ПРЕСА

Press conference in Chernivtsi at the beginning of the Summer Academy, former Hotel Bellevue, Central Square

Архітектурна академія рятує „спальні райони"

Учасники Міжнародної літньої архітектурної академії з Німеччини, Австрії, Румунії та України у захваті від історичного центру Чернівців, але перейматимуться проблемами нових районів

Вадим ПАВЛЮК
v_pavliuk@ukr.net

Професор Гюнтер Цамп Кельп у захваті від архітектури в центрі міста, але вважає, що Чернівці потребують санації спальних районів.

Цього тижня у Чернівцях розпочала роботу Міжнародна літня архітектурна академія. У роботі академії візьмуть участь студенти вузів чотирьох країн – Німеччини (Берлінський університет мистецтв), Австрії (Технічний університет міста Граца), Румунії (Університет архітектури та містопланування м. Бухарест) та України, яку представлятимуть студенти та викладачі Чернівецького політехнічного технікуму. Робота академії триватиме два тижні. За цей час студенти розроблять та представлять на розгляд фахівців та громадськості свої проекти архітектурного розвитку нашого міста на наступні роки. Як зазначив професор технічного університету міста Граца (Австрія), досвід попередніх років свідчить, що саме студенти дуже часто у своїх проектах пропонують нестандартні й оригінальні рішення.

Як зазначила представник Берлінського університету мистецтв Юлія Лінемайєр, за період роботи академії в Чернівцях її учасники переважно працюватимуть у історичній частині міста, вивчаючи можливості подальшого розвитку та використання архітектурного потенціалу міста. До речі, саме потенційні можливості старого міста і стали тим ключовим моментом, завдяки якому Чернівці приймають молодих архітекторів із чотирьох країн.

Звичайно, окрім захвату від архітектури старого міста, гості, як справжні професіонали, побачили чимало проблем, над якими, власне, і попрацюють разом зі студентами упродовж наступних двох тижнів.

– Звичайно, немає досконалого міста, зазначив професор Берлінського університету мистецтв Гюнтер Цамп Кельп. – Перше, що впало нам в око - те, що Чернівці, які складаються з двох частин – Чернівців та Садгори не розташовані безпосередньо на річці. Дуже шкода, адже річка - це дуже важливий елемент. Зокрема китайське вчення фен-шуй надає велике значення водоймам, і ми б хотіли якось наблизити місто до цієї прекрасної річки. А другий аспект, яким ми плануємо зайнятись, – санація так званих „спальних районів", які становлять великий контраст із старою частиною Чернівців.

А за словами пані Юлії Лінемайєр, сьогодні місцева влада особливу увагу приділяє переважно старому місту, в той час, як нові райони незаслужено залишають поза увагою. Але ж нові райони є більшими, аніж історичний центр, і вони мають чимало проблем, і щодо інфраструктури та інших аспектів. Пані Лінемайєр зазначила, що учасникам архітектурної академії буде що запропонувати, щоб життя мешканців цих районів стало більш комфортним.

Із результатами роботи німецьких, австрійських, румунських та українських молодих архітекторів можна буде ознайомитись на виставці, яку організатори проекту влаштують після завершення роботи академії.

Європейці планували майбутнє міста

Ярослав ВОЛОЩУК

Якими можуть бути Чернівці у майбутньому, показали студенти з Німеччини, Румунії, Австрії та України. Протягом двох тижнів вони розробляли концепцію розвитку Чернівців у міжнародній літній архітектурній школі. Після цього свої ідеї чернівчанам представили на виставці «Чернівці завтра» у художньому музеї, яка триватиме до 23 серпня.

Експозиція складається з чотирьох макетів, де чотири робочі групи студентів представили своє бачення розвитку міста.

Одна група запропонувала створити у мікрорайоні Комарова Південно-Кільцева більше різноманітних закладів, щоби розванти цанитити історичну частину міста. Ідея другої групи - поєднати між собою залізничний вокзал і університет, зробивши сходи, тераси і навіть фунікулер.

Студенти також запропонували у районі Калинівського ринку створити міжнародний центр торгівлі, а також біля нього побудувати сучасний міжнародний європейський університет. ∎

Фото Ярослава Волощука

Студенти з Німеччини, Румунії, Австрії та України працювали разом у літній архітектурній школі.

Left page

Article: Architect's academy saves 'dormitory areas', Newspaper: Pohlyad No. 61, 04.08.2006, S.2, by Vadym Pavljuk

Article: Europeans plan the future of Chernivtsi, Newspaper: Molodyj Bukowynez, 17.08.2006, S.4, by Jaroslaw Woloschtschuk

ЧЕРНІВЦІ ОЧИМА МОЛОДИХ АРХІТЕКТОРІВ

Другий тиждень в Художньому музеї експонуються роботи молодих архітекторів. Якими будуть Чернівці завтра? На це питання спробували відповісти студенти Чернівецького політехнічного технікуму, а також їхні колеги з технічного університету міста Граца (Австрія), Берлінського університету мистецтв (Німеччина), Іон Мінку університету Бухареста (Румунія).

Цього року в рамках "Архітектурної академії" об'єктом дослідження було обране саме наше місто. Ще відлунює колишня слава шляхетного, толерантного, поліетнічного культурного центру - столиці Буковини, яка подарувала світові не одну творчу особистість. Місто, яке довший час виконувало функції своєрідного моста між Сходом і Заходом, а нині поволеньки перетворюються на заштатне провінційне містечко. Жахливі дороги, жалюгідний стан будинків, як кажуть, зі слідами колишньої розкоші (сяк-так зроблений поверхневий макіяж лише підкреслює їхнє теперішнє зубожіння). Місто Чернівці пам'ятає і цінує Європа. Молоді люди протягом кількох тижнів ретельно вивчали особливості міста. Дослідження йшло трьома напрямками. Перший - створення Міжнародного Європейського Університету. Мета - відновлення багато-

Роботи молодих привертають увагу ровесників.

етнічного характеру Чернівців. Фінансування закладу передбачається з європейських джерел, приватними фундаціями. Потім - розвиток туризму. Оскільки Чернівці мають багато зразків європейської архітектури різноманітних стилів і епох, чудове природне оточення, унікальні місця для відпочинку, то є надзвичайно привабливими для туристів з усього світу. Третій напрямок - створення зони вільної торгівлі.

Команди працювали на чотирьох територіях: залізничний вокзал, північний берег Пруту, Калинівський ринок та місцевість на півдні від історичного центру. Ці території визначили як потенційно перспективні і реальні при подальшій розбудові та переплануванні міста. Молоді люди запропонували досить цікаві концепції. Так, залізничний вокзал вони бачать з розширеними функціями: там будуть залізнична та автобусна станції, торговельні пунк-

ти... На північному березі річки Прут має розміститися сучасне університетське містечко. Замість примітивного базару, Калинівський ринок бажано б перетворити на Центр торгівлі й бізнесу. А на південь від центру треба залишити споруди совіцької доби. Це, на думку майбутніх архітекторів, створить нову картину міста. Врахували учасники "Архітектурної академії і те, що Чернівці прямо-таки потерпають од величезної кількості машин – від легкових до багатотонних вантажних монстрів. Вузенькі вулиці, які будували під фіакри, екіпажі, ландо, не в змозі витримати божевільний потік автомобілів. Грунт просідає, утворюючи ями, фасади неповторних будинків з вишуканою архітектурою осипаються, відкриваючи сумні зморшки тріщин... Правда, перебудовують старе місто й українські нувориші, для яких єдиний закон – гроші. Зводять вони свої фортеці зазвичай в облюбованій заповідній частині, спотворюючи, знищуючи особливий шарм вуличок зараз з поважного віку будівлями. А деякі чиновники зайняті хіба що декларуванням де треба й де не треба своєї псевдошляхетності. Їм би (за штатом бо призначено) зберігати, доглядати місто, та вони, непохитні і принципові у дрібязках, коли йдеться про "челобітні" людей небагатих, стають напрочуд зговірливими, навіть поблажливими, коли зачують милий їхньому серцю солодкий шелест... Не в приклад чиновницькій братії, студенти таки подбали про місто. Аби зменшити транспортне перевантаження історичного центру, майбутні архітектори запропонували реконструювати вулицю Руську.

Молоді мрії – це природно. І мрії їхні не безпідставні. Достатньо уважно роздивитись плани, макети, представлені на виставці. Інше питання: чи стануть ті мрії реальністю? Можливо. Та це, як сказано у відомій повісті, зовсім інша історія...

ч. 32 /508/ четвер, 10 серпня 2006 р.

ЗАХІД НАМ ДОПОМОЖЕ?

СЦЕНАРІЙ РОЗВИТКУ ЧЕРНІВЦІВ ПІДГОТУЮТЬ ЗА ТИЖДЕНЬ

У Чернівцях розпочала роботу Міжнародна літня архітектурна академія "Tomorrow in Chernovitz" ("Завтра у Чернівцях"), у роботі якої беруть участь понад 30 студентів-архітекторів із Німеччини, Австрії, Румунії та Чернівців. З допомогою досвідчених наставників за два тижні вони мають підготувати сценарій розвитку Чернівців 2030 року, - повідомили "Добі" **в Центрі буковинознавства при ЧНУ ім.Ю.Федьковича.** Над розробкою проектів архітектурного розвитку Чернівців працюють студенти Берлінського

університету мистецтв (Німеччина), який став ініціатором проведення Міжнародної літньої архітектурної академії у Чернівцях, Технічного університету міста Грац (Австрія), Університету архітектури та містопланування м. Бухарест (Румунія) та Чернівецького політехнічного технікуму (Україна). На прес-конференції, присвяченій відкриттю Академії, професор Берлінського університету Гюнтер Цамп Кельп зазначив, що до участі у проекті були запрошені представники тих чотирьох культур, які наклали свій відбиток на

архітектурне обличчя Чернівців. Перед студентами поставлено завдання, орієнтуючись на архітектурний історичний потенціал Чернівців, розробити концептуальні проекти санації спальних районів, які поки що дисонують із старою частиною міста, а також визначити шляхи використання в планах архітектурного розвитку Чернівців річки Прут, яка поки що залишається незадіяною. Проекти-макети учасників архітектурної академії 13 серпня буде виставлено для огляду та обговорення в Чернівецькому художньому музеї.

---

above: Article: Chernivtsi through the eyes of young architects,

Newspaper: Culture, 24.08.2006, S. 18, by Larysa Artemenko, photographed by Volodymyr Cytrak

below: Article: The scenario of the development of Chernivtsi will be prepared in a week, Newspaper: 'Doba', 10.08.06, S. 2

Студенти придумають, як використати Прут в архітектурі

У Чернівцях працює Міжнародна літня архітектурна академія «Tomorrow in Chernovitz» («Завтра у Чернівцях»), у роботі якої беруть участь понад 30 студентів-архітекторів з Німеччини, Австрії, Румунії та Чернівців. Вони за допомогою досвідчених наставників за два тижні мають підготувати сценарій Чернівців 2030 року.

Над розробкою проектів архітектурного розвитку Чернівців працюють студенти Берлінського університету мистецтв (Німеччина), Технічного університету міста Грац (Австрія), Університету архітектури та містопланування м. Бухарест (Румунія) та Чернівецького політехнічного технікуму (Україна).

Перед студентами поставлено завдання: орієнтуючись на архітектурний історичний потенціал Чернівців, розробити концептуальні проекти санації спальних районів, які поки що дисонують із старою частиною міста, а також запропонувати шляхи використання в планах архітектурного розвитку Чернівців річки Прут, яка поки що залишається незадіяною. ■

МАЙБУТНЄ ЧЕРНІВЦІВ ОЧИМА ЗАХІДНОЄВРОПЕЙЦІВ

МИ І СВІТ

За яким сценарієм розвиватиметься наше місто наступних 25 років? Що може змінитися в його архітектурі та соціально-економічній функціональності? Чим цікаві ми світові? Відповіді на ці та дотичні запитання зможемо отримати за півтора тижня – по закінченні роботи Міжнародної літньої архітектурної академії, що розпочалася в понеділок, 1 серпня, і триватиме до 14-го.

У ній візьмуть участь представники чотирьох країн – Австрії, Німеччини, Румунії та України. При виборі країн-учасниць проекту керувалися тією обставиною, що всі вони історично пов'язані з Чернівцями. Їхні впливи і досі помітні в образі нашого міста.

Цікаво, що ініціаторами заходу, який проводитиметься на базі нашого рідного ЧНУ за сприяння Центру буковинознавства, виступили берлінці – професор тамтешнього університету мистецтв Гюнтер Цамп Кельп та дипломований інженер Юлія Лінемайєр. Два роки тому, бажаючи ближче познайомитися зі східною Європою, вони побували у Львові, Одесі та Чернівцях. І саме наше місто стало для них справжнім відкриттям. Тоді зародилася ідея створити дослідницький проект на тему "Зміна архітектури й ідентичності у Центральній і Східній Європі" і реалізувати його в рамках науково-практичних студій на буковинських теренах. Аби познайомити з цим чудовим, унікальним містом якомога більше західної молоді, а також привернути до нього увагу самих чернівчан – передусім тих, які досі не зрозуміли надзвичайної важливості Чернівців у загальноєвропейському контексті. Захід важливий і в плані об'єднання чотирьох країн спільною корисною справою – визначення перспективи розвитку та інтеграції українського полісу в загальноєвропейську спільноту.

Перший день перебування іноземних делегацій у столиці Буковини був присвячений екскурсії. У ролі гіда виступив місцевий архітектор Володимир Цвілюв. Гості побували в районах залізничного та автовокзалу, аеропорту, Калинівського ринку, інших торговельних зон, на горі Цецино, у передмісті Роша, подивилися на панельні будинки та сучасні котеджі, відвідали старий австрійський парк, ландшафтний заповідник "Гореча", міський пляж на річці Прут і чимало інших об'єктів.

За словами професора Технічного університету м. Грац (Австрія) пана Грігора Дойчінова, який у Чернівцях вперше, попереднє уявлення про місто він отримав завдяки матеріалам, наданим колегами з Берлінського університету мистецтв. З побаченого під час екскурсії гостя передусім вразив високий рівень збереження історичної забудови. Ця архітектурна спадщина, на його думку, таїть у собі величезний потенціал. Зацікавила і річка Прут, яка не лише прикрашає місто, а є і потенційним ресурсом для використання у сфері містобудування. Адже її береги майже не задіяні, при тому що загалом місцина дуже мальовнича й перспективна, а її забудова зробила би Чернівці ще гарнішими, вважає пан професор. Приємно було особисто відчути дух культурної поліетнічності й міжнаціональної толерантності, яким здавна славиться столиця Буковини і який знаходить своє вираження, зокрема, в університетському містечку.

Учора вельмишановне панство ходило вулицями старого міста, захоплювалося його красою і дійшло думки, що найімовірніше концепція майбутнього Чернівців базуватиметься на багатих ресурсах їхнього минулого. Намагатимуться опрацювати декілька ділянок, подивляться, які райони міста мають потенціал, перспективи для розвитку, яким з них потрібна підтримка.

На думку керівника архітектурного відділення Чернівецького політехнічного технікуму доцента Оксани Бойко, співпраця із західноєвропейськими колегами дозволить не лише розробити різноманітні варіанти перспективного образу нашого міста, а й посприяє обміну професійним досвідом між зрілими фахівцями. Особливо ж корисним буде цей захід для студентів, які матимуть нагоду реалізувати свої творчі фантазії. У чому, до речі, зацікавлені їхні викладачі, адже часто саме нестандартні рішення молодих дають вихід зі складних ситуацій. Об'єднані у змішаних робочих групах (чотири по вісім осіб із різних країн), вони досліджуватимуть матеріал особистих спостережень, дискутуватимуть, спільними зусиллями і в різних ракурсах розв'язуючи поставлені завдання.

У ході роботи академії відбудуться також лекції з актуальних проблем архітектури, а по закінченні – виставка проектів-розробок, що розгорнеться у Чернівецькому художньому музеї в неділю, 13 серпня, о 17 годині.

Валентина КУКУРУДЗ

above: Article: Students figure out how to use the river Pruth in architecture,

Newspaper: 'Molodyy Bukovynetz", 5.08.06, S. 2

below: Future of Chernivtsi through the eyes of West Europeans

Newspaper: 'Chernivtsi', 04.08.2006, S.12,

by Valentyna Kukurudz

Opening of the exhibition: Cerznowitz tomorrow – Ideas for the city of Chernivtsi, 13.08.2006, Art Museum, Central Square 10, Chernivtsi

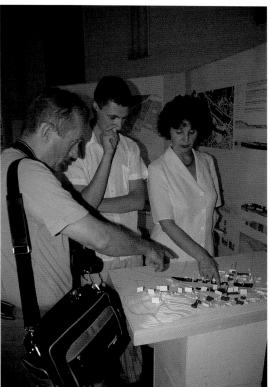

CHERNIVTSI OF THE FUTURE

ARTICLE FROM THE DAILY NEWSPAPER CHERNIVTSI
BY *LARYSA ARTEMENKO*, PHOTOGRAPHED BY *VOLODYMYR CYTRAK*,
18.08.2006

This glance into the future was ventured by the participants of International Summer Academy of Architecture and Urbanism, consisting of guests from Germany, Rumania, and Austria. The organizers of this outstanding event were the Bukovina Center for scientific research, the Chernivtsi National University, the University of the Arts in Berlin, the Technical University in Graz, the Architectural University in Bucharest, and the Chernivtsi Polytechnical School. Additionally, this project found support through the Robert Bosch Foundation, the German Embassy in the Ukraine, and the administrative body of Carinthia (Austria). The selection of the participating countries was not accidental: each of them has contributed its own part to the historic development of Chernivtsi.

Chernivtsi looks back on a 600-year history. Citizens living in Chernivtsi know a lot about its past; but what will its future be like if we try looking at least a few decades ahead? Professional architects and students from Berlin, Graz, Bucharest, and, of course, from Chernivtsi debated about this aspect in Chernivtsi. They creatively researched possible projects for the city's development, the results being displayed at the Chernivtsi Art Museum at present. The opening of the exhibition occurred only several days ago.

The usefulness and originality of this creative academy cannot be denied. Two years ago professor Günter ZampKelp, teaching at the University of the Arts in Berlin, and his teaching and research assistant Julia Lienemeyer, wished to get more closely acquainted with Eastern Europe and therefore visited several Ukrainian cities, e.g. Odessa and L'viv. On this tour, they also paid a visit to Chernivtsi. In connection with this visit, a group tour with students from the University of the Arts followed. The group seemed unanimously impressed by the town's potentials and was convinced that Chernivtsi posed as an optimal terrain for unconventional architectural solutions.

This year this step was taken. For several days, the participants belonging to the I from Austria and Rumania belonged as well, got acquainted with the most distant corners of the city, thoroughly studying them.

Some areas were especially notable in the participants' eyes. The first area links the region around the railway station with the university campus. The resulting exhibited project holds similarities to this historic area's original appearance. The flood lands near the River Pruth were not overlooked. The Western European architects cannot comprehend why the building grounds near the water remain unused, since developed European cities' structures usually concentrate around the water. The third region with just as high a potential is the area around Kalynivskyy market. The students' project is aimed towards the transformation of the trade compound into a business-center on a much larger scale and with a highly developed infrastructure. The rebuilding of the area between the axes Golovna Street, Nezalezhnosti Ave., and Chervonoarmiys'ka Street has also provoked a great interest.

Certainly, our architects have already been inspired by the exhibited projects. The head of the district administration regarding architectural disciplines and lecturer

NO. 1 CONTEMPORARY SPACES - URBAN CONTAINERS, KALINIVSKI MARKET, CHERNOWETZ

ARTICLE FROM THE ARCHITECTURAL MAGAZIN "ARHITECTURA", BUCHAREST, BY *EMIL IVANESCU*

Motto : "Containers can be turned into modern, stylish houses The Sunday Times

In academic studies, workshops have become extremely fashionable. Before the summer vacation, the student is offered a large array of such events. This summer I was invited to one event of this kind : a Summer School in Chernowetz in the Ukraine. It was organized by the Department of Architecture within the University of the Arts in Berlin and was carried out with the support of the National University of Chernivtsi. The Department of Architecture at the TU Graz and at the "Ion Mincu" University in Bucharest participated as well.

For us as Romanians, the city appeared familiar and I was anxious to find out more about it. Chernowetz was probably the most successful multicultural urban model in this part of the world. It has preserved its historic centre, built mostly by the Austrians in the 19th and at the beginning of the 20th century, but also by the Romanians during the interwar period. The most outstanding modernist construction is one designed by Horia Creang on the Theatre Square. In addition to the official monuments, Chernowitz, like every other city, owns characteristic places hidden from the public, which one comes upon serendipitously.

In the 1990s, the fall of communism and the withdrawal of the Soviet Empire from its spheres of influence could be felt everywhere in South-Eastern Europe. The Ukraine is no exception, and Chernowetz is a good example in this respect. Once an important industrial center for Russia regarding weaponry, the city has maintained only few factories that were able to change their field of production ; the rest have been abandoned. Its cultural and economic role during the 19th century, still noticeable in the old urban center, has been lost and the effects are visible in the urban fabric. A good example is the Kalinivski Market.

The Kalinivski Market (kalina = snowball tree with red fruit) developed outside town as a large shopping center on the left bank of the River Pruth, resulting from the transition period when it supported the trade market. It resembles Bucharest's Europa Complex in its function, belonging in a widely spread phenomenon in East European cities. However, its particular feature lies in the whole complex consisting of goods container constructions. Except for some recently erected structures lining the street, the complex follows some simple urban rules derived from a unique container pattern. The containers have even received a name, "japki", by now. "Japki" stands for frog in the Ukrainian language ; the containers' proportions resemble those of a frog's jaws. The containers measure 244 x 318 x 244 cm. They have been brought by ship from Odessa together with the merchandise within them. In time, a pseudo-city grew here. The one-storey or two-storey containers house shops where people spend their time from dawn to dusk, and sleep inside them as well. One special fact calls on the observer's attention : the way in which the containers are embellished. Just like a pen top, each container has an entrance-façade or a shop window façade. Various modules or partitions make them look out of the ordinary.

244 x 318 x 244 cm. Ele sunt aduse din Odessa, şi au venit odată cu mărfurile, pe mare. Cu timpul, un pseudo oraş s-a format aici. Pe un nivel sau două, simple sau suprapuse, containerele adăpostesc magazine în care oamenii îşi desfăşoară activitatea de dimineaţă şi până seara târziu, practic, ei locuind aici.

Un lucru interesant este modul în care sunt cosmetizate containerele. Asemeni unui capac de stilou, fiecare container are o faţadă-intrare sau faţadă-vitrină. Diverse tipuri de modulări şi diverse tipuri de împărţiri scot din banalitate complexul. Containere duplex (două module suprapuse) şi containere simple alternează fronturile aleilor comerciale. Cele duplex, au la interior o scară de acces la etaj , unde este amenajat un depozit-vitrină.

Terenul complexului nu este proprietate privată, ci comunală, aparţinând primariei Cernauţiului. Datorită dezvoltării şi deci extinderii rapide, au fost edificate câteva clădiri pe cadre, însă majoritatea densităţii construite o deţin containărele. Astăzi dezvoltarea a stagnat şi doar modu-

The containers at Kalinivski Market

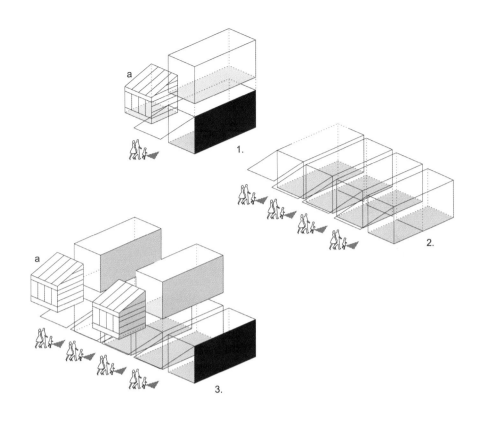

The duplex containers, stacked on top of each other, and the single ones alternate along the commercial lanes. The duplex type has a staircase to the top floor, where a storage – showcase is arranged.

The land is communal property, being owned by the Chernowetz Town Hall. Some buildings have been erected, but most of the built area is overspread with these containers. Thus, a little container town has emerged. Its streets are filled with a general hustle and bustle. The in-between spaces result from the way in which the containers are oriented, while the free spots are taken by stalls. The three-dimensional modulation demands a certain order: the chaotic space generated by stalls stays limited due to the containers. Thus, a hierarchy persists in this complex space and the container module as the most valuable structural object strongly dominates the market area.

Scheme of the containers

lele metalice mai interesează pe comercianţi. S-a creat, astfel, un mic oraş al containerelor. Pe străzile lui, comerţul generează o forfotă constantă. Spaţiile interstiţiale emerg din felul orientării modulelor, iar ce rămâne liber este ocupat de tarabe. Modularea pe trei dimensiuni impune o anumita ordine: spaţiul haotic de tip comerţ la tarabă se diminuează mult în cazul celui container comercial. Există, deci, o ierarhie a spaţiului în complex, iar spaţiul generat de modulul container este cel mai valoros.

Ceea ce te impresionează din primul moment, observând, complexul este vernacularul locului, în utilizarea unor elemente pe care mediile arhitectural-profesioniste le teoretizează continuu şi doar într-un final le aplică răzleţ şi cu mare emoţie estetică. Modul direct şi frust în care omul simplu şi-a însuşit un fapt şi l-a utilizat în real şi fără prea mult zgomot, această discreţie a funcţiunii îndeplinite, ne face să gândim ironic (oare pentru a câta oară?) cu privire la atitudinea noastră ca profesionişti atât de gureşi, uneori. Putem să încercăm chiar un zâmbet: iată un proiect modernist reuşit! Şi de ce? Pentru că, aşa cum spunea Luis Fernandes-Galiano în A.V. Monographs (no. 104 pe 2003): "la fel de primitiv ca şi modernitatea industrială, containărul combină cele două mituri fondatoare ale funcţionalismului: standardizarea şi mobilitatea. În spatele stocurilor de containere multicolore, dimensiunea standard şi producţia de masă materializează vechiul vis arhitectural al repeţiei şi eficienţei." Fără să-şi pună prea multe probleme, ucraineanul de rând a reuşit acest lucru: un mini City Containers al lui MRDRV(fără Bienala de la Rotterdam).

Deşi nu am discutat calitatea estetică şi chiar umană a exemplului dat, nu putem să nu menţionăm câteva exemple de arhitectură cultă în care containărul este elementul esenţial de design (poate un contra-argument la expunerea facută!). Exemplele sunt lucrări deja date în funcţiune şi pot reprezenta puncte de referinţă în teoria containerului. De exemplu, Nomad Museum al lui Shigheru Ban şi Keetwonen, cămine studenţeşti în Amsterdam. Ambele sunt lucrări foarte interesante în care se combină întreaga dimensiune contemporană a designului de arhitectură. Nu ştiu cum ar intra în această categorie tabăra americană de deţinuţi de la Guantanamo Bay - Cuba, unde celulele de detenţie sunt, de fapt, containere cuplate unul cu celălalt , aşezate pe două laturi paralele, cu un culoar de circulaţie la mijloc. O şarpantă generală asigură protecţia containerelor, dar şi aerisirea şi iluminarea culoarelor.

Faţă de aceste exemple, născute ca urmare a unor demersuri economico-teoretice sau concentraţionare vădite, piaţa comercială Kalinivski se desfăşoară nepăsătoare la forfota conceptelor şi ideilor contemporane. Dacă astăzi, a trăi într-un spaţiu generat de containere presupune un anumit stil de viaţă, a trăi în acest mic pseudo-oraş modulat este un firesc al locului.

The vernacular character poses as the market's most striking feature – that natural dimension which the professional world attempts to theorize but which the market's inhabitants apply randomly and, simultaneously, aesthetically. This straight-forward and crude manner in which the average person learnt and used this fact in real life without much ado, this discretion of the applied function makes us think ironically (how many times now?) about our own talkative ways. We can even smile: this is a successful modernist project! Why is it so? Because, as Luis Fernandes-Galiano has put it in his A. V. Monographs (no. 3/2003):

"just as primitive as industrial modernity, the container combines the two founding myths of functionalism: standardization and mobility. Behind the stocks of colorful containers, the standard size and mass production materialize the old architectural dream of repetition and efficiency."

Without giving much thought to it, the average Ukrainian was successful: he created a mini City Containers of MVRDV (without the Rotterdam Biennial). Although I haven't talked about the aesthetic and human qualities of the example, I cannot help mentioning some examples of cultured architecture in which the container is the key design element (maybe a counter-example to my discourse!). The examples are used now and seen as landmarks in the theory of containers, for instance the Nomad Museum of Shigheru Ban and Keetwonen and the student hostels in Amsterdam. Both are interesting and combine the whole range of architectural design. I have no idea to which category the detention cells in Guantanamo Bay, Cuba, fit into this picture; there, the containers are semi-detached, stand on two parallel sides, and are crossed by a circular lane. A general roof frame protects the containers, the air, and lights the lanes. In comparison to these examples that resulted from theoretical, economic, or obvious confinement intentions, the Kalinivski Market is a compound free from any current ideas and concepts. If living in a space generated by containers assumes a certain lifestyle, then living here, in this pseudo-modulated city comes with the nature of this place.

BRÜCKEN SCHLAGEN IN DIE ZUKUNFT
BUILDING BRIDGES INTO THE FUTURE

BY *KATJA KOLLMANN*, UDK BERLIN

Ideen und Visionen haben ideelles Gewicht. Deshalb war unser Reisegepäck zur Sommerakademie nach Czernowitz eher leicht. Die UdK-Studentin Elena Fischman nahm sich vor allem ihren speziellen Laptop für Architekten mit auf die Reise und eine lange schwarze Rolle für ihre vorbereiteten Entwürfe und Pläne. Ich brachte vor allem eine große Portion Reporter-Neugierde mit. Die geborene Ukrainerin Elena kehrte in ihre Geburtsstadt zurück, um im Rahmen dieses internationalen Projektes Vorschläge und Projektentwürfe für eine lebenswerte Stadt an Ort und Stelle zu präsentieren. Für mich als Studentin für Kulturjournalismus war diese Reise im Rahmen eines Hospitanz-projektes ein erster Besuch.

Die Architekturstudenten hatten sich gründlich darauf vorbereitet. Zwei Jahre lang hatten Berliner, Bukarester und Grazer Studenten an einer städtebaulichen Vision für diese Stadt in der Westukraine gearbeitet. Sie errichteten neue Brücken, planten Umgehungsstraßen auf dem Papier und ließen sogar schon eine imaginäre Gondel über den Fluss schweben -von einer Brücke zur anderen. Aber nur Elena Fischman kannte die Stadt vorher aus eigenem Erleben. Ihre Kommilitonen waren auf Bücher und Stadtpläne angewiesen. So hatte jeder bald sein eigenes Czernowitz im Kopf. Aber genau diese Ideen waren das wichtigste Gepäck für die Sommerakademie.

In Czernowitz angekommen, sollten die deutschen, österreichischen und ru-mänischen Studenten gemeinsam mit Studierenden des Czernowitzer Polytechnikums ein städtebauliches Konzept für die Stadt am Fluss Pruth entwerfen. Zeit: Zwei Wochen im August 2006. Ort: Czernowitz / Westukraine. Vorgehensweise: Vier Gruppen und vier Schwerpunkte. An den ersten beiden Tagen der Sommerakademie stand Feldforschung auf dem Programm. Erste Erfahrung: Stadt und Stadtplan sind nicht unbedingt das Gleiche, auch wenn für ein und dieselbe Straße ein identischer Name draufsteht. Zum Beispiel zieht sich die Altstadt von Czernowitz einen Hang hinauf. Die Straßen sind schmal und das Kopfsteinpflaster alt. Der Bahnhof liegt unterhalb vom Hang. Hinter diesen verrotten brachliegende Industrieanlagen, es führt plötzlich ein Weg in ein kleines Wäldchen. Ein Trampelpfad endet vor wildem Strand. Sonnenanbeter liegen hier auf Kies. Wilde, nicht befestigte Pfade führen vom Bahnhof steil bergauf durch ein Waldstück zur Universität. Wenn es regnet, was in diesen zwei Wochen öfter vorkommt, werden diese Wege zu lebensgefährlichen Schlammbahnen. Aber auch auf der Straße strömt das Wasser in Sturzbächen hinunter zum Bahnhof. Das alles konnte man sich alleine am Stadtplan so nicht vorstellen.

Ideas and visions possess ideal weight. Therefore our luggage to the Summer Academy in Chernowitz was rather light. The UdK student Elena Fischman decided to take her special laptop for architects as well as her black roll with the prepared project work and plans along. Above all, I carried a great amount of writer's curiosity with me. The native Ukrainian Elena returned to her hometown in order to make proposals and offer design work aimed at the creation of a more livable surrounding within the setting of this international project. I, a student of cultural journalism, partook in this journey, my first passage to Chernowitz, as part of an exchange program.

The architecture students had thoroughly prepared themselves for this trip. Students from Berlin, Bukarest, and Graz had worked on an urban vision for this town in the Western Ukraine over a time span of two years. They erected bridges, planned bypasses on paper and even determined to let a gondola float across the river – from one bank to the other. But initially only Elena Fishman was acquainted with the town through own experience. Her fellow students had to depend on books and maps. As time went by, each of them developed their own Chernowitz in their imagination. But precisely these ideas formed the most important luggage for the summer academy.

Following their safe arrival in Chernowitz, the German, Austrian, and Romanian students were to develop a town-planning concept for the city by the River Pruth in cooperation with students from the Chernowitz Polytechnical School. Time span: Two weeks in August 2006. Place: Chernowitz / Western Ukraine. Procedure: four teams and four core themes. The program for the first two days consisted of field studies.

First experience: The town and the town's map do not necessarily concur, even when the matching streets carry an identical name. For instance, Chernowitz's old town stretches out over a hillside. The streets are narrow and the cobblestone pavement old. The railway station lies at the bottom of the slope. At the rear of these abandoned industrial plants a lane suddenly leads into a little wood. A trail comes to an end at a beach with wild vegetation. Sunbathers lie on the gravel. Grassy paths steeply wind uphill through a thicket towards the university. During rainfall, which happens almost daily throughout these two weeks, these paths transmute into life-threatening courses of slurry. Moreover, streams of water gush down the streets towards the railway station in torrents. This entirety is unimaginable when solely observing street maps.

Field studies

Sunbathers lie on the gravel of the Pruth River

Aber die Spuren der wechselhaften Geschichte dieser Stadt lassen sich an vielen Stellen entdecken. Überraschenderweise auch an den Kanaldeckeln. So verschieden wie hier sind sie mir in keiner anderen Stadt vorgekommen. "Magistrat Czernowitz" steht in lateinischen Buchstaben auf den einen, auf den anderen "Cernauti". Wieder Anderen wurden kyrillische Buchstaben eingebrannt: "Chernovtsi". Die jüngsten Gullideckel sind wieder anders gekennzeichnet: "Chernivtsi". Kanaldeckel als historische Zeugen der Zeitläufe des letzten Jahrhunderts.

Die Architekturstudenten der UdK aus Berlin planen während ihrer Sommerakademie weit in das 21. Jahrhundert hinein. Nach der ersten Feldforschung beginnt die Planung. Ort: Zwei Räume mit abgetretenem Parkett und alten Schulbänken in der historischen Fakultät der Universität Chernivtsi. In jeder Gruppe arbeiten acht Studenten aus vier Ländern gemeinsam. Verständigt wird sich auf Englisch. Häuser, Brücken und Straßen entstehen auf Transparentpapier. Der Lärmpegel steigt, die Diskussionen werden immer leidenschaftlicher. Es geht um ganz existentielle Fragen eines Städteplaners: "Was soll erhalten werden? Was soll weg? Was soll umgewandelt werden?" Am Ende einigt sich jede Gruppe ganz pragmatisch auf ihren Entwurf, der in Rekordzeit bis zur Eröffnung der Ausstellung ausgeführt sein muss. Kleine Schwämmchen werden mit Hingabe waldmeistergrün gespritzt und ganz vorsichtig auf das Modell geklebt. Geduldige Hände zeichnen am Entwurf für eine internationale Universität am Fluss.

Bei der Vernissage der Architekturausstellung im Kunstmuseum Czernowitz steht Elena Fischman, die ehemalige Czernowitzerin, vor dem Modell eines neuen, umgestalteten Kalinivskij Marktes und erläutert den Besuchern in ihrer Muttersprache russisch, was in den Entwürfen zu sehen ist. Darunter auch die Vision von einem Markt, der abends zur Freilichtbühne wird. Natürlich ist das noch Zukunftsmusik. Und Veränderungen brauchen Zeit, das weiß Elena Fischman. Aber die Chancen stehen gut für "Czernowitz tomorrow".

History faculty of Chernowitz University, Sorbona Square: Two lecture halls have been the workspace for the students of the Summer Academy

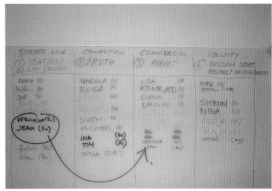

However, the traces of this town's frequently changing history may be explored in numerous settings. Surprisingly enough, this is furthermore perceptible on the manhole covers. I have not encountered such diversity in any other town. One holds the Latin inscription "Municipal Authority of Chernowitz"; another reads "Cernauti". Still others were brandmarked with Cyrillic letters: "Chernovtsi". The most recent manhole covers are marked still differently: "Chernivtsi". Manhole covers as historic witnesses of the course of the last century.

Throughout the summer academy, the architecture students of the UdK in Berlin plan far ahead into the 21st century. Subsequent to the first field study the planning is taken up. Place: Two lecture halls laid with worn out parquet and old desks in the history faculty of Chernowitz University. Eight students from four countries compose one team. Communication takes place in English. Houses, bridges, and streets come into existence on transparent paper. The noise level rises, the discussions become more intense. The focus lies on a town planner's natural and existential questions: "What should be preserved? What should disappear? What should be transformed?" In the end, each group pragmatically agrees on their well-rounded design work, which has to be detailed in record time until the exhibition's opening night. Woodruff green is applied to sponge bits with great dedication prior to their arduous application onto the model. Patient hands draw the design for an international university by the river.

During the architecture exhibition's vernissage in the Art Museum Chernowitz, Elena Fischman, a former resident of Chernowitz, stands in front of the model of a new, redesigned Kalinskij Market and elucidates the projects' core themes to the visitors in her mother tongue, Russian. Among those lies the vision of a market place that alters into an open-air stage at night. Naturally, these ideas still subsist only as dreams of the future. And change takes time, Elena Fishman knows that. But things are in good shape and chances are good for "Chernowitz Tomorrow".

above: Workspace: Discussions in front of the city plan; eight students from four countries compose one team

below: Manhole cover

EPILOGUE
EPILOG
EPILOG
ПІСЛЯМОВА

VOM VERMÄCHTNIS MULTIETHNISCHER KOEXISTENZ ZUM URBANEN MEDIATOR FÜR IDENTITÄT, SCHÖPFERTUM UND WISSENSCHAFT IN EUROPA
FROM THE HERITAGE OF A MULTIETHNIC COEXISTENCE TO THE URBAN MEDIATOR FOR IDENTITY, CREATIVITY AND SCIENCES IN EUROPE

PROF. *GÜNTER ZAMP KELP*

Im Jahr 1916 stirbt Kaiser Franz Josef 1 von Österreich, König von Ungarn. Mit seinem Tod begann das Sterben des sozialpolitischen Gefüges Alt Europa. das im Jahr 1945 mit der Kapitulation der deutscher Truppen im 2. Weltkrieg endete.

Die Bukowina als ehemaliges Kronland der K und K Monarchie existiert in den bestehenden Strukturen als Teil Rumäniens bis etwa 1940 weiter und gerät dann in die Wirren und Gewaltorgien des zweiten Weltkrieges mit ihren fatalen Ergebnissen. Chernivtzy / Czernowitz als damalige Hauptstadt der Bukowina mit seiner heterogenen Bewohnerstruktur aus Deutschen, Juden, Rumänen und Ukrainern überlebt die österreich-ungarische Monarchie etwa um 20 Jahre. Die Stadt wird ab 1945 unter russischem Mandat in einen konservatorischen Tiefschlaf versetzt, in dem der historische Stadtkern über Jahrzehnte nicht verändert werden durfte.

Während die westeuropäischen Städte zum Teil auf Grund von Kriegszerstörungen, zum Teil aus Bedarf an Erneuerung einem Modernisierungsprozess mit global gleich-artigen Tendenzen unterzogen wurden, blieb Czernowitz zumindest in seinem Zentrum von städtebaulichen Innovationsprozessen weitgehend unberührt.

Auch wenn sich die Bewohnerstruktur der Stadt auf Grund der Zerstörungen im sozialen Bereich von ethnischer Vielfalt hin zu einem vorwiegend ukrainisch, russisch geprägten Gefüge gewandelt hat, blieb der Stadtraum im Zustand von 1940 erhalten. Wir finden eine Stadt vor, die sich in ihrem Zentrum frei von Nachkriegseinflüssen präsentiert und dem alten Europa und der österreich-ungarischen Monarchie verhaftet blieb. Die sozial-archäologische Recherche bringt eine Reihe von Literaten, Künstlern und Architekten zu Tage, die als international anerkannte Träger europäischer Kultur Bedeutung erlangt haben. Die Intensität der Kultur- und Stadtgeschichte in Verbindung mit dem nahezu perfekt erhaltenen Stadtraumgefüge alteuropäischer Prägung bilden ausgezeichnete Voraussetzungen für ein wichtiges und überschaubares europäisches Experiment zur Konstituierung einer Europäischen Stadt der Gegenwart und Zukunft, fernab der gleichmachenden Globalisierungstendenzen, denen Mittel- und West-europäische Stadt- und Kulturlandschaften ausgesetzt waren und sind.

In 1916 Emperor Franz Josef I of Austria King of Hungary passed away. His death initiated the decease of the "Old Europe" sociopolitical order, which came to an end in 1945 with the German troops' capitulation in World War II.

Bukovina, as the K & K Monarchy's former crown land, within the persisting structures as part of Rumania until about 1940 and inevitably became engrossed in the confusions and orgies of violence of the Second World War with its fatal results. Chernivtsi / Chernowitz, as Bukovina's capital at that time with its heterogeneous composition of inhabitants of Germans, Jews, Romanians, and Ukrainians outlives the Austrian-Hungarian Monarchy for about 20 years. In 1945, the town is forced into a conserving deep sleep under the Soviet mandate, during which the historic town center could not be altered for several decades.

While Western European cities underwent a process of modernization with globally similar tendencies, partly due to war damages, partly due to a demand for renewal, Chernowitz – that is its center – remained extensively untouched regarding innovation processes in urban development.

Even though the town's habitational structure transformed itself due to destructions in the social sphere from ethnic diversity to a structure shaped predominantly by Ukrainian, Russian culture, the urban space prevailed in the state of 1940. We come upon a town, which presents itself in its center as free from post-war influences and abides with the old Europe and the Austrian-Hungarian Monarchy.

The social-archaeological research unearths a range of authors, artists, and architects who have achieved international recognition as representatives of the European culture. The intensity regarding cultural and urban history combined with an almost immaculately preserved structure of the urban space's old European imprint, offer excellent prerequisites for an important and straightforward European experiment: An attempt to constitute a "European City of the present and the future", distant from leveling globalization tendencies to which Central- and West-European urban and cultural landscapes were exposed.

Ziel unseres Forschungsprojektes ist es, ausgehend von der historischen Architektur der Stadt und im Wissen um ihre Geschichte, ein soziokulturelles Experiment anzuschieben, das Wesenszüge und Möglichkeiten künftiger Entwicklung europäischer Lebensart untersucht und produktive Schwerpunkte für einen Beitrag im Blick auf eine Weltgesellschaft voller Vielfalt auslotet.

Im Rahmen der Sommerakademie 2006 in Chernivtzy / Czernowitz wurden 3 Handlungsfelder ausgemacht, die eng aufeinander bezogen, in der Stadt innovative Impulse auslösen. Es sind dies die Bereiche Handel, Tourismus, sowie der Block Kultur und Wissenschaft, die aktuell und in der Tradition der Stadt verankert sind.

Die Gründung einer internationalen europäischen Universität steht dabei im Mittelpunkt. Durch den Ausbau einer solchen Institution kehrt die einstmals selbstverständliche ethnische Vielfalt in die Stadt zurück und das soziale Gefüge der Stadt wird durch neue Potentiale in Lehre und Forschung sowie der Bewohnerstruktur aufgewertet.

Hier gilt es zunächst die universitären Inhalte, die vermittelt und in denen geforscht werden soll, bezogen auf die lokalen Bedürfnisse in der Ukraine und bezogen auf das Thema Europa zu erarbeiten.

Parallel dazu können die städtebaulichen und gebäudeplanerischen Untersuchungen zu Standort, Architektur und Identität der Institution weiter entwickelt werden. Zu klären wird auch sein, wie die Universität im Bewusstsein der Stadtbewohner verankert werden kann. Dabei werden bestehende und neu zu gründende kulturelle Einrichtungen als vermittelnde Elemente eine entscheidende Rolle spielen. Auch erscheint es in diesem Zusammenhang sinnvoll, die aus Czernowitz hervorgegangene, Kultur tragenden Persönlichkeiten aus der Vergangenheit ins Bewusstsein zu rücken.

Die Einrichtung einer lokalen Freihandelszone war eine Idee, die während der Sommerakademie 2006 entstanden ist und dann auch kürzlich im Bereich des politischen Diskurses in der Europäischen Union, als eine mögliche überregionale Perspektive im Annäherungsprozess zwischen EU und der Ukraine ihre Bestätigung fand. Geografischer Ausgangspunkt dieser Überlegungen, im lokalen Umfeld, ist der weit in die Region wirksame große Kalinivski Markt an der nord-östlichen Peripherie der Stadt, jenseits des Flusses Pruth.

Our socio-cultural experiment regards the comprehension of the town's history and is based on its historic architecture and on the knowledge of its history. This experiment investigates the characteristic traits and possibilities of a European way of life and its future development and explores how his can contribute a view of a diverse global community.

Hereby the foundation of an International Europe-University stands in the center of attention. The projected expansion of such an institution would secure the return of the formerly self-evident ethnic diversity into the town. The city's social configuration will be enriched by the new potentials in teaching, applied research, as well as residential structure.

The first step incorporates drafting the academic contents, which are to be subject to teaching and research based on the regional requirements in the Ukraine and based on the topic "Europe".

In addition to the former, the urban and architectural analyses regarding the institution's location, architecture, and identity may be developed. It is also necessary to clarify how the university can be anchored within the consciousness of the town's inhabitants. In the course of this alteration, existing and newly established cultural institutions will play a significant role. In this context, it appears reasonable to move to bring back leading personalities from chernowitr's past cultur into the inhabitants' consciousness.

During the Summer Academy 2006, the idea of a regional free trade zone developed. This notion found support in the European Union where it was integrated in political debates. It found consent as a possible trans-regional perspective within the process of approach taking place between the EU and the Ukraine. The geographical focal point within the region is the large Kalinivski market which has a great impact on this region. It is located along the Northeastern periphery of the city on the opposite side of the River Pruth.

Tourismus war, während der Zeit als die Ukraine Teil der Sowjetunion gewesen ist, ein wichtiger wirtschaftlicher Faktor und beginnt sich nun langsam wiederzubeleben. Nach wie vor kommen die wesentlichen Touristenströme aus den östlich gelegenen geografischen Gebieten des Kontinents. Die Stadt, mit ihrem städtebaulich intakten historischen Kern und mit ihrem literaturhistorischen Hintergrund, ihrer Nähe zu den Karpaten, aufgewertet durch eine Internationale Europauniversität, wird auch für mitteleuropäische Touristen Anziehungskraft haben.

In Czernowitz verdichtete sich seinerzeit das multiethnische, strategische Modell der Donaumonarchie zur überschaubaren Realität. Überschaubarkeit ist ein wichtiger Aspekt für die Entscheidung für die Auseinandersetzung mit dieser Stadt. Mit Ihrer alteuropäischen Substanz und mit ihrer schicksalhaften, bewegten Vergangenheit, bietet Czernowitz / Chernivtsi beste Voraussetzungen, den Bedarf an Identität und Lebensart, hervorgehend aus der Geschichte, für ein künftiges zusammengewachsenes Europa zu erforschen.

Aus diesen Überlegungen ergeben sich die Forschungsziele einer anstehenden Phase der Vertiefung. Dabei werden die Zukunftspotentiale Internationale Europa Universität, Freihandelszone und Tourismus, Standort bezogen zu untersuchen sein.

Die Entwicklung einer auf lokale und internationale Bedürfnisse und Studienangebote abgestimmte universitäre Struktur ist dabei ebenso thematischer Schwerpunkt, wie die Ermittlung von städtebaulich relevanten Positionen für darauf bezogene gebäudeplanerische Maßnahmen im Stadtgebiet.

Zu untersuchen sind weiterhin mögliche Aktivitäten der Wirtschaft und des Tourismus als Faktoren, die vor allem im Breitspektrum des sozialen Gefüges der Stadt wirksam werden: In wiefern sich deren enge Beziehung zu universitären Einrichtungen, zum einen, auf dort angesiedelte Lehr- und Forschungsinhalte auswirkt, zum anderen, wie diese universitären Angebote die wirtschaftlichen und touristischen Bereiche beeinflussen werden.

Nicht zuletzt wird zu untersuchen sein, wie solche synergetischen Prozesse zwischen Wissenschaft, Wirtschaft und Tourismus die Atmosphäre und Lebensweise in der Stadt neu definieren können, um auf diese Weise Modellfunktion für die Entwicklung von gesellschaftlichen und städtebaulichen Vorgangsweisen im europäischen Raum zu übernehmen.

While the Ukraine was part of the Soviet Union, tourism was an important econo-mic factor and is only now experiencing a gradual revival. Similar to the past, a substantial amount of tourists originates from the Eastern part of the European continent. In the future, however, the city will also attract tourists from Western Europe. Czernowitz's with its intact historical town center and its literary background, the vicinity to the Carpathians would be further enhanced by an International Europe-University.

In the past, the multi-ethnic strategic model originating from the Danube Mo-narchy intensified. A clear structure is an important aspect with regard to looking closely at the city. Considering the latter's historical European core and the town's fate-stricken, moving past, Czernowitz / Chernivitsi offers important prerequisites. The requirements of a specific identity and way of life, which have developed over time, are fulfilled. Thus a future intertwined Europe can be explored in this city. Thus, a future integrated Europe can be explored.

The research aims for an upcoming phase of in-depth analyses have developed from these notions. In addition, the future potentials, namely the "International Europe University", "Zone of Free Trade", and "Tourism", will have to be examined in the context of the location.

There will be two main measures to be considered. Firstly, there is the thematic emphasis of developing an array of courses, which consider both local and international needs, as well as placing them within the university's structure. Secondly, possible building sites must be considered where construction could take place with the town itself.

Furthermore, one must examine possible alterations in the economy and tourism, regarding them as factors which are important within the town's social structure. Specifically their close relationship to the university facilities and in turn how the university's faculties and courses influence the economy and tourism, are of impor-tance. Last but not least, one must explore the synergetic processes, which take place between the sciences, the economy, and tourism and which have the power to redefine the atmosphere and way of living in Czernowitz.

By doing so, the town functions as a model for the development of social and architectural approaches in Europe.

CREDITS
ABSPANN
FINAL
ПРО УЧАСНИКІВ

`ION MINCU´ University of Architecturte

PROFILS OF THE PARTICIPATING UNIVERSITIES:

"ION MINCU" UNIVERSITY OF ARCHITECTURE AND URBANISM IN BUCHAREST
Stefan Ghenciulescu

"Ion Mincu" University of Architecture and Urbanism in Bucharest (IMUAU) is the oldest and by far the largest academic institution in its field within Romania. The school of architecture was founded in 1892 as a private school belonging to the "Romanian Society of Architects". In 1897 it was transformed into the public "National School of Architecture" within the "School of Fine Arts" and in 1904 it became in- dependent. From 1952 to 1997 the institution functioned under the name of "Ion Mincu" Institute of Architecture - IAIM, Ion Mincu being the founder of the "Neo-Romanian" movement, the Romanian variant of National Romanticism. It managed to preserve its leading status and its prestige even though it was exposed to right-wing dictatorship and, after 1947, the socialist regime.

The École des Beaux-Arts served as the model upon the foundation of "Ion Mincu" and remained as such, even if between wars the Neo-Romanian style was reigning, to be replaced after the 40s by modernism, reinstated after a Stalinist break. Starting with the late 50s until 1989, the mixture between the Beaux-Arts tradition and enthusiastic functionalism shaped the character of education.

And now? Reforms have changed many things after 1989 and the school undergoes a permanent (r)evolution. Modern architecture is still undisputed, but one can say that the school is now the ground for two very different tendencies. One of them tries to keep the venerable (and successful) tradition described above; the other tries to promote the process rather than the result, the context and not the universal solution. Slowly but firmly, the character of education changes.

The "Ion Mincu" School is proud not to belong either to a Technical or to an Arts University, but that it is a university of its own. Trying to cope with the general trend towards specialization, the university now offers degrees in all architecture-related subjects: Architecture, Interior Design, Urbanism, etc. To pay more attention to the social and environmental sides of our profession, and the ability to compete on a now pan-European market could be some of the most important challenges in the near future.

CHERNIVTSI POLYTECHNICAL COLLEGE
Oksana Boyko

The Chernivtsi Polytechnical College was founded in 1944, resulting from a need to rebuild the country after the war. The first students to graduate from the college were Civil engineers. Today, the college incorporates six different departments: Programming of computers and computerized systems, Construction, production and maintenance of wireless devices, Materials' processing in machines and automated lines, Business management, Construction and maintenance of buildings, and Architecture.

Architecture has been taught at the college since 1992. Chernivtsi, Bukovina's picturesque capital, has been famous for its cultural heritage at all times. Lucky not to experience destruction during the wars, the city has preserved unique samples of architecture from many epochs. Chernivtsi's town center forms an organic synthesis of modernism, classicism, constructivism, and the Gothic period. This served as a strong foundation for future art critics in studying architectural styles and the history of architecture.

The department of architecture strongly focuses on the artistic component in their studies. The design work concentrates on working with specific building sites of varying sizes and functions, but it also encompasses subjects such as urban planning, interior design, landscape planning, and graphic presentation techniques.

The architectural studies last four years; each year 25 to 30 young architects graduate from the college. Half of the graduates continue their studies at the Lviv Polytechnical School or at the Kyiv University for Building and Architecture. The other half finds work in architecture studios, as project organizers, or works for municipal authorities. Nowadays, there is a high demand for architects because of the Ukraine's and, with that, Chernivtsi's rapid development; building and refurbishment processes experience an economic revival. Our graduates make their noticeable contribution to this process.

THE TECHNICAL UNIVERSITY OF GRAZ (TU GRAZ)
Prof. Grigor Doytchinov

Founded by the government of the federal state of Styria in 1864 and situated in the heart of Styria's capital, the Technical University of Graz defines the centre for studies and research in engineering for Southern Austria. The TU Graz holds 21 departments and possesses both outstanding research facilities and excellent contacts to the industry.

The TU Graz forms an integral part of Graz's flair where different, partly contradicting cultural influences are interspersed. Symbols of modern architecture preside next to the historic centre listed as cultural heritage by the UNESCO. The publicity regarding Graz as Europe's Cultural Capital of 2003 also focused on the co-existence of old and new edifices and promoted its importance as a cultural symbol for the whole region. Marking Graz as the secret capital of Austrian architecture formulated the climax of one generation's persistent striving towards establishing a modern architecture characteristic for Styria.

The Faculty of Architecture at the TU Graz develops its teaching and research activities on these fruitful grounds. The curriculum focuses on an all-round architectural training. Its project-based education promotes a natural balance between architectural work and theory. The architecture department's teaching staff orientate their studies towards interdisciplinary work. Within the frame of possibilities, each student's main interests and their emphasis on certain areas of their studies are motivated. The students are called upon to assist shaping their field of study through taking an active role within it.

THE UNIVERSITY OF THE ARTS AND THE DEPARTMENT OF ARCHITECTURE
Edith Wunsch

The University of the Arts Berlin (UdK) stands among the leading and largest European institutions for education in art. Based on a history that reaches back for more than 300 years, the UdK holds approximately 4000 students today and incorporates four faculties: Fine Arts, Design, Music, and Drama. It consists of over 30 departments, which cover almost the entire spectrum belonging to education in art and art-related subjects. The UdK originates from the "Royal Prussian Academy of the Arts", founded in 1696. This academy embodied not only an educational institution, but primarily functioned as the universal Prussian authority regarding all issues in and related to art.

Following WWII, the UdK's predecessor developed towards its present shape in three significant stages. Around 1950, Max Taut created the architecture department's new profile as is still largely continued to the present day. The school crystallized two significant principles at this time: firstly, the intense interaction between different disciplines and, secondly, the admission exclusively on the grounds of the students' artistic skills rather than their academic records. This possibility regarding admissions resulted from the German academic post-war situation. The next drastic change occurred in 1975. This involved merging the "Public College for Fine Arts" and the "Public School for Music and Drama", resulting in the creation of the "College of the Arts", the HdK. This newly founded institution received university status following another restructuring process in the 2000, marking the presently last step in the institution's development into the "University of the Arts".

The selection process based upon the students' aptitude for the arts still remains as an elementary characteristic. The admission to nearly all fields of study still takes place on the grounds of the applicant's artistic skill. The process for admissions to the Department of Architecture includes an initial portfolio-based assessment and, if successful, an art assessment test. The Department of Architecture, one of the largest departments within the UdK and integrated into the Faculty of Design, holds about 400 students, nevertheless a fortunate size. The UdK's Department of Architecture continually appeared among the top three German universities in rankings published during the past ten years.

SHORT VITA OF THE AUTHORS

PROF. DR. GRIGOR DOYTCHINOV

Born 1950 in Sofia, Bulgaria. 1968-1974 Studies of Architecture in Aachen and Sofia. 1974-1991 Collaboration with the planning and research institute "Sofprojekt" and at the International Academy of Architecture in Sofia. 1979-1980 PhD-Scholarship of the German Academic Exchange Office (DAAD) at the RWTH Aachen. 1974-1992 planning practice in Sofia and Karlstadt/Main. Since 1992 Lecturer in Urban Design at the Graz University of Technology. 2001-2004 Guest Professor at STU Bratislava and RWTH Aachen. Memberships: International Council of Monuments and Sites (ICOMOS), Paris. Grazer Alterssachverständigenkommission. Jury European Union Prize for Cultural Heritage/Europe Nostra Prize. Honours: 1998 Scholarship of research at the foundation of architecture, austria.

STEFAN GHENCIULESCU

Born 1972. Editor-in-chief of "Arhitectura", review of the Union of Romanian Architects, founded in1906. Lecturer at the "Ion Mincu" University of Architecture and Urbanism, Bucharest (UAUIM). PhD Cum Laude in Urbanism at the UAUIM. Author and co-author of architecture and exhibition projects and publications. Current research interests: Urban identity and its mechanisms, urban culture and morphology in Europe and in the Orient, modernism and contemporary developments forms in architecture and city planning.

VOLODYMYR GYNDYCH

Born in Chernivtsi, on 27 September 1959. He graduated from Chernivtsi Art School and Kyiv Art-Industrual Institute, faculty of design. He works as an art designer and as an expert of public consulting council for issues of preservation of architectural and cultural heritage of protected areas in the historic parts of Chernivtsi.

EMIL IVANESCU

2004 graduated University of Architecture and Urbanism "Ion Mincu" Bucharest; 2003 Erasmus Grant -Liege "Saint Luc de Wallonie" Belgium; Phd University of Architecture and Urbanism "Ion Mincu" Bucharest; Prizes Architectural Competitions: 2003 First Prize International Competition in Luxembourg together with Polaris Architects: "Skip Pavilion"; 2005 Third Prize National Competition together with architect Carmen Tanase: "Kretzulescu Kindergarden"; Honorable Mention International Competition IAAC Institute Barcelona: "Self Sufficient Housing". 2007 Nominated, together with architect Carmen Tanase, in National Architectural Annual Competition with "Kretzulescu Kindergarden project". Workshops: 2006 architectural student workshop organizer: "Corbii de Piatra" Romania; guest Lecturer in Chernivtsi Summer Academy 2006.

KATJA KOLLMANN

Born 1972 in Cham in Eastern Bavaria. After finishing school, she moved to Berlin and studied history and Russian literature at Humboldt University. Katja Kollmann is now a journalist. She writes about cultural life in Berlin – especially in Russian newspapers. Two years ago she decieded to become a student once more and now studies cultural journalism at University of the Arts Berlin.

PAVLO KOLYADINSKY

Born in Chernivtsi, Ukraine, 13.01.1983. He currently works as an acting director of the marketing department of Karavan shopping mall in Chernivtsi. He also works as a scientific colleague of the Bukovina Center at Chernivtsi National University and as a member of nongovernmental youth public organization "Krok". He has studied geographical ecology, international economics and cultural management. His scientific interests includ the ecological problems of regional development in Chernivtsi.

IRYNA KOROTUN

Architect, Doctor of Philosophy, PhD Born in Chernivtsi, Iryna Korotun graduated from architect faculty of Lviv Polytechnical Institute. Worked in private institutions and bodies of local government. She dedicated more than 20 years to researching of the architectural heritage of Chernivtsi city. Author of more than 40 articles, dedicated to the historical architectural heritage of Chernivtsi. Architect of more than 100 objects of public meaning, including 20 religious buildings, trade and public centers, apartment houses, erected on the territory of Chernivtsi and Chernivtsi region. Prize-winner of Joseph Glavka prize in the nomination "Restoration of historical heritage". Member of the National Association of Architects of Ukraine, member of regional and city architect-town-planning council.

PROF. DR. JOSEF LEHNER

Architect, was born on the 31st of October 1894 in Czernowitz. 1913-1923 he attended the Technical University of Vienna to study architecture. 1923 he began his work as an architect in Czernowitz; simultaneously he accepted a position as a Professor at the Public College for Construction in Czernowitz / Cernauti. Romania. In October 1940 he re-settled with his family to Austria; lecturer at the Public College for Building in Deutsch-Krone (Pomerania). 1942-1946 director of the newly foundet College for Building in Krems, Austria. 1947 move to vienna. dissertation and graduation. 1952 move to the Federal Republic of Germany. 1953 he became director of the School of Architecture, Regensburg.1966 move to Grenzach. He dies on the 30 October 1980 close to Lake Constance.

PETER A. LEHNER

Architect, born 10 October 1926 in Cernauti, lived in the House on the Barleon Lane until the age of fourteen. Following expulsion by the Red Army in 1940, a new chapter began in his and his family's lives in Vienna. Following in his father's footsteps, he studied architecture at the Technical University in Vienna from 1945 to 1951. He married in 1951 and left Vienna with his wife in 1953. With stops in Regensburg and Frankfurt / Main, he eventually settled in Basel, Switzerland where he ran his own architecture office for over forty years. Since 2002 he has lived in eastern Switzerland and Berlin. He travels frequently, one of his favoured destinations being Chernowitz.

JULIA LIENEMEYER

Architect, scientific assistant at the UdK Berlin; born 1968 in Frankfurt / Main. During 1989-1996 studied Architecture at the UdK Berlin. During 1996–2002 collaboration at the Hufnagel Pütz Rafaelian office of architecture, Berlin. Since 2002 freelance architect in Berlin. Since 2003 scientific assistant at the chair of building planning, interior design and switching technology at UdK Berlin. Focus of Research: "Architecture and Urban Regeneration as Link between Past and Future Development of Eastern European Cities instancing the city of Chernivtsi, Ukraine". Working on her dissertation: "Identity-oriented Urban Development – The Example of Chernivtsi, Ukraine". 2006 Initiator and Organizer of the International Summer Academy of Architecture in Chernivtsi, Ukraine.

DR. WERNER SEWING

Sociologist of Architecture, 2003-2005 Visiting Professor at the University of the Arts Berlin, Sociology of Architecture, Architectural Theory. 2004 Visiting Professor at the Technical University Braunschweig, History and Theory of Architecture. 2004 Alcatel / SEL Visiting Professor at Stuttgart University. 2002 / 2004 Visiting Lecturer at the Berlin Studio, University of Kentucky. Since 2003 Lecturer for Sociology of Architecture, postgraduate studie course Real Estate Management (REM), TU Berlin. 1995-2001 Assistant Professor Technical University Berlin, Institute of Social Sciences Sociology of Architecture. 2000 Visiting Lecturer at University of Berkeley, Architectural History. 2001 / 2002 Guest critic Architectural Association in London and Bauhaus University Weimar. 1992-1995 Lecturer Bauhaus University Weimar, Department of Design, Urban Sociology. He teached at the Free University Berlin Sociology and Urban Sociology, Sociology of Architectureat the Technical University Berlin. Member in numerous advisory committees, for example the BDA Berlin and the Stiftung Baukultur.

VOLODYMYR TSVYLYOV

Born 06.11.1957 in Kiev. 1980 he entered Kiev State Art Institute. 1984-86 he served in the Soviet Army. 1988 he graduated from the Institute and in May he moved to Chernivtsi city to work as the chief architect in the Department of the city of Chernivtsi. Married, one son, 11 years. He is a member of the Association of architects of the Ukraine. Chernivtsi impressed him during a visit with friends on an excursion. At that time he was 19 years old and he fell in love with the city, where he still lives.

PROF. GÜNTER ZAMP KELP

Was born 1941 in Bistrita, Transsylvania. 1959-1967 Degree in Architecture at TU Vienna. 1967-1969 Assistant of Prof. Dr. Karl Schwanzer at TU Vienna, Building planning and design. 1967 Foundation of Haus-Rucker-Co, Vienna; group of architects and artists. 1970 Move to Düsseldorf, Member of Architektenkammer NRW. 1971-1972 Constitution of Haus-Rucker-Studio in New York. 1981 Visiting professor at Cornell University, Ithaca, division architecture and Visiting professor at Academia of fine arts, division design, Berlin. 1987 Independent studios in Berlin and Düsseldorf, Member of Architektenkammer Berlin. 1988 Visiting professor at Städelsche Kunstschule, Frankfurt, division architecture. Professor at University of Fine Arts, Berlin, Building planning and interior desion. 1993 Director of building planning, interior design and switching technology at Hochschule der Künste, Berlin. 1996 Visiting professor at TU Wien, division architecture. 2001 Member Advisory Commitee, division design, Linz, Austria. 2002 Director of the class of Architecture at the Internationale Sommer-akademie, Salzburg. 2004 Visiting professor Bauhaus University Weimar. 2006 Chairmen Advisory Commitee, division design, Linz, Austria. Initiator Summeracademy for Architecture, Chernivtsi, Ukraine.

ORIGINAL POSTERS OF THE EXHIBITION: "CZERNOWITZ TOMORROW – IDEAS FOR THE CITY OF CHERNIVTSI"

TOMORROW IN CZERNOWITZ

David Bürger, Irina Bogdan, Sasha Chebni, Kostja Chebni, Raluca Davidel, Joachim Maier, Matthias Tscheuschler
Coordination: Emil Ivanescu, Jule Lenzenmeyer

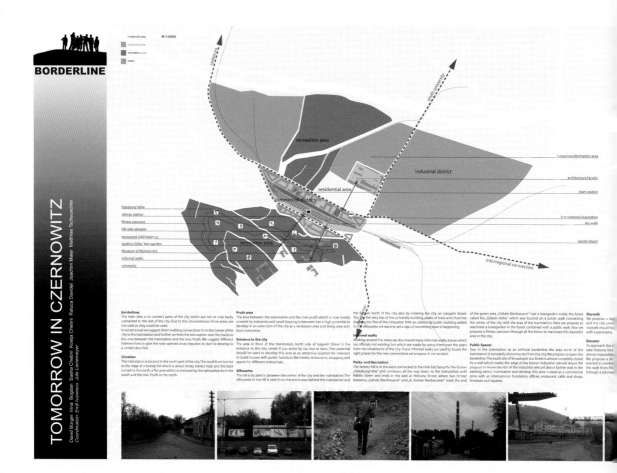

residential area
industrial area
recreation area
water

M 1:5000

recreation area

future transformation area

industrial district

architecture faculty

tram station

residential area

international busstation

commercial district

sky walk

habsburg höhe
railway station
fitness parcours
hill-side elevator
restaurant (old brewery)
goebels höhe beergarden
Museum of Modern Art
informal walks
university

recreation area

goods depot

interregional connection

borderlines
The main idea is to connect parts of the city which are not or only badly connected to the rest of the city. Due to this circumstances these areas are not used as they could be used.
In our proposal we suggest direct walking connections from the Center of the city to the trainstation and further on from the trainstation over the tracks to the area between the trainstation and the river Pruth. We suggest different interventions to give the now opened areas impulses to start to develop in a certain direction.

Situation
The trainstation is located in the north part of the city. The southfront turned to the north, a flat area which is enclosed by the railroadtracks in the south and the river Pruth in the north.

Pruth area
The area between the trainstation and the river pruth which is now mostly covered by industries and small housing in between has a high potential to develop in an extension of the city as a recreation area and living area with local commerce.

Entrance to the city
The area in front of the trainstation, north side of Gagarin Street is the entrance to the city center if you arrive by car, bus or train. This potential should be used to develop this area as an attractive location for investors to build houses with public functions like hotels, restaurants, shopping and spaces for different enterprises.

Silhouette
The hill is located in between the center of the city and the trainstation. The silhouette of the hill is seen from the entire area behind the trainstation and

the further north of the city, also by entering the city on Gargarin Street. You see the very top of the university building, peaks of trees and churches drawing the line of the silhouette. With an additional public building added to the silhouette we want to set a sign of something new is happening.

Informel walks
Walking around the areas we discovered many informel walks, traces which are officially not existing but which are made by using them over the years from the inhabitants of the city. These informel walks we used to locate the right places for the new connections we propose in our project.

Parks- and Recreation
The foresty hill is in the west connected to the Park Fed'kovychy the former "Habsburghöhe" and continues all the way down to the trainstation until Nikitin Street and ends in the east at Holovna Street, where two former brewerys "Göbels Bierbrauerei" und "A. Steiner Bierbrauerei" mark the end

of the green area. "Göbels Höhe" had a beergarden inside the forest called the "Göbels Höhe" which was located on a public walk connecting the center of the city with the area of the trainstation. Here we propose to reactivate a beergarden in the forest combined with a public walk. Also we propose a fitness parcours through all the forest to reactivate this beautiful area in the city.

Public Spaces
Due to the trainstation as an artificial borderline the area north of the trainstation is completely disconnected from the city. We propose to open this borderline. The south site of Sevastopol'ska Street is almost completly closed by a wall which marks the edge of the former industrial railroad depot. We propose to move the rest of the industrial railroad depot further east to the existing switch trainstation and develop this area instead as a commercial zone with an international busstation, offices, restaurant, cafés and shops, terrasses and squares.

Skywalk
We propose a sky and the city centre skywalk should be with a panoramic area in the city.

Elevator
To approach the t take Holovna Stre almost impossible. We propose a dir erected in combin the walk from Filk through a pituresc

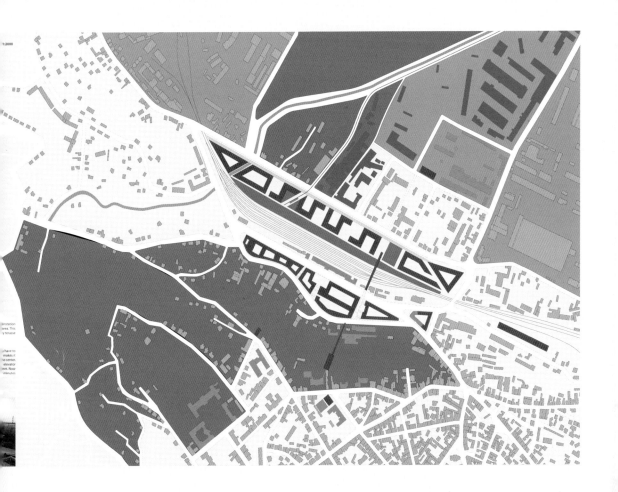

TOMORROW IN CZERNOWITZ

David Bürger Irina Bogdan Sasha Chebni Kostja Chebni Raluca Davidel Joachim Maier Matthias Tscheuschler
Coordination: Emil Ivanescu, Jule Lienemeyer

0 | ELEV
1 | NEW
2 | GOE
3 | OLD
4 | RAIL
5 | SKY
6 | OLD
7 | CHI
8 | RAIL
9 | MUS
10 | UNIV
11 | HAB
PAN
FITN
EAT
REL
BEE

ONNECTING THE CITY WITH THE RAILWAYSTATION

e main idea was to connect the city with the railwaystation along two existing ways through the forest. The main way is
fined by the new museum of modern art [MOMA] and the skywalk over the trainstation to the new built Shopping City. The
er way connects the university with the railwaystation.

MUSEUM OF MODERN ART AND SKYWALK

the area of the institute for music will be a new museum of modern art which should become a new
RADEMARK] - [LANDMARK] for the whole city, as a symbol for changing and modern development. From the Museum,
restaurant and cafe you will be able to view the hole area to the Pruth, like a terrasse for the city. The Museum will be
nnected through an elevator which can be accessed through a tunnel from the old Railwayroad and the [SKYWALK], which
uld be more than a bridge, it is a place with bars, cafes and places for events. The old brewery could be rebuild and
ablished as a hotel.

RUNNING THROUGH THE FOREST

ross the forest on the hill a [FITNESS PARCOURS] with several stations / walking paths is created to bring back human life
he woods.

EW TERRASSES FOR THE CITY

ng the fitness parcours / walking paths there will be serveral places with cafes and little restaurants from where you will
ve a panoramic view over the city. For example the old Goebls Höhe or the new cafe/ restaurant in the museum.

[MOMA]]]]]]]

Museum Of Modern Art for Czernowitz

239

BORDERLINE

TOMORROW IN CZERNOWITZ

David Burger Irina Bogdan Sasha Chebini Kostja Chebini Raluca Davidei Emil Ivaniescu Joachim Maier Matthias Tischeuschler
Coordination: Julie Lienemeyer

THE UNTAMED NATURE - THE MAN - THE CITY AS AN ORGANISM - THE ECONOMIC FACTOR - THE FORCE OF NATURE - THE WILL OF MAN

The evolution of the area in time

Important factors which shaped and developed the site   -the natural element
                                                         -the nearby RAILWAY STATION

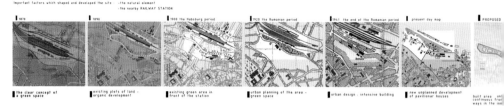

| 1879 | 1890 | 1900 the Habsburg period | 1920 the Romanian period | 1941 the end of the Romanian period | present day map | PROPOSED |

| the clear concept of a green space | existing plots of land - organic development | existing green area in front of the station | urban planning of the area - green space | urban design : intensive building | new unplanned development of pavilionar houses | built area unt continuous fro ways in the inn |

Proposed development of the area in the context of the growing city

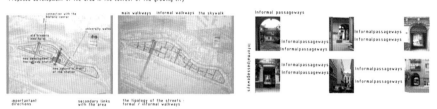

connection with the historic center
university walks
old brewery
new hotel
new development of the railway station
new square in front of the station

main walkways   informal walkways   the skywalk

Informal passageways

informalpassageways
Informalpassageways   Informalpassageways
Informalpassageways   Informalpassageways
Informalpassageways   Informalpassageways
Informalpassageways   Informalpassageways

importantant directions

secondary links with the area

the tipology of the streets : formal / informal walkways

Panoramic view of the railway station street

Nikitina street -view towards east/view towa

Panoramic view of the area in front the railway station

Conceptual image of the proposed constructed area

Sketch plan scale 1/1000

Proposed functions : - shops and caffees - groundfloor level
- living spaces - first level
- offices - second level

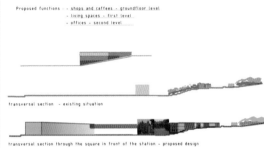

transversal section - existing situation

transversal section through the square in front of the station - proposed design

CONNECTIONS VS. BORDERS

TOMORROW IN CZERNOWITZ

David Bürger Irina Bogdan Sasha Chebrii Kostja Chebrii Raluca Davidel Joachim Maier Matthias Tscheuschler
Coordination Emil Ivanescu Julia Lienemeyer

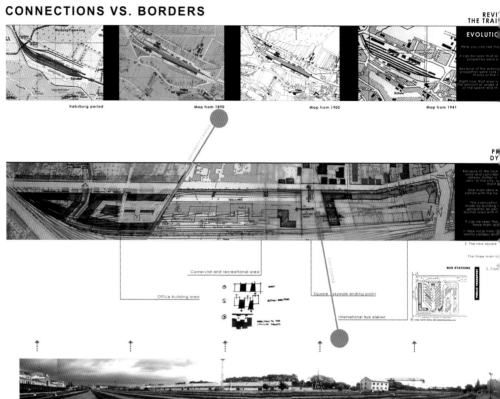

Habsburg period — Map from 1890 — Map from 1900 — Map from 1941

Comercial and recreational area

Office building area

Square askywalk ending point

International bus station

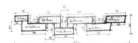

OFFICE AREA

The office building area is divided in two built sectors. The dividing element is the river leading to the Pruth river and by the pedestrian walkway leading to the green area/to the University campus park.

This proposal tries to implement also a parking place for the local residents and for the comercial area.

Another proposal would be to build two typical "hof" buildings.

Another important point that connects this area with the rest of the city is the new tram railway. The actual station connecting the "Bahnhof" to the other side of the Pruth is placed between the office building area and the commercial and leasure area.

The image of the "hof" type buildings is a continuous built front that generates an urban image needed in this unstructured area.

B A H N H O F   P R O M E N A D E

LEASURE

BIKING

OUT FOR A WALK

COMMEERCIAL AND RECREATIONAL AREA

The comercial area is ment to bring a dynamic movement to the already existing image of the area.Comerce means in fact a dynamic process.

This irregular shape of the comercial building actually rests to the former unstructured building style of the area; volumes with different highs and placed closer of futher away from the walking ways.

This whole area is ment to have two main characters:

1 **Comercial character** - on the front side of the site
2 **Leasure character** - facing the railway station and offering panoramas towers the old part of the city

The comercial area communicates with the street through a sequence of terraces and public spaces.

The leasure area is designed as a promenade with areas reserved to restaurants pubs etc.

Here you can find also the tram station from where people can reach the Pruth, the new University Campus and other facilities.

This comercial area is connected directly to the new market and commercial center of Czernowitz, creating a comercial axis.

CONNECTION SQUARE

This square represents an ending point for the general axis formed by the exterior lift connecting the University and the railway station and the skywalk that connects the old part of the city with the new one.

This square represents actually a transit area between the comercial zone and the international bus station.

The "agora" is continued on the other side of the street, creating a visual connection between both sides of the street.

From this point you can directly reach the international bus station and the shop area.

INTERNATIONAL BUS STATION

Taking in account the future city development of the city we reach the conclusion that Czernowitz will become an international city. This leads to comunication, international transport facilities etc.

One important link towards the international development of the city would have to be the building of an international bus station.

One point that can be taken in account as a good argument towards building such a facility is the fact that today Ucranian people use the bus in a percentage of 70-80%(inner country traveling).

The visual impact of this facility would have to respond to the already proposed solutions. Therefor the fist important characteristic should relate to the front side:

>building an urban image>forming a continuous front

SIGNAL

HERE WILL BE THE INTERNATIONAL BUS STATION

THE FRONT LINE

After annalysing the already existing front on the other side of the street it can be easily seen the fact that the front is irregulated.To create a visual connection between the two sides of the street the new built front responds to the already existing one.Therefor an irregular front side is created.

The composition of the front follows the concept.

THE SHAPE OF THE FRONT

FRONT

243

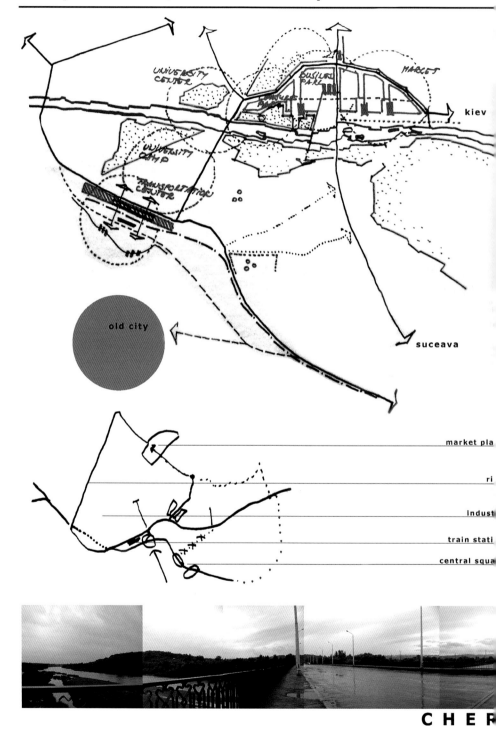

DOYTCHINOV GRIGOR (AU)   DUNDICH OLGA (UA)   GALUSHKA NATASHA (UA)   DIETERSDORFER LISA (AU

of the Chernivcy Trade and Business Centre is located on the northern shore of the river Prut. The Centre is of re-international importance. The development of the Centre is based on the existing Kalinivski Market. The direct con- the traditional City Centre and to the future Transportation Terminal (the existing railroad station and the future al, located north of the station) is guaranteed by a new bridge over the Prut. The location of the Trade and Business Centre is also directly connected to the network of regional and national highways.

ivski Market is a booming economic area founded in the 1990's which development has won in the last years a self he market has established itself as the most important trade area of the city of Chernivcy and as a economic link to ncl. the region in an European scale. The dynamic of the market is to be used for modernisation and future develop-ment of the location.

ivcy Trade and Business Centre is divided into an eastern and a western part by the existing tangential highway of e concept is viewing a modernisation and reorganisation of the eastern part of the Kalinivski Market by keeping the functions. A modern development of the area west of the tangential highway is proposed in the concept. The west-nsists of the Trade Centre (supermarket and office buildings as well as a new multifunctional place supporting the n with the area), a Business Park and a recreation zone (hotel complex, swimming pools and sport area). The place ication is used at daytime for market functions and in the evenings for cultural events. The stations of the public transport are in a direct connection with the place.

m of streets and parking places is organised the way that it is not dividing the Centre from the river Prut. Axes of for pedestrian walkways are open to the south including on this way the green belt of the river Prut into the image of the Centre.

TSI SUMMER ACADEMY - 2006

NRAD (AU)   TUDOR VERONICA (RO)   CRAIU JENICA (RO)   FISCHMANN ELENA (D)   BECHTLOFF BASTIAN (D)

CHERNIVTSI TRADE AND BU
Чернівецький торговий та б

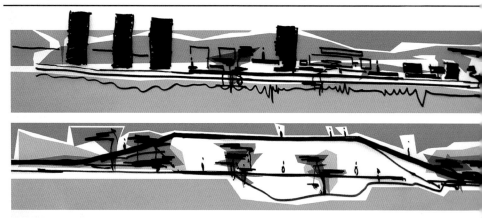

Територія Чернівецького торгового та бізнес - центру розташована на північному схилі ріки осередком регіонального та міжнародного значення. Центр створено на базі Калиновського ринку. язки зі старим центром міста та майбутнім транспортним терміналом (залізничний вокзал та майбутн станція, що буде розташована на північ від вокзалу), що спонукає до будівництва нового моста чер Розташування торгового та бізнес - центру є передумовою досягнення регіонального та національного

Калинівський ринок, який засновано в 90-х роках, є територією інтенсивного економічного розвитку прийшовся на останні роки. Станом на сьогодні ринок є найважливішим торговим центром міста Черн центром економічного зв"язку регіону з сусідніми регіонами, включаючи регіони європейського масшта ринку використовувалась для модернізації та майбутнього розвитку місцевості.

Чернівецький торговий та бізнес - центр поділяється на західну та східну частини за тенденціє міста. Розробка концепції зосереджена на модернізації та реорганізації східної частини Калинівсько виконує традиційні торгові функції. Пропозицією концепції є модернізація розвитку західної території тенденціями розвитку. Західна частина складається з Торгового центру (супермаркет та офісні спор нові, що будуть збудовані у майбутньому на цій території), бізнес - парк та рекреаційна зона (готель плавальні басейни та спортивні майданчики). Місця, які призначені для денного використання рин використовуються для дозвілля та масових заходів. Головним місцем сполучення з містом є зупинка транспорту.

Система шляхів та місця для парковки не відокремлюють Центр від ріки Прут. Пішохідні дор зеленими насадженнями, ведуть на південь до ріки Прут.

CHER

DOYTCHINOV GRIGOR (AU)   DUNDICH OLGA (UA)   GALUSHKA NATASHA (UA)   DIETERSDORFER LISA (AU

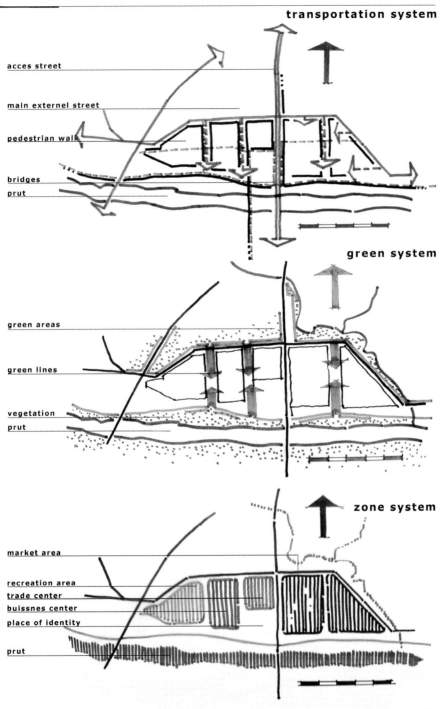

transportation system

- acces street
- main externel street
- pedestrian walk
- bridges
- prut

green system

- green areas
- green lines
- vegetation
- prut

zone system

- market area
- recreation area
- trade center
- buissnes center
- place of identity
- prut

TSI SUMMER ACADEMY - 2006

)NRAD (AU)   TUDOR VERONICA (RO)   CRAIU JENICA (RO)   FISCHMANN ELENA (D)   BECHTLOFF BASTIAN (D)

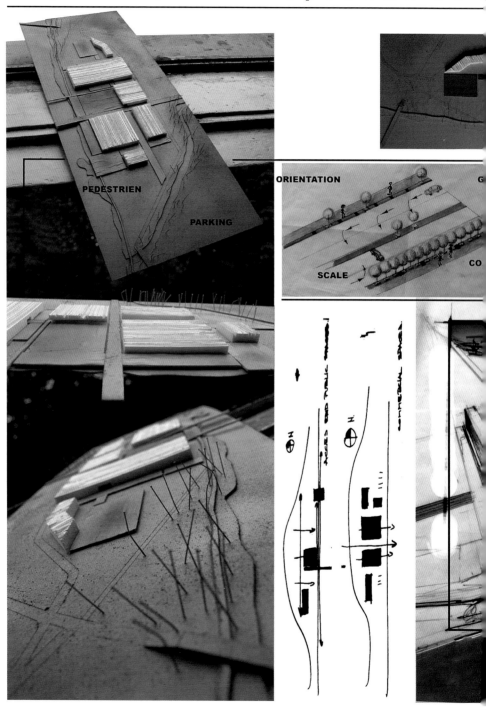

PEDESTRIEN

PARKING

ORIENTATION

G

SCALE

CO

C H E R

DOYTCHINOV GRIGOR (AU)　　DUNDICH OLGA (UA)　　GALUSHKA NATASHA (UA)　DIETERSDORFER LISA (AU)

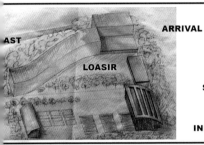

AST

ARRIVAL

LOASIR

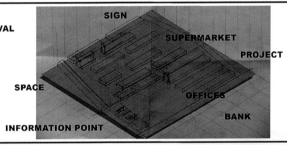

SIGN

SUPERMARKET

PROJECT

SPACE

OFFICES

INFORMATION POINT

BANK

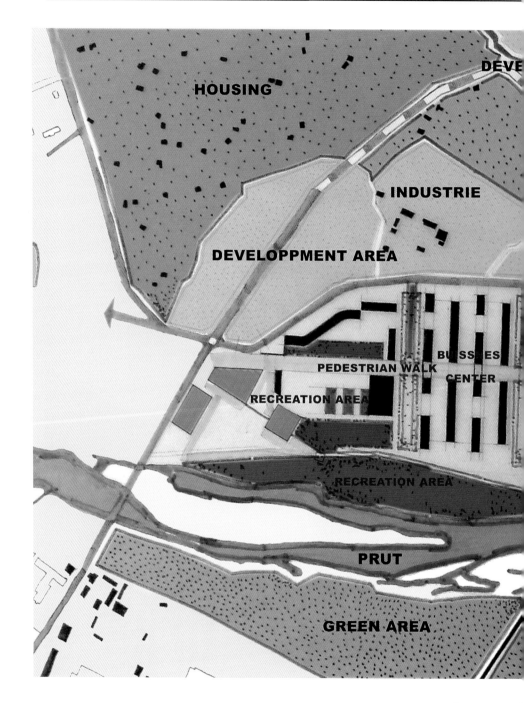

HOUSING

DEVE

INDUSTRIE

DEVELOPPMENT AREA

BUSSES CENTER

PEDESTRIAN WALK

RECREATION AREA

RECREATION AREA

PRUT

GREEN AREA

DOYTCHINOV GRIGOR (AU)   DUNDICH OLGA (UA) GALUSHKA NATASHA (UA) DIETERSDORFER LISA (AU

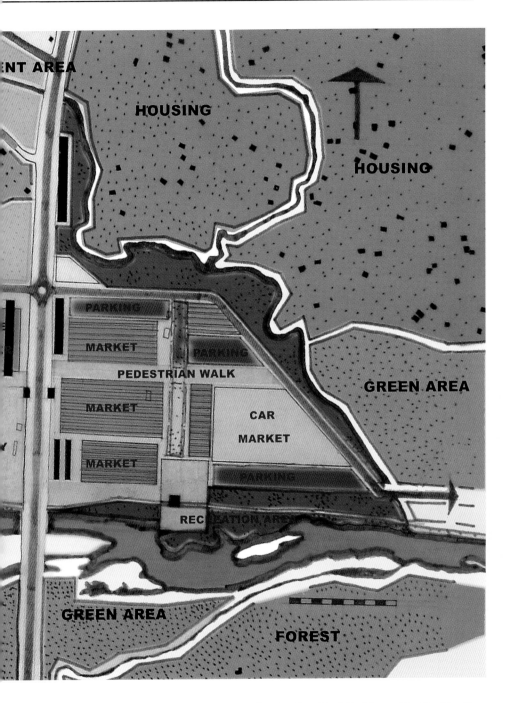

NT AREA

HOUSING

HOUSING

PARKING

MARKET

PARKING

PEDESTRIAN WALK

MARKET

CAR
MARKET

GREEN AREA

MARKET

PARKING

RECREATION AREA

GREEN AREA

FOREST

TSI SUMMER ACADEMY-2006

ONRAD (AU)   TUDOR VERONICA (RO)   CRAIU JENICA (RO)   FISCHMANN ELENA (D)   BECHTLOFF BASTIAN (D)

Legend:

REFURBISHED BUILDINGS
будинки під реконструкцію

NEW BUILDINGS
нові споруди

EXISTING BUILDINGS
існуючі споруди

GREEN SPACE
зелена зона

PUBLIC SPACE
громадська зона

PROPOSED INTERVENTIONS:

Holovna street:
• Opening of the central park
• Opening of the military complex
• Rehabilitation of the Bukovina stadium, some of the buildings of the military complex, insertion of new buildings; we create a new sports centre and a complex of offices, exhibition halls, hotels, apartments, restaurants and cafes.
• Insertions of new buildings in the existing structure: offices or apartments with shops on the ground floor
• Restructuring of the crossing between Holovna Street and Chkalova Street: replacing of a street, creation of a square and a dominant element on the axis

Chervonoarmiys'ka and Prospekt Nezhalezhnosti:
• Rehabilitation of the prison as a public building (administration, offices, shops)
• Opening of the military complex and the hospital towards the street; rehabilitation of the old buildings and insertion of new, dynamic functions: offices, ateliers and exhibition spaces, apartments and shops.
• Creation of a new park, with a belvedere over the city
• The new apartment buildings connect the different existing structures
• Insertions of new buildings in the existing structure: offices or apartments with shops on the ground floor
• Re-organisation of the socialist living areas: private gardens, extensions, balconies, parking spaces, commercial spaces
• New centre around the Prospekt and Chervonoarmiys'ka Street: offices, cinema, entertainment, shopping, apartments create a real boulevard.
• The clinic area on the Prospekt will become a big public park, with public functions (entertainment, hotels and hostels, administration) located in the 19th. Century pavilions.

Map labels:

OPENING – ripping down the walls (central park Holovna street) and bringing the houses to the street
ВІДКРИТТЯ – знесення стін (центральний парк по вулиці Головна)

NEW HOTEL AND HOSTEL
ГОТЕЛЬ & ГУРТОЖИТОК

RE-MODELLING OF SOBORNA-PLATZ
РЕКОНСТРУКЦІЯ СОБОРНОЇ ПЛОЩІ

URBAN SQUARE – temporary market and a remodeled park
ВІДКРИТТЯ – міськопалаці парк

REFURBISHMENT OF THE OLD COMMERCE BUILDINGS
ВІДНОВЛЕННЯ СТАРИХ КОМЕРЦІЙНИХ БУДИНКІВ

NEW OFFICES
ОФІСНА ЗОНА

CONNECTING
- creating the new front (4 storey buildings with commerce at ground floor)
ПОЄДНАННЯ
- поєднання фасадів (5-типоверхові будинки з магазинами першому поверсі)

OPENING – the Central Park
ВІДКРИТТЯ(парк)

SPACEPOCKETS – creating green, public space in front of some buildings along the Holovna street
ПРОСТОРОВІ КАРМАНІ - створення зелених зон, громадського простору перед деякими будинками по вулиці Головна

MUSEUM
МУЗЕЙ

LIBRARY
БІБЛІОТЕКА

THEATRE
ТЕАТР

GALLERIES
ГАЛЕРЕЇ

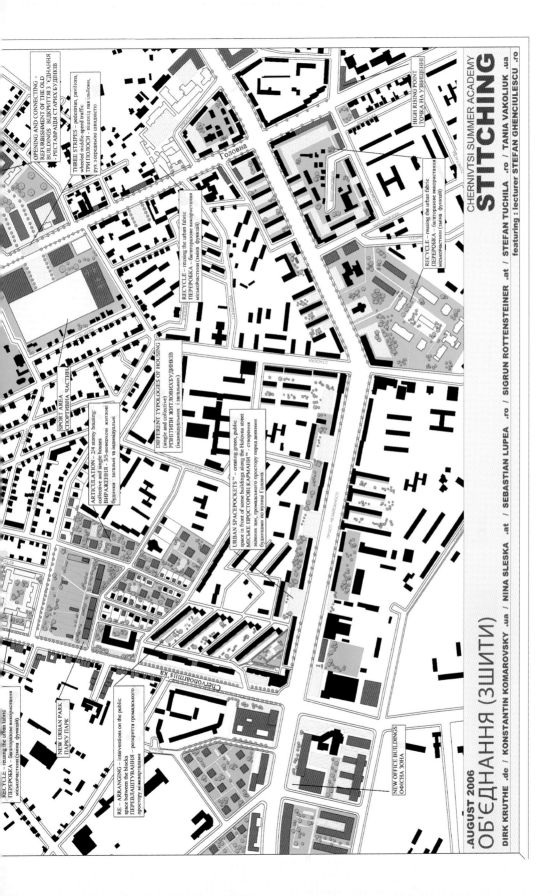

CHERNIVTSI SUMMER ACADEMY
STITCHING

OPENING AND CONNECTING -
REFURBISHMENT OF THE OLD
BUILDINGS - ВІДКРИТТЯ З'ЄДНАННЯ
- РЕСТАВРАЦІЯ СТАРИХ БУДІНКІВ

THREE STRIPES - pedestrian, pavilions,
wheeled middle-speed traffic.
ТРИ ПОЛОСИ - пішохід, пав`ільйони,
рух з зеркалою швидкістю

Головна

HIGH RISING POINT
ТОЧКА НА УЗВИШЕННІ

RECYCLE - reusing the urban fabric
ПЕРЕРОБКА - багаторазове використання
міськоївластині (зміна функцій)

SPORT AREA
СПОРТИВНА ЧАСТИНА

RECYCLE - reusing the urban fabric
ПЕРЕРОБКА - багаторазове використання
міськоївластині (зміна функцій)

ARTICULATION - 2/4 storey housing
collective and single houses
ВИРАЖЕННЯ - 3/5-поверхові житлові
будинки : загальні та індивідуальні

DIFFERENT TYPOLOGIES OF HOUSING
(single and collective)
РІЗНИТИТИ ЖИТЛОВИХБУДИНКІВ
(індивідуальних і загальних)

URBAN SPACEPOCKETS" - creating green, public
space in front of some buildings along the Holovna street
МІСЬКЕ ПРОСТОРОВІ КАРМАНИ" - створення
зелених зон, громадського простору перед деякими
будинками по вулиці Головна

STADSKA

ПРОСП. НЕЗАЛЕЖНОСТІ

RECYCLE - reusing the urban fabric
ПЕРЕРОБКА - багаторазове використання
міськоївластині (зміна функцій)

NEW URBAN PARK
ПАРКУ ПАРК

RE - ARRANGING - interventions on the public
space between the blocks
ПЕРЕБЛАШТУВАННЯ - розкриття громадського
простору міжквартальним

Сельопоштитьк.

NEW OFFICE BUILDINGS
ОФІСНА ЗОНА

.AUGUST 2006
ОБ'ЄДНАННЯ (ЗШИТИ)

DIRK KRUTHE .de / KONSTANTIN KOMAROVSKY .ua / NINA SLESKA .ua / SEBASTIAN LUPEA .ro / STEFAN TUCHILA .ro / TANIA VAKOLIUK .ua
featuring : lecturer STEFAN GHENCIULESCU .ro

253

BELVEDERE PARK СТВОРЕННЯ ПАРКУ ТА ОГЛЯДОВОЇ ПЛОЩАДКИ У ЦЬОМУ ПАРКУ Chervonoarmijs'ka street вулиці Червоноармійської

A COURTYARD IN THE HOUSING AREA ВНУТРІШНІЙ ДВОРИК

254

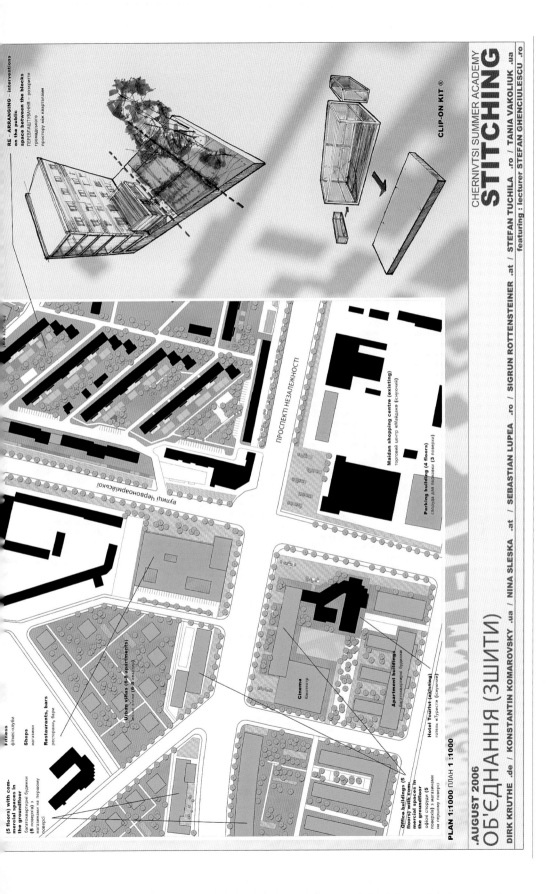

RE - ARRANGING - interventions on the public space between the blocks
ПЕРЕПЛАНУВАННЯ – розкрити громадського простору між кварталами

CLIP-ON KIT ®

CHERNIVTSI SUMMER ACADEMY
STITCHING

featuring : lecturer STEFAN GHENCIULESCU .ro
STEFAN TUCHILA .ro / TANIA VAKOLIUK .ua

ПРОСПЕКТІ НЕЗАЛЕЖНОСТІ

вулиці Червоноармійської

Maidan shopping centre (existing)
торговий центр «Майдан» (існуючий)

Parking building (4 floors)
споруда для парковки (3 поверхи)

Cinema
Кінотеатр

Apartment buildings
багатоквартирні будинки

Hotel Tourist (existing)
готель «Турист» (існуючий)

Urban villas (6-8 apartments)
міські вілли (6-8 квартир)

(5 floors) with commercial spaces in the groundfloor
багатоквартирні будинки (5 поверхів) з магазинами на першому поверсі

Fitness
фітнес-клуби

Shops
магазини

Restaurants, bars
ресторани, бари

Office buildings (5 floors) with commercial spaces in the groundfloor
офісні споруди (5 поверхів) з магазинами на першому поверсі

PLAN 1:1000 ПЛАН 1:1000

.AUGUST 2006
ОБ'ЄДНАННЯ (ЗШИТИ)

DIRK KRUTHE .de / KONSTANTIN KOMAROVSKY .ua / NINA SLESKA .at / SEBASTIAN LUPEA .ro / SIGRUN ROTTENSTEINER .at

255

THE NEW STADIUM НОВИЙ СТАДІОН

URBAN SPACEPOCKETS™ МІСЬКЕ ПРОСТОРОВІ КАРМАНИ™

SECTION M 1:1000

urban villas

market

business & shops

theatre

startup-office-lofts

hotel

PLAN 1:1000 ПЛАН 1:1000

.AUGUST 2006
ОБ'ЄДНАННЯ (ЗШИТИ)
DIRK KRUTHE .de / KONSTANTIN KOMAROVSKY .ua / NINA SLESKA .at / SEBASTIAN LUPEA .ro / SIGRUN ROTTENSTEINER .at / STEFAN TUCHILA .ro / STEFAN VAKOLIUK .ua

CHERNIVTSI SUMMER ACADEMY
STITCHING
featuring : lecturer STEFAN GHENCIULESCU .ro

257

OPENING MILITARY STRUKTURE AND RECREATING OF THE STADIUM

The old military area and the recreation area with the Stadium offers a great potential to the city, witch is not used. Most of the cities put there military outside. There is the chance, to give the people this space back, and open it to the public. This interventions are able to define a new point of interest in between the old town and the area of the prospect.

Step 1

Recreation and renovation of the sporting area and the Bukowina Stadium: The old stadium gets a new covering of a semitransparent glassing structure. The new structure creates a new indoor -space, witch contains function like shops, café, dressing-rooms and sanitary. T he new structure build a roof over the sitting places. In this way, the new stadium will become a landmark for this in between area of the city and give it a new identity. The recre-ation area around the stadium will be filled up with other functions for sport and health like a multifunction- hall, a swimming-bath and a wellness-center. The new buildings will create a large space, witch defines the new entry area.

Step 2

We open up the military complex. The area and the buildings of the military will be given to the public and redefined as offices, markets, stores and so on. The arrangement of the old and new buildings in this area define a new green but urban square. We decided to offer a big parking space, created as a large carport. The roof of the carport is designed as a large plate standing on several abutments.

Step 3

Connected to the new defined center we will create new urban villas. We define a new kind living space with urban villas, mixed with old existing houses.

RE-ARRANGING. The socialist housing from the 60s

Today, people make their own interventions: they close the balconies, extend the ground floor apartments, make private gardens. It is maybe illegal and not beautiful, but it shows the problems these neighborhoods have. Why not try to design, to order – to RE-ARRANGE – these operations?

Step 1.

We define private gardens around the blocks, for the people which live on the ground floor. A system of transparent metal fences or greenery. The rest of the space remains public. Shops are badly needed. A modular system will be designed and they will be placed only along the main streets (especially around the Prospekt).

Step 2.

We define the extension area of the ground floor apartments. A building system could be proposed for these extensions.

Step 3

One of the biggest problems of collective old housing today is the usage of the balconies. The needs are divers and complex: living space, sound insulation, temperature insulation, drying space for clothes and, why not, looks. Because one's balcony could represent that persons life.

But, fear no more, all these problems can be resolved by the CLIP-ON KIT ®. Thought as a flexible and simple concept, this structural concept satisfies all the wishes one could have. The walls of the balcony are built out of a rigid metal frame. On this frame it is possible to mount any of the offered options: storage boxes, windows, different types of closure (from different materials), grills for drying clothes and many others.

Through its modular form the system can provide a unitary image to the building blocks, making also possible a better way of living.

PROMENADE ON THE CORSO. NEW CENTRE ON PROSPEKT

Why make a complete new centre isolated from the old one? We propose a big concentra-tion of functions at the crossing of the Prospekt with Chervonoarmiys'ka street. The city de-velops naturally along the 2 boulevards.

OPENING AND CONNECTING. BELVEDERE PARK

Inside the 2 boulevards (Holovna and Chervonoarmiys'ka), different worlds come together: old villas, socialist blocks, free areas. We propose the creation of a park with a belvedere and the building of urban villas (3 storeys – 6 or 8 apartments) A stepped apartment build-ing is placed along the park. A higher building (10 storeys) marks the highest point of Chervonoarmiys'ka street.

громадськості. Цвключення можуть створити новий пункт зацікавленості між старим містом районом проспекту Незалежності

Крок 1

Перетворення та оновлення спортивної зони і стадіону "Буковина". Старий стадіон залишається громадським. Нова структура отримує нове перекриття з напів-прозорою скляною структурою. Нова структура створює новий внутрішній простір, яке включає в себе функції магазинів кафе, гардеробів та санітарні функції. Новаструктура маєвигляд даху над місяцидля глядачів.

Таким чином стадіон стане цікавиммісцемзавдяки свой новій формі у цьому середньому районі міста! надасть йому нового ідентифікації. Рекреаційна зона навколо стадіону буде наповнена новими функціями як і здоров'я як багатофункціональний зал, купальний басейн і велнес-центр. Нова будівля створить великий простір, що визначить новий вхід умісто

Крок 1

Крок 2

Ми розкриваємо військовий комплекс. Зона військової забудови буде віддана громадськості і змінить своє призначення на офісний район, ринки, магазини і ін. Нове облаштування старих і нових будівель вільому районі визначать нову зелену, проте міську площу. Ми вирішили запропонувати великий простір для паркування, оформлений у формі "авто-порта". Дахавто -порта матиме вигляд великої тарілки, як аєтоть на кількох підпорах

Крок 3

Пов'язавши із новоствореним центром ми створюємо нову зону міських котеджів. Ми визначаємо новий тип життєвого простору з міськими віллами які доповнюють собою старі, вже існуючі будинки.

Крок 1

Ми визначаємо приватні сади навколо блоків для людей, які живуть на першому поверсі. Система прозорих металевихзаборів або рослинності. Інша частина місцевості залишається громадською. Стоянка можлива тільки на спеціальних о відведених місцях. Магазини дуже необхідні. Модульнасистема буде розроблена таким чином, що вони будуть розміщені тільки по головним вулицям (особливо врайоні Проспекту.)

Крок 2

Ми визначаємо область розширення (продовження) квартир першого поверху. Будівельна система могла бути запропонована для цих розширень (продовжень)

Крок 3

Одна з найбільших проблем старі житлові забудови – це використання балконів. Потребічих балконів різноманітні та складні, це і житлова площа, і звукоізоляція, і теплоізоляція, і простір для сушіння одягу та багато іншого. Тому конкретний балкон може виразити (показати) життя конкретної людини, сім'ї. Але не бійтеся, всі ці проблеми можуть вирішитись з допомогою CLIP-ON SYSTEM* Хоча концепція є простою і гнучкою, вона задовольняє всі можливівимоги.

Стінки балконів виконані з жорсткого металевого каркасу. Напьому каркасі можливно запропонувати такі речі: стелажі, вікна різні типи балконних рам (з різнихматеріалів).

Система, через її модулярну форму, може забезпечити и єдиний образ житловий кварталів, роблячи можливимтакож кращий спосіб життя

ПРОГУЛЯНКА ШИРОКИМ ПРОСПЕКТОМ НОВИЙ ЦЕНТР НА ПРОСПЕКТІ НЕЗАЛЕЖНОСТІ

Чому роблять повий новий центр ізольований від старого? Ми пропонуємо велику концентрацію функцій на перехресті Проспекту Незалежності та вулиці Червоноармійської Місторозвивається, звичайно, по цим двом великим вулицям, продовжуючи деякий громадський простір, який можна було знаходити і в старому центрі

ВІДКРИТТЯ З'ЄДНАННЯ СТВОРЕННЯ ПАРКУ ТА ОГЛЯДОВОЇ ПЛОЩАДКИ У ЦЬОМУ ПАРКУ.

Між вулицями Червоноармійська та Проспект Незалежності різноманітні «світи» знаходяться разом : старі будиночки, соціалістичні блоки (так звані «хрущовки»), вільн місця Ми пропонуємо створення парку з оглядовою площадкою і будівництво невеликих будинків (3 поверхи – 6 або 8 квартир). Ступінчаті житлові будинки, розміщений вздовж парку. Висока будівля (10 поверхів) відмічаєнайвищу точку вулиці Червоноармійської

Ідея операцієюи ми думаємо, щоможемо зробити більшактивним так званий «спальний район», принесем туди трохи більшеміськогожиття це нетількиторгівля, а йінше розміщення житла з з'єднання функціональних зон

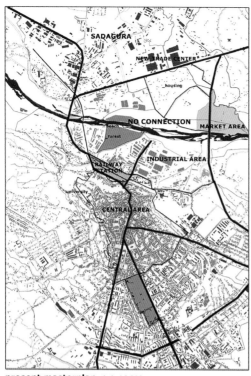

present masterplan / 1_16 000

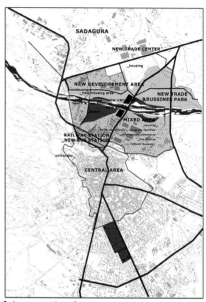

future masterplan / 1_20 000

local masterplan / 1_5 000

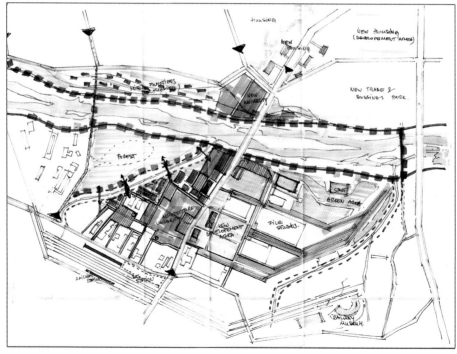

sven marx _de / michael wirdak _de / elisa hernando villar _au / vanessa sartori _au

vitsi Summer Academy
:ting sadagura & new university center

y District

nnecting the new territories in the north
dustrial zone between the old city-center and
important and starting-point for future devel-
ea. The plan to build here a new and
pean University at the north end of the
able potential and will create a new urban
the new parts of the city will grow in direc-

nter stays in direct connection with the new
center in the east and a high standard living
e river in the west.

of the university district is designed in two

ows the university- complex integrated in the
dam, with spaces opening up to the river.
ses a 2 lane bridge with moderate traffic in-

tive proposes the building- structure of the
le distance to the river and leaves the dam
w bridge in this concept will be developed in

grate cultural and administrative facilities
niversity- library on the other side of the
n. In this way vivid pedestrian activities will
the scenery, beside the individual and public
s.

emy of Architecture 2006 proposes to keep
ed chimneys of the former industrial areas as
racteristic cluster of landmarks for the sites
he south side of the river. There for both
architectural towers of different use, which
ith the chimneys of a former epoch.

ian _ro / adrian timaru _ro / dina socur _ua / natasha patroboy _ua / ina palka _ua

zamp klep

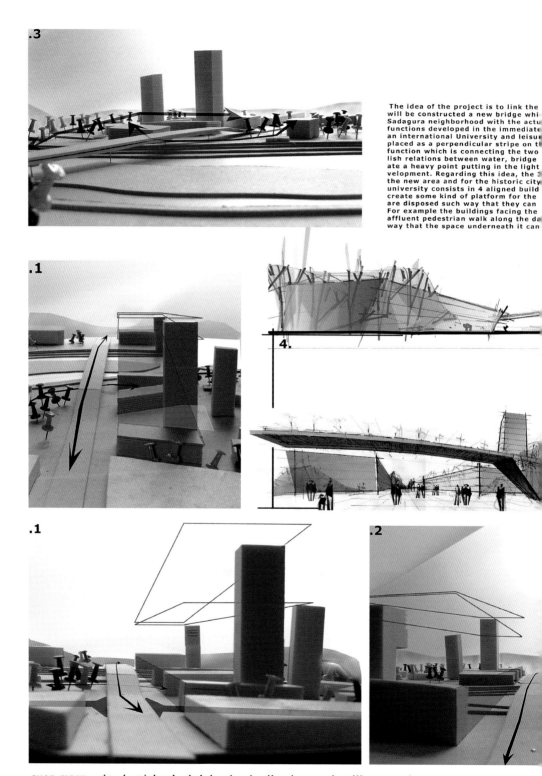

.3

The idea of the project is to link the
will be constructed a new bridge whi
Sadagura neighborhood with the actu
functions developed in the immediate
an international University and leisur
placed as a perpendicular stripe on t
function which is connecting the two
lish relations between water, bridge
ate a heavy point putting in the light
velopment. Regarding this idea, the 3
the new area and for the historic city
university consists in 4 aligned build
create some kind of platform for the
are disposed such way that they can
For example the buildings facing the
affluent pedestrian walk along the da
way that the space underneath it can

.1

4.

.1

.2

sven marx _de / michael wirdak _de / elisa hernando villar _au / vanessa sartori _au

Chernivitsi Summer Academy

connecting sadagura & new university center
University _ spread stones complex

e river. Here it
functionally the
ea. The main
e bridge will be
e university is
nd is the main
decide to estab-
This will gener-
he new area de-
dmarks both for
m visually. The
me high which
. The buildings
public spaces.
larged areas for
s designed such
blic purpose.

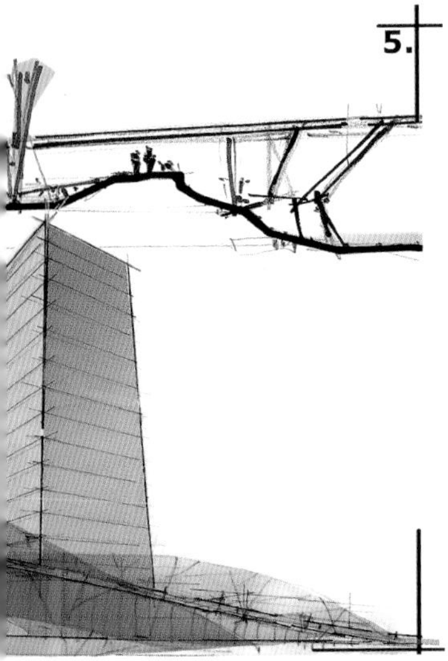

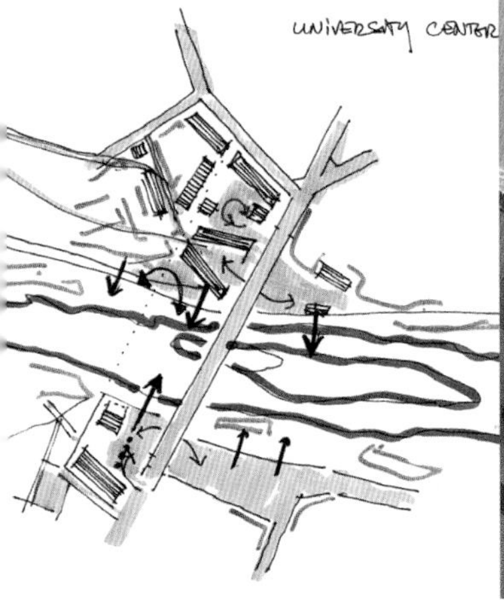

university plan   /   1_1000

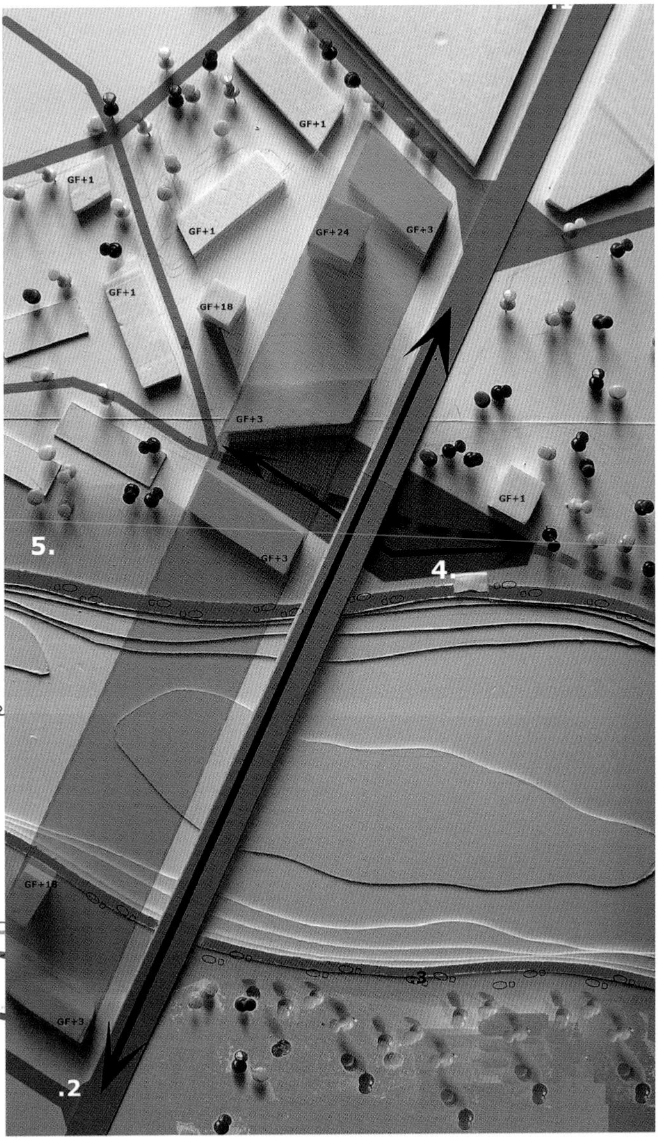

GF+1
GF+1
GF+1
GF+24
GF+3
GF+1
GF+18
GF+3
5.
GF+3
4
GF+1
GF+18
GF+3
.2

UNIVERSITY CENTER

ian _ro / adrian timaru _ro / dina socur _ua / natasha patroboy _ua / ina palka _ua

zamp klep

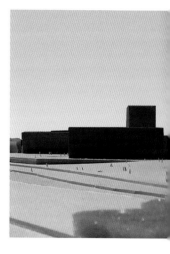

Looking to the west: The two towers and the promenade on the north side which follow to the sloping place.

From above: The three places; one from the library in the south, one from the culture and the place from the University in the north, the dam and the bridge build one unite with the river.

The sloping place brings the different rectly to the users. This place is the e is closely linked with the university

sven marx _de / michael wirdak _de / elisa hernando villar _au / vanessa sartori _au

Chernivitsi Summer Academy
connecting sadagura & new university center
University on the Pruth

University integrated in the dam

The river makes this sites between the ancient center of Cernowitz and Sadagura to a particularly place. We saw this as a chance to go deep in this necessity in our concept. From the hill, where the old city is situated you will recognize the two towers, which lead to the University. Through the old and redeveloped Industrial zone lead the main street over the bridge to Sadagura. But actually before you cross the bridge the University opens with the library and culture buildings on one level. It is the level of the dam which we need to protect the city or the industrial area against float. The dam is build as a promenade on the river. The river keep the new area together, he is the center of our work. He gravitates and arrange the to sides. The different river highs are always recognizable, noticeable and in contact with the users.

plan 1_5000

om the river di-
a culture way and

ɔian _ro / adrian timaru _ro / dina socur _ua / natasha patroboy _ua / ina palka _ua

zamp klep

Wir danken den Sponsoren beim Zustandekommen dieses Projektes:

Mr. Willie Nagel, CMG, London
geboren in Czernowitz,

Prof. Dr.h.c. Karl Wilhelm Pohl, Köln und Salzburg

Frau Sorea Wammers,
stellvertretend für die Nachkommen der Familie Bendak

EDITION SALZGEBER

Die Volker-Koepp-Kollektion

Sechs Filme von Volker Koepp mit ausführlichem Werkgespräch
Deutschland, 1999–2006, insgesamt ca. 700 Minuten, Farbe

Volker Koepp, einer der Großen des deutschen Dokumentarfilms und vielfach ausgezeichnet, verschafft sich und uns Zeit und Raum für Begegnungen mit Menschen und Landschaften, er lässt reden und die Kamera schweifen, hört und sieht genau hin, frei von Folklore, fern von Ideologie. Seine Filme schlagen Brücken zwischen Gestern und Heute, zwischen Vergessen und Erinnern, zwischen großer Geschichte und dem Schicksal des Einzelnen.

Sechs Filme, sechs DVDs, die sowohl einzeln als auch zusammen in einem Schuber erhältlich sind, mit umfangreichen Hintergrundinformationen und einem gut einstündigem Werkgespräch: Die VOLKER KOEPP KOLLEKTION ermöglicht erstmals einen umfassenden Überblick über die Koepp'schen Wieder- und Neuentdeckungen der Regionen des östlichen Europas.

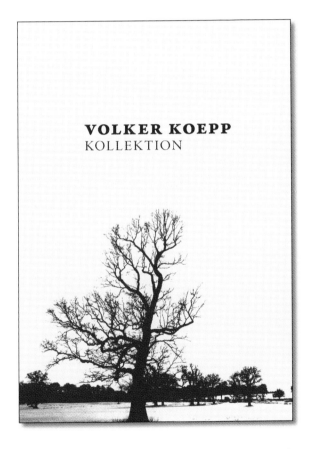

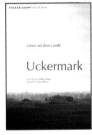 

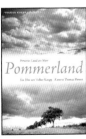 

Mit den Filmen:
Herr Zwilling und Frau Zuckermann, Kurische Nehrung, Uckermark, Dieses Jahr in Czernowitz, Pommerland, Schattenland
Bestell-Nr. D240 · www.salzgeber.de · www.delicatessen.org/shop · Bestell-Hotline 030 / 285 290 43

www.infolines.de

Fachwissen online

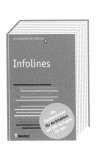

Akustik | Altbaumodernisierung | Aufzüge und Fahrtreppen | Barriere-
freies Bauen | Beschläge | Beton | Bodenbeläge | Dämmstoffe |
Elektro | Energieeffizientes Bauen | Fassade | Fenster und Türen |
Flachdach | Fliesen und Platten | Fußbodenkonstruktionen | Geneigtes
Dach | Glas | Haustechnik | Heizung | Licht | Mauerwerk | Schalungen
und Gerüste | Schiefer | Sicherheitstechnik | Solar | Sonnenschutz |
Treppen | Türautomation | Zukunftsfähige Bürogebäude

Boommärkte im Blick